# New Playwriting at Shakespeare's Globe

# New Playwriting at Shakespeare's Globe

*Vera Cantoni*

Bloomsbury Methuen Drama
An imprint of Bloomsbury Publishing Plc

BLOOMSBURY
LONDON · OXFORD · NEW YORK · NEW DELHI · SYDNEY

**Bloomsbury Methuen Drama**

An imprint of Bloomsbury Publishing Plc

Imprint previously known as Methuen Drama

| | |
|---|---|
| 50 Bedford Square | 1385 Broadway |
| London | New York |
| WC1B 3DP | NY 10018 |
| UK | USA |

**www.bloomsbury.com**

**BLOOMSBURY, METHUEN DRAMA and the Diana logo are trademarks of Bloomsbury Publishing Plc**

First published 2018

© Vera Cantoni, 2018

**British Library Cataloguing-in-Publication Data**

A catalogue record for this book is available from the British Library.

| ISBN: | HB: | 978-1-474-29824-7 |
|---|---|---|
| | ePDF: | 978-1-474-29826-1 |
| | eBook: | 978-1-474-29825-4 |

**Library of Congress Cataloging-in-Publication Data**

A catalogue record for this book is available from the Library of Congress.

Cover design: Adriana Brioso
Cover image: *We The People* by Eric Schlosser. Pictured: John Stahl. 2007.
(© Johan Persson/ArenaPAL)

Typeset by Integra Software Services Pvt. Ltd.

To find out more about our authors and books visit www.bloomsbury.com. Here you will find extracts, author interviews, details of forthcoming events and the option to sign up for our newsletters.

# CONTENTS

# LIST OF TABLES

# ACKNOWLEDGEMENTS

The whole Foreign Languages and Literatures Section of the Department of Humanities of Università di Pavia and its English branch in particular is a most inspiring environment in which to work. I am very grateful to all the people there who make every encounter professionally fruitful and personally pleasant, especially Lia Guerra, for her supportive mentoring, her generous help and her essential Socratic questioning, and Silvia Granata, who never tires to listen and read and give useful feedback with a smile.

I also wish to acknowledge the contribution provided in terms of advice and reading suggestions by some academics from the neighbouring fields in which I have here and there trespassed: Fabrizio Fiaschini, Tommaso Piazza and especially Luisa Bonesio.

My research would not have been possible without Shakespeare's Globe Library and Archives and their ever-helpful staff; I wish to thank in particular Ruth Frendo, Shauna Barrett, Rosie Fielding and Mathilde Blum, who were everything I could have wished for in a team of archivists and librarians and much more. When I came back to update my research after a nearly two-year gap, many of them had moved to other jobs, but I was happy to discover they had been replaced by other pleasant, generous and competent professionals such as Victoria Lane and Jacqueline Grainger.

Moulding academic research into a book can be a very tricky process, but I have had the chance to benefit from the reliable and patient support of Bloomsbury's Mark Dudgeon and Susan Furber, to whom I am especially thankful for being always there when some help or a reminder is needed while never becoming an intimidating presence.

Last but certainly not least, my heartfelt gratitude goes to the playwrights who have provided me with some very precious material: Jessica Swale and Chris Hannan, who have helpfully answered my questions, and even more Howard Brenton, who has also allowed me to preview the script and an article on which he was working. May their audiences always be as well disposed as they have been to me.

# LIST OF
# ABBREVIATIONS

HW     David Eldridge, *Holy Warriors. A Fantasia on the Third Crusade and the History of Violent Struggle in the Holy Lands*, London: Bloomsbury Methuen Drama, 2014

IE     Howard Brenton, *In Extremis. The Story of Abelard and Heloise*, London: Nick Hern Books, 2006

L     Glyn Maxwell, *Liberty*, London: Oberon Books, 2008

LC     Ché Walker and Arthur Darvill, *The Lightning Child*, London: Shakespeare's Globe, 2013

LDT     Simon Armitage, *The Last Days of Troy*, London: Faber and Faber, 2014

M     Tony Harrison, *Plays 1 – The Mysteries*, London: Faber and Faber, 1985

NG     Jessica Swale, *Nell Gwynn*, London: Nick Hern Books, 2015

NW     Trevor Griffiths, *A New World*, unpublished script, 2009, Shakespeare's Globe Library and Archives ref. GB 3316 SGT/THTR/SM/1/2009/NW

O     Rory Mullarkey, *The Oresteia*, London: Bloomsbury Methuen Drama, 2015

P     Richard Bean, *Pitcairn*, London: Oberon Books, 2014

S     Peter Oswald, *The Storm*, London: Oberon Books, 2005

TAT     Trevor Griffiths, *These Are the Times. A Life of Thomas Paine*, Nottingham: Spokesman, 2005

UBF     Simon Bent, *Under the Black Flag*, London: Oberon Books, 2006

WP     Eric Schlosser, *We the People*, unpublished script, 2007, Shakespeare's Globe Library and Archives ref. GB 3316 SGT/THTR/SM/1/2007/WTP

# Introduction

Although it is seen mainly as a monument to the dramatic art of Shakespeare and his contemporaries, the reconstructed Globe is also a theatre operating in its own time, that is from 1995 on.[1] Besides staging Elizabethan and Jacobean plays for twentieth- and twenty-first-century audiences, since 1999 it has offered a rather steady flow of premières. The twenty-seven new texts thus produced under the direction of Mark Rylance (1995–2005) and Dominic Dromgoole (2006–2015) constitute a consistent corpus because they have been written specifically for this unique context. Some have been adapted from pre-existing versions, but most of them have been especially commissioned for Shakespeare's Globe, and many have been created by authors who had already taken part in its 'theatrical experiment',[2] whether as actors, directors or playwrights. The result is a very interesting collection of works shaped by the peculiarities of this replica theatre: its characteristic architecture, the complex set of cultural and historical references it carries and the heterogeneous audience it attracts.

The present study is aimed at analysing some features shared by the majority of these plays in connection with the uncommon context in which they originated, so as to investigate how writers have responded to the specificities of Shakespeare's Globe. Since its goal is not so much to describe the reconstructed theatre's new dramaturgical output as to show how the scripts have been shaped by the unique environment of their creation, they will not be examined individually but as a corpus. Rather than emphasizing the different choices of each author, their discussion will stress the similarities that testify to the venue's impact on the plays' conception and development. Examples will show particular occurrences of a theme or the various ways a device has been used, mainly in order to let the playhouse's imprint emerge from the diversity of styles, approaches and subjects the scripts display.

Arguing that these texts share more than their birthplace in consequence of being produced by Shakespeare's Globe is relevant to the identity of the reconstructed theatre itself. That is why their analysis will be preceded here by a brief exploration of the Globe's complex nature as a monument referring to the past but also a theatre operating in the present. In this perspective the new plays it produces are evidence of an artistic fruitfulness that transcends not only the hollowness of a theme park but also the limits of an exclusively historical experiment.

After a short overview of how the Globe's new scripts have been commissioned and written or selected and adapted, the analysis will get into the details of the influence this unique destination has had on their creation. The features that seem to define them will be described so as to suggest a possible ex-post theorization of how their authors have harnessed the opportunities and faced the challenges they were met with. Although most of the characteristics that emerge from an investigation of this kind will not be found in all of the works under scrutiny, their frequent presence and their connection with the theatre's needs and possibilities make them worth analysing. Generally speaking, these recurring traits can be expected to match the two main aspects that make the Globe unique: the complex net of time frames and cultural references it evokes and the extraordinary visibility of its diverse audience. Therefore, the plays will be analysed in relation to these two focal points.

The theoretical premise for the exploration of how the new scripts interact with the playhouse's many references will be a discussion of the multiple time planes that coexist in the Globe. The texts will then be examined as regards such historically and/or culturally marked features as: the opportunity to evoke Shakespeare's spiritual presence; the use of a heightened language; the comic possibilities of fool figures and anachronisms; the overwhelming prevalence of historical and mythical subjects; the representation of contemporary hot issues by means of past situations; how ballads have been used by three of the Globe's new writers to bring the action near to the spectators while distancing it through a process of historicization. This last specific but exemplary case will provide a thematic bridge between this chapter and the one dedicated to the audience's role.

The following section will begin by questioning received ideas on the Globe's patrons. Then the playwrights' expectations on this subject will be outlined, because the wide, diverse crowd of theatregoers and their visibility in the reconstructed playhouse are both a challenge and an asset for artists. The scripts will be examined in accordance with this ambivalent reality by focusing first on devices aimed at attracting and securing the potentially wandering attention of the spectators and then on how these plays address, cast and represent the people in the auditorium so as to capitalize on the conspicuousness of their presence.

While the first part of the book deals with the Globe's new plays as a corpus, the second is dedicated to the exemplary case of Howard Brenton's extremely fruitful collaboration with the reconstructed playhouse, highlighting the productive connection between the dramatic poetics and politics of the theatre and of the playwright. Evidence of their consonance can already be found in the chronological development of this relationship: after the success of *In Extremis* (staged in 2006 and again in 2007), Dominic Dromgoole asked Brenton to write what was to become *Anne Boleyn*, that was exceptionally performed during three consecutive years (2010, 2011 and 2012) and the 2014 season has included a new play of his on the topical subject of the First World War, *Doctor Scroggy's War*.

Howard Brenton's works for the Globe display an ideal interaction between the author's art and the theatre's features with reference to the focal points presented above, i.e. the permanence of the past in the present and the centrality of the audience. Since the playwright has displayed a remarkably constant sensibility for these themes throughout his career, the visibility of the spectators and of the historical dimension which characterizes the Globe's architecture did not cause a radical transformation in his writing. It rather presented him with an optimal environment for some experiments quite in keeping with his previous output; he evidently considered both the audience and the echoes of history as part of the picture his plays were to draw and harnessed the new opportunities their visual prominence offered. *In Extremis*, *Anne Boleyn* and *Doctor Scroggy's War* will therefore be analysed also in relation to the rest of his oeuvre, so as to show that they are part of an ongoing artistic discourse and at the same time they respond to the theatre's specificity. This doubly harmonious relation will be foregrounded first in connection with the historical genre, to which all three plays belong, and then in the way they manifest an insightful and complex consideration of the audience's centrality.

Up to now, the main essays on Shakespeare's Globe have focused either on the building itself or on how the theatre has staged its eponymous author's works (see e.g. Mulryne and Shewring 1997; Kennedy 1998; Orgel 1998; Kiernan 1999; Worthen 2003; Conkie 2006; Carson and Karim-Cooper 2008), while the abundant and varied issues raised by the production of new texts in the reconstructed playhouse have been rather neglected.[3] In this study I do not presume to cover such a wide and manifold subject in its entirety. By charting some key recurring features of this growing dramatic corpus and focusing on the outstanding example of Howard Brenton's plays, I intend to show the influence of the theatre's unique characteristics on the artistic choices of its twenty-first-century playwrights and to point out the potential of this connection.

Consequently, the method I mainly employ here to examine the relationship between playtext and theatre is what Judith Milhous and Robert Hume have described as 'production analysis' of the scripts, that is 'the interpretation of the text specifically aimed at understanding it as a performance vehicle' (Milhous and Hume 1985: 10). It is essentially the approach a creative team takes in view of a production (hence its name) and its interest lies precisely in the opportunity to highlight the connections between the written page and the performances it can engender. In Milhous and Hume's work, it is one of the main techniques employed to outline a 'producible interpretation' of a playtext, one that can be actually conveyed to a theatre audience; here, I will focus more specifically on the stagings that seem to be envisaged by the author, those Milhous and Hume would define not only 'producible' but also 'valid' (ibid.: 17). This does not necessarily mean to espouse the directorial choices that characterized the actual première of the play, but to look for the multiple readings the script offered in the context for which it was conceived. The nearness in time and space of these plays' composition and the wealth of evidence concerning the process of their genesis allow for such speculations, which would not be warranted in the case of Restoration plays.

The point of view is thus shifted from the creative team interpreting the text to the writer presenting them with a wide range of opportunities. The fundamental premise of such a perspective's meaningfulness is the assumption that the playwright's work is based on a well-grounded understanding of and a sensitive attention to specifically theatrical features such as rhythm of speech and action or basic blocking. Consequently, this kind of production analysis can be a fruitful instrument of academic research whenever the dramatist is fully conscious of the processes and characteristics of stage performance, whether directly, as a theatre practitioner, or by means of a close collaboration with the company for whom the play is written. This is precisely the case of the new texts penned for Shakespeare's Globe, as the story of their creation shows; furthermore, because they were shaped for a very peculiar theatre, the fact that they should fit a specific space was granted special prominence in the playwrights' work. The natural outcome of this mindfulness is a script in which non-verbal aspects of the spectacle are tellingly encoded, either explicitly, by means of stage directions, or implicitly, in the characters' words. The tight relationship between playtext and stage practice that ensues has been analysed more than once in the case of Shakespeare's works (see e.g. Pasternak Slater 1982), both for their outstanding richness and because we often lack any more direct evidence of Elizabethan theatre productions. In the case of twenty-first-century drama, there are plentiful records of shows, so there is no need to reconstruct them on the basis of textual hints, but a clear performability is still a hallmark of conscious playwriting. As Keir Elam has pointed out in the concluding comments of *The Semiotics of Theatre and Drama*, 'the written text ... is determined by its very need for stage contextualization, and indicates throughout its allegiance to the physical conditions of performance, above all to the actor's body and its ability to materialize discourse within the space of the stage' (Elam 2002: 190), so when authors envisage performances in a specific playhouse, it is fair to assume that traces of its singularity will appear in their works.

The scripts are not the only documents on which this study is based, though. Thanks to the archives of Shakespeare's Globe, I have been able to consider beside the published plays a rich set of materials that witness their history: other versions of the texts; some correspondence and notes concerning their development; 'bible' prompt books and video recordings that show how they were actually first staged (thus confirming or challenging the results of production analysis); programmes and advertising leaflets exemplifying how they were marketed and presented; evidence of their reception in reviews and front-of-house reports. Furthermore, I have had the opportunity to ask some questions to three authors of plays that are particularly relevant to the present study, Howard Brenton, Jessica Swale and Chris Hannan, whose answers have provided me with valuable information, clarifications and comments on their works for the Globe. These are all precious traces of the fleeting life of drama besides the printed page and, more relevantly in the perspective of the research summarized here, of the complex relationship between dramaturgy and performance.

# New Plays at Shakespeare's Globe Theatre

| Year | Playwright | Title | Director |
|------|-----------|-------|----------|
| 1999 | Peter Oswald | *Augustine's Oak* | Tim Carroll |
| 2002 | Peter Oswald | *The Golden Ass* | Tim Carroll |
| 2005 | Peter Oswald | *The Storm* | Tim Carroll |
| 2005 | Jack Shepherd, Oliver Cotton | *Man Falling Down* | Jack Shepherd, Oliver Cotton |
| 2006 | Simon Bent | *Under the Black Flag* | Roxana Silbert |
| 2006 2007 | Howard Brenton | *In Extremis* | John Dove |
| 2007 | Jack Shepherd | *Holding Fire* | Mark Rosenblatt |
| 2007 | Eric Schlosser | *We the People* | Charlotte Westenra |
| 2008 2009 | Ché Walker | *The Frontline* | Matthew Dunster |
| 2008 | Glyn Maxwell | *Liberty* | Guy Retallack |
| 2008 | Seamus Heaney | *The Burial at Thebes* | Derek Walcott |
| 2009 | Frank McGuinness | *Helen* | Deborah Bruce |

| Year | Playwright | Title | Director |
|------|-----------|-------|----------|
| 2009 | Trevor Griffiths | *A New World* | Dominic Dromgoole |
| 2010 | Nell Leyshon | *Bedlam* | Jessica Swale |
| 2010 2011 2012 | Howard Brenton | *Anne Boleyn* | John Dove |
| 2011 | Chris Hannan | *The God of Soho* | Raz Shaw |
| 2011 | Tony Harrison | *The Globe Mysteries* | Deborah Bruce |
| 2013 | Samuel Adamson | *Gabriel* | Dominic Dromgoole |
| 2013 | Jessica Swale | *Blue Stockings* | John Dove |
| 2013 | Ché Walker, Arthur Darvill | *The Lightning Child* | Matthew Dunster |
| 2014 | Simon Armitage | *The Last Days of Troy* | Nick Bagnall |
| 2014 | David Eldridge | *Holy Warriors* | James Dacre |
| 2014 | Howard Brenton | *Doctor Scroggy's War* | John Dove |
| 2014 | Richard Bean | *Pitcairn* | Max Stafford-Clark |
| 2015 | Helen Edmundson | *The Heresy of Love* | John Dove |
| 2015 | Rory Mullarkey | *The Oresteia* | Adele Thomas |
| 2015 | Jessica Swale | *Nell Gwynn* | Christopher Luscombe |

# PART ONE

# The New Globe Plays

# 1

# Something Old, Something New

When first hearing of the new plays produced by Shakespeare's Globe Theatre, most people are surprised, many to the extent that they think there must be a misunderstanding; some even start fantasizing about new Shakespearean texts, presumably the result of an extraordinary manuscript find. The reconstructed theatre is so strongly connected with the idea of something historical and therefore old (or maybe rather 'olde', that is, of doubtful age but inextricably linked with the heritage industry) that relating it to the production of new values appears to be difficult. Yet joining something old and something new is not an unusual way to foster change, as even wedding superstitions remind us. It can actually be a very fruitful procedure, when the 'old' structure is conceived for future use and the new contents specifically tailored to suit its characteristics, and this is the case of Shakespeare's Globe Theatre and the twenty-first-century drama it has hatched, as a detailed analysis of their origins and development can show.

## A reconstructed theatre

Shakespeare's Globe was conceived by American actor Sam Wanamaker as a tribute to the genius of William Shakespeare and to the richness of the sixteenth- and seventeenth-century English drama in general, and with this aim it was built according to the latest finds in the study of Elizabethan theatre architecture.[1]

It has been and still is constantly updated in compliance with new research on historical issues. So much so that, although the building's foundations were laid in 1989 and the theatre was first used in 1995 and then officially opened in 1997, the construction process may be said to have started in 1970, when Wanamaker formed the Globe Playhouse Trust, and not to have ended yet, since the Architecture Research Group is still working on its interior decorative scheme and considering the possibility of changing the lower gallery's structure and measures.[2] Despite this constant focus on the careful reconstruction of a past model, Shakespeare's Globe was always meant to look to the future too. In 1997 Andrew Gurr, Wanamaker's principal academic advisor, described the building as 'a test-tube, the basis for experiments aimed at getting a better idea of how Shakespeare expected his plays to be staged' (Gurr 1997b: 159). From this scholarly perspective, the replica's realization was the first step in a long-term project in the context of which future action would be aimed at understanding the past; on the contrary, the theatre practitioners in the Artistic Directorate were moved, in the words of actor and artistic-director-to-be Mark Rylance, by the 'desire to explore old structures for new theatre' (Rylance 1997: 169). Sam Wanamaker saw it as an instrument for theatrical innovation, a possible way to revive stage practice, thus answering the twentieth-century need to shake the conventions of performance. 'He linked his dream to the theatre's own rediscovered urge to take acting back into the audiences whence picture-frame staging had for centuries removed it, in the long retreat into its own scenic realm behind the footlights.... Such theatre would be new and old at the same time' (Gurr 1997a: 32–3).

    The theatre's twenty-first-century productions have been actually used as a source of information, and the performers' feedback has contributed to the reconstruction's improvement too. The most conspicuous examples of this experimental procedure took place during the Workshop and Prologue seasons (1995 and 1996), when the main features of the building were still under construction and could therefore be modified in response to the comments of the practitioners: the stage pillars were moved back and towards the centre so that actors could easily turn around them, and the side doors were distanced further in order to widen the space for entrances and exits (Greenfield 1997: 94–6). Since the fabric's completion, this kind of macroscopic change is unlikely to occur,[3] but the research department keeps monitoring the artists' reactions to the playing space, from 2006 by means of systematic End of Season Interviews (EOSI) with cast and creatives.[4]

In other words, the double nature of Shakespeare's Globe, its being both a historical replica and a working theatre, is far from being contradictory. Although during the first stages of the project these two aims were often considered diverging, especially because the lack of modern comforts and facilities could discourage spectators (Gurr 1997a: 33–5), in time they have proved to be mutually beneficial: performances have provided valuable evidence as to the venue's possible structures and usages, and audiences seem to have been attracted, rather than repelled, by the adventurous dimension of an open-air 'uncomfortable' theatre experience.

The theatre's utilization can be seen as a requirement, rather than an obstacle, in the quest for authenticity that animated Wanamaker's project since its early stages. Had it not been used, the replica would have become a huge museum exhibit, ceasing to be a playhouse at all. This risk could jeopardize the meaning of the whole enterprise no less than the temptation to compromise between the features of Elizabethan architecture and the expectations of the twentieth-century audiences, thus giving up the aim of reproducing Shakespeare's theatre faithfully. In order to assess the nature and importance of these two dangers, it may be useful to consider the new Globe in the context of the contemporary debate concerning genuine and fabricated cultural heritage and to examine the implications of the terms with which the Bankside playhouse has been defined.

In 1994, paragraph 11 of the *Nara Document on Authenticity* stated in the authoritative framework of the World Heritage Convention that it is 'not possible to base judgements of values and authenticity within fixed criteria. On the contrary, the respect due to all cultures requires that heritage properties must [be] considered and judged within the cultural contexts to which they belong'.[5] Unsurprisingly, the positive assertion that such a fundamental concept is not absolute but relatively triggered, precisely in the years in which the new Globe was built and opened, a very lively theoretical and practical debate, although one that has unfortunately not continued with the same widespread interest in the following decade, despite the many unsolved problems (Labadi 2010: 66).

Shakespeare's Globe was always peripheral to this discussion, that focused mainly on the appropriate conservation of extant monuments, because the question of reconstructions was addressed often, but in the context of extreme forms of restoration. Such discourses only referred to what the *OED* presents as the first meaning of the verb 'to reconstruct', i.e. 'to construct or put together again, especially following damage or destruction, or by way of renovation', while the Elizabethan-like playhouse is in many ways more precisely the outcome of the action described in its second definition, 'to form a mental or visual impression of (a past event, phenomenon, etc.) based on assembled evidence'.

In other words, the lack of information concerning its long-lost antecedent makes the new Globe peculiar as a copy; nevertheless, because of the question of its authenticity, it is interesting to compare the reconstructed theatre's situation to those considered for instance by Gus Gerneke in his analysis of architectural duplications (1995, 1996). It is certainly not a 'fake', in that it involves no fraud (even though some of its visitors seem to trick themselves into believing it is really a more than 400-year-old building). At the same time, since it does not actually replicate an existing original, Shakespeare's Globe is no proper 'copy', being on the contrary itself unique. It has often been called a 'replica': maybe it is just an imprecise use of the term, like the one quoted by Gerneke himself, as a synonym of 'reconstruction' (Gerneke 1996: 27), but it may hint at something more. Antiquarians and art dealers call 'replica' 'a reproduction, as of a picture or statue, especially one by the maker of the original and assumed to be of equal value' (Gerneke 1995: 26). So the choice of this word may point to the fact that the playhouse has been built, if obviously not by the same people, with the same techniques and materials employed in the creation of the original Globe Theatre, and may thus be considered of equal value – of the value the first Globe had in 1595, that is to say, before it could acquire the patina of time, because 'notwithstanding the perfection of copies produced by the latest techniques, the mystique of the old and original is still overwhelming' (ibid.: 21). The amount of historical research on which its realization was based and the firmness with which its creators stuck to the best information available and eschewed concessions to the twentieth-century concepts and tastes are what make the definition of 'imitation' inappropriate too, together with the fact that Shakespeare's Globe is a working theatre: there is no simulation either in the aspect or in the functioning of the playhouse.

The term that best applies to the reconstructed building, among those discussed by Gerneke, seems to be 'model', 'a representation in three dimensions of some projected or existing structure, or of some material object, showing the proportions and arrangement of its component parts' (ibid.: 26). Models are very often made with the same material of the present, past or future structure they represent, and they can be full scale. Crucially, they are meant to show how their object 'works', and for this reason they have often played a role in the design process of engineering and architecture projects. In the light of this definition, the reconstructed Globe displays once more an interesting duplicity: on the one hand, it is an exploration of the past, like the 1:1 ship models cited by Gerneke (1995: 21–2) or, even more, like the jewellery Honoré d'Albert, Duc de Luynes, realized in the nineteenth century in order to test some scientific hypotheses on ancient crafts (Hellmann 1988: 43–4); on the other, it is part of a forward-looking experiment with theatre techniques.[6]

Gerneke concludes the first part of his essay by stating that 'even an accurate full-scale model of a historical building can never attain more than a relative monumental value' (ibid.: 26), and the reason for this assertion is pretty obvious: no matter how valuable, beautiful and skilfully executed, a reproduction will always lack what Benjamin called the aura of the original (1936), something which cannot be obtained or recovered, because it is precisely the essence of an object being unique and unrepeatable. If Shakespeare's Globe should be destroyed, for example, from this point of view the loss would not be irrecoverable, since it could be rebuilt, and the new fabric would only lack what the previous one did not have either, i.e. the right age and the experience, so to speak, of the 1595 (or 1614) theatre.

Nevertheless, Gerneke himself quotes an interesting exception, the case of a duplicate that can be said to have acquired absolute monumental value: Hadrian's villa at Tivoli, an architectural ensemble based on the *evocatio* of several styles that had impressed the emperor during his travels throughout the ancient world (ibid.: 25). Nowadays, these buildings are a UNESCO World Heritage Site, preserved and visited as precious monuments witnessing not so much the cultures that inspired them as the grandeur and the antiquarian taste of second-century Rome and the influence this complex has had in turn on later artists.[7] This example may suggest a fruitful reading of Shakespeare's Globe too, namely the possibility to consider it representative not of late-Elizabethan architecture but of the historical knowledge, craftsmanship and interest at the turn of the millennium, a meaningful product of an age that sees itself as very consciously standing on the shoulders of giants. In this perspective, the ability with which it has been planned and realized employing the forms, materials and techniques of a past epoch paradoxically contributes to make it a valuable monument of today. Nevertheless, its relevance to the present rests also, in a more direct way, in the fact that it is actually used as a theatre, to stage, according to the customs of late twentieth- and early twenty-first-century Britain, both revivals and new plays.

This complex situation may be clarified by means of Alois Riegl's theorization of the values monuments express. His essay on *The Modern Cult of Monuments* is more than a hundred years old and is once again centred on the preservation of existing works of art, but the concepts it outlines are still quite relevant to the debate on cultural heritage,[8] and the reconstructed Globe seems to embody several specificities it discusses.

First of all, Shakespeare's Globe is an intentional monument, one built in order to convey to the present and hopefully to the future the merit of a specific aspect and moment in human history, and not one the 'commemorative value' of which has been determined by the passing of time (Riegl 1903: 1). As such, it is meant to exist in an eternal present rather than to acquire and display the patina that confers 'age value', i.e. the marks of time with their inherent capacity to foster a reflection on the ephemeral nature of all things human (ibid.: 38–9). It may defy the 'newness value' of completeness (ibid.: 46–7), but not in the sense of pointing to the past by displaying the absence of something that once was there; on the contrary, it hints at the possibility of adjustments and additions in the future, for instance by means of some as yet unpainted wooden parts.

What makes the status of Shakespeare's Globe difficult to pinpoint is the contrast between its manifest 'historical value' (ibid.: 29–30) and its total lack of 'age value' (ibid.: 22). It explicitly, obviously and to the best of our knowledge correctly refers to a specific moment of our past, while it seems to deny the passing of time, the gulf that separates that age from the present, confronting its twenty-first-century visitors with the paradox of a new sixteenth-century building. Although he somehow deprecatingly presents 'historical value' as typical of a previous epoch in the 'cult of monuments' and therefore more primitive than 'age value' (ibid.: 10–21), Riegl sanctions a situation such as the reconstructed theatre's in two different ways. First of all, he stresses the importance of copies and of educated attempts to remove all signs of decay not from original documents but from duplicates or hypothetical descriptions as a way to investigate history and art (ibid.: 30, 37–8).[9] Furthermore, even though in the same passage he denounces 'an insoluble conflict with "age value" when the copy is not offered as a sort of auxiliary instrument for the purposes of scientific research, but as a complete substitute of the original with a claim to historical-aesthetical appreciation' (ibid.: 38),[10] in the section of his work dedicated to 'contemporary values' he implicitly explains the reason why a replica can even be the object of aesthetic appreciation. 'Relative art value', in Riegl's terms, is what enables us to enjoy products of the past for their specific conception, form and colour (ibid.: 57), thanks to their concordance with the present *Kunstwollen* (ibid.: 41). This feeling of proximity to an art of the past and the desire to get closer to it are precisely what has animated the adventure of Shakespeare's Globe, since Sam Wanamaker's dream (Gurr 1997a: 32) and up to the enthusiasm of the practitioners that have been experimenting with it.[11]

So according to Riegl's ideas the meaning of the reconstruction resides in the present and in the way it relates to its Elizabethan heritage, but not in the field of architecture per se, because the art with which our *Kunstwollen* appears to resonate is Shakespeare's, i.e. the theatre. Once again, in order to be a valuable monument, the Globe must be first of all a working playhouse. Moreover, the presence of a visible and recognizable twenty-first-century audience, together with the 'anachronisms' it entails, such as 'emergency exit' signs or 'no photographs' announcements, naturally foregrounds the building's time displacement, and thus contrasts the risk of the reconstruction unwittingly posing as an ancient fabric.[12]

To conclude this overview of some possible theoretical perspectives on the connection between the new Globe's authenticity and its activity, the importance of usage is actually stressed by the World Heritage Convention itself, which lists 'use and function' as one of the eight sets of attributes that have the potential to truthfully and credibly express a property's cultural values and thus to manifest its authenticity.[13]

# Specially constructed plays

Shakespeare's Globe Theatre is unquestionably very specialized in its offer: with very few exceptions, it features only plays by Shakespeare and his contemporaries or world premières. As a result, nearly all the texts it produces have been especially written for its Elizabethan-like structure. From the theatre's opening to 2015, the only three twenty-first-century texts staged by the Globe that had premièred elsewhere were Simon Armitage's *The Last Days of Troy* (Royal Exchange Theatre, Manchester, 8 May 2014; Shakespeare's Globe Theatre, 10 June 2014), Richard Bean's *Pitcairn* (Chichester Festival Theatre, 22 August 2014; Shakespeare's Globe Theatre, 22 September 2014) and Helen Edmundson's *The Heresy of Love* (Swan Theatre, Stratford-Upon-Avon, 2 February 2012; Shakespeare's Globe Theatre, 31 July 2015). The first two were nevertheless created with the Globe in mind: even though they were initially conceived for the other playhouses, which asserted their right of precedence by hosting the plays' debuts, they were produced in association with Shakespeare's Globe, where they opened only a month later. It is therefore fair to assume that Armitage's and Bean's works were tailored to suit both their original venues and the reconstructed theatre.

Some other scripts were enacted before their premières in workshops or theatre courses, but this sort of staging can be considered part of the dramaturgical creative process rather than its issue's first presentation, not only for its informal and sometimes almost private context, but mainly because after these performances the texts were significantly reworked. So *The Heresy of Love* was the only revival proper among the Globe's new plays up to 2015, and only time will tell whether this single and very recent occurrence will mark the beginning of a new trend in the theatre's artistic policy or remain an exception in its output.

For the time being, new writing is usually commissioned by the artistic director, so it is influenced not only by the architecture in which it is going to be presented, but also by the season it is going to be part of. The contiguity with a specific set of Shakespearean works can bear both on general themes and on details of the 'new writes'. An example of the former kind is Ché Walker's *The Frontline*, portraying the variety of people who inhabit the streets of London, which was staged in the 2008 season, entitled 'Totus Mundus', that 'aimed to celebrate the diversity of Shakespeare's voice, and the comprehensive inclusiveness of the Globe' (Dromgoole 2008: 6). The latter type of influence can be exemplified by the *Hamlet*-based pun in *The Storm*, 'I'm more an antique Roman than a dame' (*S* 74).[14]

Furthermore, texts can be developed or adjusted while they are being mounted, by means of the cooperation between playwright, cast and creative team, an interaction that takes the form of dialogues, at various stages of the process, and sometimes of staged readings or rehearsals attended by the author. The most frequent alterations, very often attested by the prompt books, are minor word changes and more or less extensive cuts; in this case, the playwrights' participation[15] is just a sign of the healthy collaboration they have with Shakespeare's Globe. While this sort of modification is quite common in theatre productions generally, though, sometimes adjustments are made specifically in view of the reconstructed playhouse's peculiarities.

A very interesting case is that of Jessica Swale's fictional account of some late-Victorian female Cambridge students' university years and of the fight for their right to graduate, *Blue Stockings*. The play was already entirely written when Dominic Dromgoole chose it for the 2013 season, but the author, who had previously directed Nell Leyshon's *Bedlam* for the Elizabethan-style theatre (2010), was able to rework it very knowledgeably to make it fit that stage. Generally speaking, she trusted the artistic director would 'never say yes to doing a play that didn't work at the Globe' (Swale 2014)[16] because 'he knows that building really well' (ibid.), so she relied on his judgement for the themes and characters to suit that space, but in developing the text she kept the playhouse well in mind. The changes Swale made were of different kinds. Some, such as the choice to focus more on one of the four students portrayed, were part of a dramaturgical elaboration quite independent of the venue; some responded to needs of the staging, but have later proved useful elsewhere too (e.g. the version of 2.4 without the cart);[17] finally, some were intended specifically to match the Elizabethan stage's strengths and weaknesses. The main example of this last category recalled by Swale is a change of setting: several dialogues that were supposed to take place in Tess's room were moved to the college's orchard because in her experience 'the plays that work best at the Globe are plays where scenes are set outdoors or in spaces that don't need walls' (ibid.).

Trevor Griffiths's *A New World. A Life of Thomas Paine* is worth special consideration because it is the re-writing, specifically designed for the reconstructed theatre, of a screenplay by the same author, *These Are the Times*.[18] The playwright himself summarized this reworking in three main points: the piece's length was reduced to three hours including an interval; a dozen songs were added; Benjamin Franklin's role as narrator was considerably extended (Robins 2009: 2). These changes might have benefited the play's staging irrespective of the venue (and in the case of duration, of the medium too), but conspicuous musical moments and characters directly addressing the audience are recurring features of the new plays produced by the Globe that dovetail with its peculiarities, as remarked explicitly by another dramatist, Ché Walker (Tripney 2008). Anyway, as attested by the three 'Script Development' boxes in the archives of Shakespeare's Globe, Griffiths carefully optimized the text for the space and context that hosted its première.

This 'fitting' phase is fundamental in the less frequent case of ready-made plays that are chosen to be adapted for the Globe, but it is important for specially written works too, both because the playwright may be willing to adopt permanently ideas that originated on stage and in consideration of production details that could not be foreseen, such as the actors' physical appearance. Howard Brenton wrote *Anne Boleyn* for the Globe, for instance, but he could not know that Henry VIII would be played by brown-haired Anthony Howell, and so had a character refer to his red hair (possibly in 2.3 or 2.4, by describing newborn Elizabeth as having inherited this trait of her father's). The line was then changed, with the author's permission; actually, it does not even appear in the printed playtext (where in those passages the king repeatedly says the baby has eyes like his, *AB* 84 and 86).[19] Commissioned plays can go through more substantial adjustments too. More than one has been recorded in the case of Ché Walker's *The Frontline*, for example: a rehearsal note relates that the playwright himself was penning a pre-show announcement that would match the text's style;[20] in his 2007 EOSI, the writer stated that after attending a reading of the play artistic director Dominic Dromgoole had two requests: 'more songs and ... an interval'.[21]

Dromgoole, who has also directed two of the new plays produced by the Globe (*A New World* in 2009 and *Gabriel* in 2013), is of course a key figure in this creative process. At the helm of Shakespeare's Globe Theatre since 2006, he has constantly fostered new writing there as he had previously done in very different contexts, most notably at the Bush Theatre between 1990 and 1996. Of the twenty-seven plays investigated in the present study, twenty-four were staged in his ten seasons. He had already collaborated with several of the authors, directing their plays (Eric Schlosser's *Americans* at the Arcola Theatre in 2003; Frank McGuinness's *Someone Who'll Watch over Me* at the Ambassadors Theatre in 2005; Samuel Adamson's *Clocks and Whistles* at the Bush Theatre in 1996 and *Grace Note* at the Old Vic in 1997) or supervising their production as artistic director of the Bush Theatre (Simon Bent's *Bad Company*, 1994, and *Goldhawk Road*, 1996; Chris Hannan's *The Evil Doers*, 1990; David Eldridge's *Serving It Up*, 1996; Helen Edmundson's *The Clearing*, 1993) and of the Oxford Stage Company (the revival of Trevor Griffiths's *Comedians* in 2001) and when he was in charge of the new plays for the Peter Hall Company at the Old Vic (Chris Hannan's *Shining Souls*, 1997). The form and extension of his participation in the scripts' creation and fine-tuning obviously vary, but Nell Leyshon's account, in her 2010 EOSI, of Dromgoole's few interventions in the making of *Bedlam* outlines also what seems to be his fairly constant overall attitude, helpful and supportive but never intrusive:

> he read the script a couple of times and gave me a note, or rang me up or emailed me and gave me some really great feedback ... I could have asked him at any point for more help. He came to the run through, very supportive all the way through, but he really just lets you get on with it.[22]

Dromgoole's new writing policy has undoubtedly characterized his artistic direction of Shakespeare's Globe, but his predecessor, Mark Rylance, had already initiated this strand of the theatre's activity, which was, in fact, among the intentions he announced in his press conference on being appointed (Day 1996: 292). The first collaboration between the reconstructed Elizabethan playhouse and a twentieth-century writer took quite a different form, though, because it focused on one author who became playwright in residence for a while, Peter Oswald.

A file consisting of three full paper bags in the archives of Shakespeare's Globe gives abundant evidence of his extensive work for this theatre, as it contains material relating to ten more projects besides the three that made it to the stage. There are translations, adaptations and original plots; some are represented only by more or less detailed synopses, but at least one full-length draft is included for most of the titles. Multiple versions, sometimes accompanied by notes or messages, bear witness to the continuity and fruitfulness of the collaboration between playwright and creative team on the scripts that went through longer development processes, and especially on those that ended up in the Globe's seasons, *Augustine's Oak* (1999), *The Golden Ass* (2002) and *The Storm* (2005).

Another aspect of this cooperation emerges from the research bulletin compiled for *The Golden Ass*:[23] Peter Oswald took part in the rehearsals, so that his dialogue with actors and practitioners was not only a mediated, long-distance conversation possibly interspersed with occasional meetings, but a continuously shared artistic endeavour. Such a constant presence of the playwright is even more impressive because it extends beyond his residency in the 1998/1999 season. Not only did Oswald's involvement in the Globe's activities continue after that experience but it had already begun quite earlier: a note in pen on the synopsis of *Paul* (a play that did not reach the stage of composition, it seems) points out that it was written just after seeing the 1997 season, i.e. the Opening Season.

This pre-existing and protracted collaboration makes it clear that the goal of the Globe's management in applying for a Resident Dramatist Attachment Award in 1998 was something more complex than the mere getting in touch with a playwright and commissioning a text. In their request, three main purposes were stated, two of which are probably rather usual – the advancement of a play made-to-order and the development of other writing projects; the possibility to employ a poet's competence in adapting classic texts when needed – but the central one is characteristic of this context only: 'to provide Peter [Oswald] with a first hand insight into the whole process of playmaking for the unique Globe space' (p. 1). The motivation goes on to explain that the playwright would attend rehearsals of all the 1998 season's productions and that his work could be workshopped with members of the current company. Later on, the theoretical foundations of this scheme are outlined, i.e. that 'a space as unique as the Globe calls for a peculiar writing style' (p. 2), and 'the closer a writer is associated with the playing company (in the way in which Elizabethan writers were associated with their players) the better his/her understanding of the best way to write for the space' (ibid.).

As a matter of fact, the mutual usefulness of a playwright's residency at the reconstructed Globe had already been advocated by John Russell Brown nearly twenty years before the theatre's opening:

> Perhaps it is our playwrights who most need a restored Globe. We must find enough money to allow promising and already accomplished writers to be attached to the theatre and its company over a period of time, so that the third Globe and its new relationship between actor, stage, and audience can also be a challenge to writers. (Russell Brown 1981: 27–28)

Even though Oswald's residency has remained a unicum up to now, the need to ensure that the authors of new plays know how this peculiar theatre works, and can therefore draw up texts that suit it perfectly, has constantly shaped the artistic director's policy in the following years. Four more playwrights have worked for the Globe repeatedly like Peter Oswald, their subsequent pieces profiting from the previous experience: after *In Extremis* (2006), Howard Brenton was commissioned *Anne Boleyn* (2010) and *Doctor Scroggy's War* (2014); Jack Shepherd's *Holding Fire* (2007) followed *Man Falling Down* (2005), which he had co-authored with Oliver Cotton; after *The Frontline* (2008), Ché Walker wrote *The Lightning Child* (2013); Jessica Swale penned *Blue Stockings* (2013) and then *Nell Gwynn* (2015). And for three of them even the first play was not the debut at the Elizabethan playhouse: Shepherd had already directed *The Two Gentlemen of Verona* in 1996 and Thomas Dekker's *The Honest Whore* in 1998 and acted in the 1998 *Merchant of Venice* as Antonio; Walker had played a minor role in the 2007 *Othello*; and Jessica Swale was the director of Nell Leyshon's *Bedlam* (2010).

What is more, the consciousness of these choices is confirmed by the fact that Ché Walker was actually cast as a Senator and a Soldier in *Othello* after being commissioned what was to become *The Frontline*, precisely in order to make him experience the theatre's space (Curtis 2008). Walker wrote his play during the run of the

Shakespearean production; in his words, 'I was in three scenes in the first Act, then had a two-and-a-half hour break during which I'd sit in the attic, wearing my doublet and hose and bushy beard, writing' (Neill 2008: 2), 'with a sword as well. And I wrote it by hand, with *Othello* pulsing away through the floorboards' (Westenberg 2009). If this image may sound a little mythologizing, there is no doubt that both the playwright and the theatre management did all they could to embed the new script's roots in the playhouse.

When the new authors are full-time writers and can fill no other role in the Globe, there is evidence that they are strongly encouraged to attend performances as members of the audience. To quote but a few, Howard Brenton (2007, 2014b), Chris Hannan (2011) and Nell Leyshon (2010 EOSI) in talking about their work have explicitly referred to their experience as spectators reflecting on how this particular stage works from the point of view of the playwright.

These choices and practices show that the members of the management board keep Sam Wanamaker's vision alive in that they still see Shakespeare's Globe as first and foremost an opportunity to experiment in the present with a theatre architecture that has hatched one of the greatest flourishings of English drama and has never been quite reproduced since. Their policy concerning new playwriting is consequently aimed at producing texts that are specifically conceived for the playhouse's peculiarities, so as to test its possibilities in the twenty-first century just as Shakespeare and his contemporaries did in the sixteenth and seventeenth.

# 2

# Presenting the Past

The complex condition of Shakespeare's Globe Theatre as a possible monument and its sometimes-bewildering artistic mix of old and new elements or aspects are consequences of the elaborate relationship this cultural enterprise tends to establish between the present and the past, one that asserts continuity and stresses similarity or even identity rather than distance.

Tradition is obviously foregrounded by a playhouse built with accurately researched designs, materials and techniques of a past age and explicitly dedicated to the genius of an immortal author. The reconstructed working theatre may almost be read as an emblem of the 'invented traditions' described by Eric Hobsbawm (1983) for the careful creation of a continuity between its activity and the life of its predecessor, in spite of the centuries-long gap that separates them. In contrast with most of Hobsbawm's examples, its constructions – material and symbolic – are based on accurate historical research, but its driving force is unquestionably the desire to form a bond between a present reality and a past perceived as glorious.

As a result, the Elizabethan-style playhouse tends to create an intricate web of references to different time frames that goes beyond the discrepancies in date and duration between the fictional setting and actual realization of most performances. The new scripts written for the Globe are a lively hub of such multiple chronologies, both because they often include more time layers and for the playwrights' conscious reactions to this elaborate context. Dramatists face the challenge of a theatre explicitly dedicated to Shakespeare and engage with this connection, ever-visible in the venue's architecture and décor, but they also harness the historical sensibility conjured up by such a locale. So it is worth investigating both the nature of this unusual time machine and the ways in which it has been employed.

# Multiple time planes

In order to appreciate the twenty-first-century playwrights' creative responses to the complex system of time frames evoked by the Globe, it is first necessary to clarify this web of references itself, and to analyse the kind of relations it tends to establish between various presents and pasts, especially when the reconstructed playhouse hosts new drama.

Raised as near as possible to the site of a building destroyed nearly 400 years before, with techniques of that age, and bearing the name of its predecessor, the Globe seems to be a perfect example of what Pierre Nora termed 'lieux de mémoire', sites of memory (1989). These objects (not necessarily places) 'anchor, condense and express the exhausted capital of our collective memory' (ibid.: 24) and the reconstructed theatre speaks volumes about the desire to live 'hallucinations of the past' (ibid.: 17) that characterizes a time in which the powerful, unconscious, social continuity of memory has been almost completely replaced by the questioning, consciously subjective distance of history and even of historiographical reflection.

Still, though clearly informed by 'a will to remember' (ibid.: 19), Shakespeare's Globe is certainly among 'those composite sites in which the commemorative element is only one amid many symbolic meanings' (ibid.: 23). What is more, some of those other symbolic meanings point unequivocally to the present, since not only the playhouse operates in the context of the twenty-first century, but it is also specifically devoted to the most ephemeral of arts, the theatre. A working creative space, with its unusual architecture it marks a distance, and distance is enough to distinguish history from memory, as Nora remarks: 'with the appearance of the trace, of mediation, of distance, we are not in the realm of true memory but of history' (ibid.: 8). Yet, while the typical *lieu de mémoire* emphasizes a fundamental discontinuity, denouncing the fact that 'it is no longer genesis that we seek but instead the decipherment of what we are in the light of what we are no longer' (ibid.: 18), the

Globe's ostensible antiquity does not entail a radical difference, it rather seems to highlight the fact that today's spectators can enjoy the same things that their ancestors appreciated. So if on the one hand the reconstructed theatre may be described as a 'devotional institution' (ibid.: 12) characterized by its 'nostalgic dimension' (ibid.), on the other it does not 'seem beleaguered and cold' (ibid.). The 'faith' that founded it has apparently succeeded in reviving the spirit of its predecessor – or rather in giving this new embodiment a new vitality, because while obviously referring back to Elizabethan and Jacobean drama it keeps attracting audiences and even staging plays that belong to the third millennium.

Nevertheless, today's spectators experience a sort of temporal displacement in Shakespeare's Globe, where they perceive not only, as in any theatre, the two times of fiction and performance, but also at least a third one, the original playhouse's. The result may be compared to the bewilderment Marc Augé sketches as arising from the sight of places that match the descriptions in well-known and beloved novels, which turn out to be '"uchronias", not outside history ... but enmeshed in too many histories (memories of the author's and of the narrator's, the protagonist's time-line, general and specific historical references) and therefore belonging at the same time to the past, to the present and to the future'[1] (1989: 129–30). Similarly, theatregoers can feel the superposition of the Elizabethan age, the characters' timeline and their own present, all equally lively and visible in the sunlight.

Precisely because the actuality of fellow spectators and actors does not give way completely to the fiction either of the play or of the reconstruction, Shakespeare's Globe does not belong, on the contrary, to the category most studied by Augé, that of 'non-places' (1992, 1997). While theme parks are such, because they encourage visitors to ignore the anomaly constituted by each other's presence and plunge into the alternative reality evoked by scenery and costumed figures, thus isolating themselves rather than creating connections, the open-air amphitheatre tends to emphasize the participation of audience-members and almost to introduce them to each other. Several phenomena bear witness to its success in fostering relationships, from the ephemeral community constituted by the queuing groundlings to the Friends of Shakespeare's Globe, who share specific activities,[2] to the sense of belonging that endows the playhouse with hundreds of volunteer stewards.[3]

Shakespeare's Globe can then be only in part described as a *lieu de mémoire* and not at all as a non-place; it shares the temporal complexity of a uchronia, but it does not exactly fall into this category, which Augé has moreover only briefly outlined; it may perhaps be more usefully and precisely defined as 'heterotopia'. In Michel Foucault's words, heterotopias are, together with utopias, 'Spaces which are linked with all the others, and yet at variance somehow with all the other emplacements'[4] ([1967] 1994b: 178); while utopias have no real place, though, heterotopias are

> Real places, actual places, places that are designed into the very institution of society, which are sorts of actually realized utopias in which the real emplacements, all the other real emplacements that can be found within the culture are, at the same time, represented, contested, and reversed, sorts of places that are outside all places, although they are actually localizable. (ibid.)[5]

Theatres are among the most conspicuous examples of heterotopias because of the double reality they enclose, simultaneously fictional and actual, but Shakespeare's Globe conjures up another aspect of Foucault's concept, i.e. the temporal discontinuity that he terms 'heterochronia' ([1967] 1994b: 759–60). This break in the linear perception of time's flow takes two main forms: in libraries and museums, an accumulation of tokens that virtually eternalizes different moments; in festivals or similar exceptional events, the creation of a separate, strictly ephemeral world. The working reconstruction of an Elizabethan playhouse in the twenty-first century seems to offer a third template, linking two distant eras in a way that combines the fleeting nature of an experience and the permanent bulk of a building.

Foucault had already described what was then a new heterochronia that conjoins the two main ones: those holiday resorts that provide a reconstruction of primitive lifestyles, which are 'in one sense akin to the libraries and the museums, for, by rediscovering Polynesian life one abolishes time, but time is also regained, the whole history of humanity goes back to its source as if in a kind of grand immediate knowledge' ([1967] 1994b: 183).[6] Both these artificial villages and Shakespeare's Globe can be reasonably placed somewhere between the 'eternitary' and the 'chronic' heterotopias, because they enable people to temporarily step out of their time and get in touch with a meaningful moment in the past, but some fundamental differences keep them clearly distinct.

While the two 'time-travels' share the same direction from the historical-chronological point of view, heading towards the past, their cultural-geographical trajectories appear to be inverse: the Elizabethan theatre is visited as a temple of high culture, whereas the Polynesian villages cited by Foucault seem to attract the patronizing 'hegemonic white Eurocentric gaze' analysed by Susan Bennett as a constant threat to intercultural performances (1997: 189–91). In other words, the lurking colonial attitude that identifies a foreign lifestyle, perceived as exotic and primitive, with its own remote past, cannot be confused with the prospect of approaching a major cultural icon, even though they are both based on the opportunity to inhabit a reconstructed alien setting.[7]

What is more, the status of the actions tourists can observe in these two environments is quite different, as can be seen in the extensive comparison between Shakespeare's Globe and Plimoth Plantation (and other reconstructed historical sites) drawn by W. B. Worthen (2003: 79–116), and Penelope Woods's reflections on the same subject in relation to issues of community- and identity-building (2012: 266). The holiday village can offer a re-enactment of traditional activities,[8] in which the visitor may be allowed, or even invited, to join. Shakespeare's Globe, on the contrary, operates as a regular twenty-first-century theatre, in which people (cast, crew, creatives, security and front-of-house staff, stewards, food vendors) do the jobs they have been trained for, not as a way to present what would be done in a specified context but as their work in itself. The difference may appear to be blurred by the fact that actors are central to both heterochronias, but in one case they pretend to be part of a different age, and usually to practise another profession, while in the other they come on stage as straightforward contemporary players who impersonate characters of any time. Things get even more complicated in the case of 'original practices' performances, i.e. when Shakespeare's Globe produces a play with techniques as near as possible to those of Elizabethan theatres (employing hand-made costumes and props, sixteenth-century musical instruments or, most conspicuously, an all-male cast), so that one may wonder whether the role of an actor is, for instance, Hamlet, or Burbage-in-Hamlet. The answer may be found in the performer's purpose, that is to come across to his actual, contemporary audience, rather than to reproduce a previous rendering which might appear faulty nowadays.

The spectators' position, both literal and metaphorical, highlights the difference from another point of view. Tourists are usually encouraged to take part in holiday-resort historical reconstructions, e.g. by wearing more or less appropriate clothes or by trying their hand at some simple activities, and their inclusion in the fictional world is manifested by their sharing the performers' space. In the Globe, on the contrary, audience members cannot join the actors by climbing on stage or by somehow pretending to be Elizabethan spectators, and while the former prohibition may appear obvious, the latter has been enforced in sharp contrast to other theatres' policy: during the Prologue season the management refused admittance to people in sixteenth-century costumes (Keenan and Davidson 1997: 147; Kennedy 2009: 107), in spite of such dressing up being elsewhere entirely accepted or even promoted.[9]

On the other hand, the fact that spectators actually did turn up in Elizabethan garb, and the Globe's staff needed to repress this behaviour, points to the replica's possible ambiguity. In the words of Siobhan Keenan and Peter Davidson, 'before the structure was even finished, it had been appropriated, theme-parked (by its visitors) and (at the same time) reified, all in direct contradiction to the stated aims of those who have worked for the project' (1997: 147); this reading – and use – of the building was immediately condemned and checked by the management's reaction, but its spontaneous appearance among the Globe's visitors testifies to its viability. The status of the reconstruction has been repeatedly questioned, and although its creators keep defending it from such associations, critics often compare it to theme parks, even to utterly fictional ones like Disneyland (Kennedy 2009), with reference to the audience's composition, attitude and perceptions. These relations are certainly traced as part of a wider reflection on the increasingly strong links between stage productions and tourism industry (Bennett 2005), but they also have a specific aspect, that can be seen to focus on the Globe's unique heterochronia and on its similarity to that of the holiday village described by Foucault.

The core of the problem seems to be the fact that Shakespeare's Globe is a replica, not an authentic Elizabethan playhouse:

this difference keeps it apart from the ancient Greek theatres of Epidaurus and Syracuse, for instance, where classical tragedies and comedies are produced for twenty-first-century audiences. In this perspective, the Globe would be a sort of fake monument, but it seems unreasonable to consider it a sham when it is avowedly a reconstruction, and all discourses introducing it focus on Sam Wanamaker almost as much as on Shakespeare, so that its position is far clearer than that of many heavily restored artworks.

A potential source of confusion is that the theatre is architecturally and institutionally connected to a permanent exhibition focused on Shakespeare, on the context of his works, and on the stage techniques of his times: although written and spoken explanations point out that many of the items showcased, including the playhouse where the tour ends, are not original period pieces, the habitual connection between historical display and actual heritage site may somewhat mislead the less attentive visitors.

The spectators' perception lies, of course, at the heart of all these arguments, and it is interesting to notice that such different (almost opposite) analyses as Dennis Kennedy's and Penelope Woods's – the first one centred on the Globe as a tourist attraction, the second highlighting the audience's complex negotiations – share the same core remark: at least some visitors, though aware that the playhouse is a replica, choose to regard it as a genuine Elizabethan building, applying a 'willing suspension of disbelief' analogous to the one required by the fictive performance (Kennedy 2009: 112; Woods 2012: 72). They behave almost as if, overwhelmed by one of Augé's uchronias, they pretended to have come by the villa once inhabited by a novel's characters. This observation suggests that a shift of focus might be advisable in investigating this phenomenon, from the object of such a complex attitude to the contradictory need for reality – so strong as to embrace an openly artificial one – this voluntary illusion seems to reveal.

However, Shakespeare's Globe is apparently the ideal site for such a superposition of different realities because of the heterochronia it constitutes: it was built in the last decade of the twentieth century with materials and techniques in use 400 years earlier, and still more layers of history overlap in the playhouse. A very conspicuous, though not constant, one is provided by the time in which the plays are set, that may not coincide with either Shakespeare's or the spectators'. In some architectural and decorative features of the theatre lies, on the contrary, a fixed but subtle reference to antiquity: its round shape was originally influenced by Renaissance interpretations of Roman theatres as described by Vitruvius, and the wood painted to look like marble projected Tudor constructions into the majestic opulence of the classical world. Although this connection is probably lost on the majority of spectators nowadays, because these characteristics are no longer prominent in the popular image of antiquity and taken together they would rather spell 'Elizabethan' to most, it was quite clear in the late sixteenth century.

Therefore, to Shakespeare's contemporaries the Globe was a reconstructed classical theatre, and so 'itself a reading of the past and a living theatrical space' (Keenan and Davidson 1997: 148), just like its replica is to us. This 'double signal' (ibid.: 147–8) was then and is now constantly in sight of every spectator, even when the play is set in the same age the architecture refers to, because the audience takes four fifths of the 'wooden O' (and nearly the whole circle if the Lords' Rooms are occupied), in the sunlight, so that each of its members has several others in view. The Globe's heterochronia thus offers a spectacle of up to four superimposed time planes:

1. The punters' present;
2. The past the reconstruction points to;
3. The age in which the performance is set (if different from the previous);
4. Only in the modern replica, antiquity as seen in Tudor England, and represented in the architecture and decor of the playhouse.

In order to make the distinction between the different time planes clear, it may be useful to consider some examples: Table 2.1 lists them from the perspective of spectators attending different performances, namely Shakespeare's *Henry VIII* in 1613 and 2010, *Julius Caesar* in 1599 and *The Comedy of Errors* in 2006, and Jessica Swale's *Blue Stockings* in 2013.

Not all spectators in the reconstructed Globe actually perceive the reference to antiquity in its design, of course, but the number of those who do may be less small than expected, since guided tours of the theatre or the exhibition point it out.

*Table 2.1 Time planes that can be perceived at Shakespeare's Globe Theatre*

| Time plane | Audience's time | Reconstructed time | Fictional time | Previously reconstructed time |
|---|---|---|---|---|
| *Part of the spectacle that evokes the time plane* | *Other spectators* | *Playhouse* | *Production* | *Playhouse in perspective* |
| Example 1: 1613 viewer of *Henry VIII* | 1613 | Antiquity | 1520–1533 | – |
| Example 2: 2010 viewer of *Henry VIII* | 2010 | Late sixteenth century | 1520–1533 | Antiquity |
| Example 3: 1599 viewer of *Julius Caesar* | 1599 | Antiquity | Antiquity | – |
| Example 4: 2006 viewer of *The Comedy of Errors* | 2006 | Late sixteenth century | Antiquity | Antiquity |
| Example 5: 2013 viewer of *Blue Stockings* | 2013 | Late sixteenth century | Late nineteenth century | Antiquity |

The main objection to this parallelism between what the Globe was in the sixteenth century and what its reconstruction is now concerns its programmes, that are deeply different, paradoxically, because they mostly bill the same titles: while Burbage's theatre produced exclusively contemporary plays and never mounted the classics its architecture referred to, Wanamaker's replica is mainly devoted to performances of Elizabethan texts, the same that made up its model's seasons. Yet this dissimilarity can be ascribed to their contexts, since nowadays revivals of evergreen masterpieces are quite common and attract wide audiences, but in Shakespeare's age no drama of previous eras was ever staged. In other words, both playhouses' programmes are in tune with their times, the old one producing only contemporary work, the new one presenting both plays that belong to the canon and new ones, its specificity being that the only classics it features are Shakespeare and other Elizabethan or Jacobean authors.

This comparison foregrounds the importance of new playwriting at the reconstructed Globe, because producing contemporary drama is part of the way it operates in the twenty-first century, so as to be neither a museum display nor a theme park but a working theatre. Thus, its duplicity is indisputable, and the way spectators perceive it and inhabit it is consequently complex, but while its connection with the past is structural, in that it resides essentially in its architecture, its functional dimension appears to be firmly grounded in the present.

## Shakespeare's ghost

Even when producing new drama, Shakespeare's Globe tends to establish connections with the works and times of its eponymous author; after all, its architecture and décor are a visible enough memento that new scripts must necessarily take into consideration. Moreover, the reconstructed theatre's seasons are usually billed as a structured whole, under a general title, so that Elizabethan or Jacobean and newly written texts appear to be necessarily linked in one way or another.

It is not surprising that the reconstructed Globe has never produced re-writings of Shakespeare's works: showcasing new versions side by side with acclaimed masterpieces in a place dedicated to their author might hurt some devotees' feelings, as it could seem to imply that the original texts are not quite universal, and it would certainly put the playwrights in a very difficult position, suggesting direct, close comparisons. Yet connections and similarities between the new texts and the Bard's are bound to be remarked anyway, and most of the Globe's twenty-first-century authors have embraced this situation instead of fleeing it, fairly often by highlighting some points in common themselves. References to Shakespeare and his plays tend to cast the new writers as heirs rather than rivals of their predecessor. At the same time, they offer plenty of occasions for jokes built on a knowledge base at least part of the audience is likely to share and on an interest it has shown by visiting the theatre.

The basic technique of this kind is to cite the playhouse itself, either explicitly (as in the flowing patter of *Gabriel*'s waterman, G 32) or by playing on its name. Puns on 'the globe' are obviously more funny and fascinating when the whole sentence fits both the world and the homonymous venue, as in *Under the Black Flag*'s description of a ship that sets the scene for the following events while describing the adventurous condition performers and spectators share on another plane:

> this wooden hull The Lion's Whelp our vessel, her deck below a stage for all the world to see, cast upon the waters of this orb we call the Globe, in transport and suspension across the Seven Seas and beyond the Seven Wonders to stories not yet told – in search of distant shores – some remembered, others half forgot, some lying in wait we come at through a mist, and suddenly crashed upon their rocks. (*UBF* 29)[10]

If Bent's lines refer to a performance, Oswald's apocalyptic vision, centred on the moment when 'the entire globe goes up in flames, / With all its blessings and its blames' (*S* 60), is apparently inspired by the fire that destroyed the first Globe in 1613 and is still seen as a menace to the reconstructed wooden building. This is a clear allusion to something theatregoers cannot see but are very likely to have read in the programme or heard on a visit to the exhibition (if they did not know it beforehand).

Chris Hannan went even further by writing a dialogue that links the well-known question of the reconstructed playhouse's authenticity with the themes of identity and appearances:

**Natty**  D'you like my house though?
**Teresa**  It's mock-Tudor? Is it a copy of summing?
**Natty**  It's not a copy, Teresa. Every little thing you see is an authentic reproduction. Cept the white marble. That's real.
**Teresa**  Thass the only reason I'm here, case you was losing touch with reality. I got nothin material things but I got the streets and the realness.
...
**Natty**  Iss the spiritual things in life that's important in life. *(Pointing to her ceiling.)* Thass the gods up there. All them gold bottoms. I said I want the gods done in gold or it won't be realistic. (*GS* 38–9)[11]

The phrase 'authentic reproduction', especially in opposition to 'mock-Tudor' and 'copy', obviously recalls the disputed status of the venue itself. Natty's eagerness to specify that the white marbles are real distances the conversation from the playhouse with a further joke: the Globe's 'marbles' are prevalently coloured, so the white ones are part of the more evidently fake production set; what is more, it is easy to see that the structural elements of the theatre are all wooden and painted to look like marble, so the stone is the only thing that cannot be considered in any way authentic. The distinction between Natty's house and the venue is established by this paradox and by the consideration on the realistically golden-bottomed gods on the ceiling (a humorous allusion, once again, to the roof that covers part of the stage, which is called 'heaven', although it is painted with the zodiac, not a pantheon). Nevertheless, the two sisters' dialogue is likely to trigger reflections on the meaning and value of the reconstructed Globe. It probably constitutes the most felicitous employment of such references to the performance's visible environment because it links the play's core themes with the spectators' present situation and implicitly questions their own attitude while entertaining them with a series of funnily paradoxical allusions.

The association with the celebrity's nouveau-riche villa somehow questions the building's taste, but the implications of the dissimilarities emerging from the lines quoted above will be crucially confirmed in a Shakespeare-themed exchange. When Baz states he has nothing to say, a Lear-like[12] incensed Natty protests that 'we have the privilege to speak the language of William so-called Shakespeare innit; the least you can do is aspire to that privilege by saying something English that we'll remember. Just quote some Shakespeare if you can't make nothing up original' (*GS* 51). Asked for an example, she promptly recites the refrain of a song from musical *Oliver!* ('food glorious food hot sausage and mustard', *GS* 52) and misquotes a Winston Churchill speech ('never in the whole upsetness of human history have so many been twatted by so few', *GS* 52). For Natty, Shakespeare is only a buzzword, ultimately interchangeable with any other cultural, popular or historical cliché of Britishness. It is then up to the spectators to ask themselves whether they share this attitude or they expect something more substantial from their visit to the reconstructed theatre. Anyway, Hannan humorously addresses the issue of heritage by playing on the literary as well as architectural ghosts that haunt the Globe and thus puts to use the playhouse's uniqueness in a meaningful and effective way.

Elsewhere, references to Shakespeare and his works are much less consequential and might even sound perfunctory if they were not quite in keeping with the situation (e.g. in *Blue Stockings*'s university setting, *BS* 18, 24, 52). Sometimes a quotation may reveal a character's unexpected knowledge (Benny's 'methinks the lady doth protest too much', *F* 13, using not a pop song but *Hamlet*, 3.2.219, to make a comment) or lack thereof (when Paine does not recognize *Measure for Measure*, 3.1.118–19, in Danton's words 'Aye, but to die, and go we know not where, To lie in cold obstruction till we rot', *TAT* 176). In other situations, Shakespearean material is only employed for fun, as in the already discussed 'I'm more an antique Roman than a dame' (*S* 74).

A much more extensive presence of the Bard's works can be found in *Under the Black Flag*, an adventurous tale of piracy and revenge rooted in its historical setting, the Cromwellian Commonwealth, that purports to portray the early years of Long John Silver's buccaneering career. Simon Bent, intrigued by the discovery that off the Gold Coast around 1650 slaves on sale were made to perform an adaptation of *Hamlet* as a way to showcase them (Woddis 2006: 9), has two of his characters – the protagonist himself and Hamlet, named so after the role he has been assigned – try to free themselves during the play (*UBF* 41, 43, 45, 50–3). The result is a metatheatrical scene which often employs the tragedy's text to comic effect: when Hamlet is left alone on stage because the ghost is missing and an audience member comments 'he doesn't know what to do' (*UBF* 51), quoting the abridgement's prologue ('Hamlet, the prince, suspects foul play and doesn't know what to do', *UBF* 50), the actor begins 'To be or not to be ...' (*UBF* 51; *Hamlet* 3.1.58); the mention of 'the oppressor's wrong' (*UBF* 51; *Hamlet* 3.1.73) is immediately followed by the entrance of his companion fighting the slave traders; when the pirate captain Kees intervenes in order to stop the attempted escape, he takes on the role of Gertrude in her dialogue with Hamlet (*UBF* 52; *Hamlet* 3.4.9–12), thus recalling also the prince's addressing Claudius as his mother (*Hamlet* 4.3.51–5); the telltale who has revealed the plan is involuntarily killed with the words 'a rat. Dead' after he has cried for help from behind the arras where he is hiding (*UBF* 52; *Hamlet* 3.4.22–3); the performance is definitively closed by Tom shouting 'stop the play. Lights, lights, lights' (*UBF* 53; *Hamlet* 3.2.256–8).

   This conspicuous metatheatrical moment is not the only passage that reminds spectators of Shakespeare, though. After learning that John Silver's previous acting experience was as Julius Caesar, Kees gives him some advice that brings to mind Hamlet's recommendations to the players (*UBF* 45; *Hamlet* 3.2.1–45). Even without referring to stage practices or drama, several situations or images in the play point to a well-known Shakespearean precedent. The description of the Sultan's barge, for instance, recalls that of Cleopatra's (*UBF* 46; *Antony and Cleopatra* 2.2.198–204) and Isabelle's insistence that the only safe place for young Ann would be a nunnery echoes Hamlet's words to Ophelia (*UBF* 62; *Hamlet* 2.1.123, 2.1.138–9, 2.1.142, 2.1.152). Silver's observation that 'the sea is no respecter of persons' (*UBF* 140) paraphrases the Boatswain's 'what cares these roarers for the name of king?' (*The Tempest* 1.1.15–16), and the desperation engendered by the storm in passengers and seamen aboard the ship more generally recalls the opening scene of *The Tempest*. Ann's cross-dressing (*UBF* 96) follows that of several Shakespearean heroines; like Rosalind, she adopts this disguise in order to rejoin her father (*As You Like It* 1.3.103–21), although the menacing atmosphere that surrounds her and her entering an all-male group of outlaws bring her closer to Imogen (*Cymbeline* 3.4,

3.6, 4.1, 4.2). Most conspicuously, the ghost that demands revenge (*UBF* 103, 112, 114–16, 119–21) is significantly named Hamlet, like the dead king of Denmark (*Hamlet* 1.5, 3.4.93–105).

In conclusion, *Under the Black Flag* displays a remarkable array of references to and quotations from Shakespeare's works, not to mention the more general analogies with *Hamlet* and *King Lear* entailed by the themes of madness, loss, vengeance and regret (and the father–daughter relationship in the case of *King Lear*) that both the writer and several reviewers have stressed (Connor 2006; Irvine 2006; Shuttleworth 2006; Woddis 2006: 9). But they do not add anything to the text's meaning, their function is rather to amuse the knowing spectators, sometimes with specifically funny connections and otherwise with the quiz-like pleasure of recognizing the undeclared allusions.

A jocular mood seems to pervade other Shakespearean references too. Such is the case of the innuendo recognizable in *The Golden Ass*'s gag of the bear (*GA* 81), one of the myriad interlinked adventures that make up Peter Oswald's dramatization of Apuleius's *Metamorphoses*. In the Latin novel a she-bear frightens Lucius, the man turned into a donkey in consequence of his reckless curiosity, who runs away (7.24); later on, the shepherds find the corpse of the boy who was in charge of the ass, presumably killed by the beast (7.26). In the play, the protagonist has a short, absurd dialogue with the bear, who says it is the boy who is going to die but denies Lucius any explanation as to why; then the donkey flees and the bear leaves with its destined victim. The final stage direction 'Exit **Bear** with **Timinos**' (*GA* 81) is bound to remind Shakespeare lovers of the well-known 'Exit, pursued by a bear' (*The Winter's Tale* 3.3.57) with which Antigonus is dispatched to a considerably sudden violent death. The stage business spectators witness is essentially the same: a bear appears out of the blue and immediately leaves again with its victim to be. So the beast's refusal to motivate the boy's fate sounds like a humorous comment on the episode in *The Winter's Tale* as well as on the innumerable unexpected plot twists of *The Golden Ass*.

Not only are there dozens of short and not too consequential allusions to Shakespeare in these plays, but also sentences that could very well stand without any such reference tend to acquire one in the reconstructed theatre, and their authors are likely to exploit this effect. When *Bedlam*'s Narrator begins his speech on the fall into insanity (*B* 70–2) with 'I wasn't always Tom o'Bedlam' (*B* 70), for instance, the Globe's audience tends to think of Edgar's choice to take on the role of a mad beggar under that stereotyped name (*The Tragedy of King Lear* 2.2). The monologue is thus made more moving both by the image it has evoked of 'the basest and most poorest shape/That ever penury in contempt of man/Brought near to beast' (*The Tragedy of King Lear* 2.2.170–72) and by the contrast between the assumed identity of a man who is destined to become king after all and the bleak future that awaits the destitute deranged people represented by the Narrator.

Samuel Adamson's *Gabriel*, a collection of playlets set in the heyday of the natural trumpet, presents a much more extensive connection with a Shakespearean comedy, although mediated by a reworking, because the interlinked episodes 'The Fairy Queen' (*G* 55–60), 'Lucky Kate' (*G* 78–83) and 'The Lost Score' (*G* 83–94) are based on Henry Purcell's opera derived from *A Midsummer Night's Dream*, *The Fairy Queen*. Actress-singer Kate, actress Hannah, virtuoso trumpeter John and underling Peter make up a tangled quartet of lovers just like Hermia, Helena, Lysander and Demetrius, although with a different structure (Kate and John are in love with respectively Paul and Hannah, who are engaged to be married) and their problems are solved by a flower's juice, squeezed in the eyes of the two fiancés, that leads them to requite the affections of the other two (*G* 93–4). Their last speeches, in which they express the doubt their new-found harmony might be just a dream (*G* 94), recall the lovers' uncertainties at the end of the bewildering midsummer night (*A Midsummer Night's Dream* 4.1.186–97). There are also more specific similarities between their utterances and those of Shakespeare's characters: John quotes Helena's lines 'Use me but as your spaniel: spurn me, strike me,/Neglect me, lose me; only give me leave,/Unworthy as I am, to follow you' (*G* 58; *A Midsummer Night's Dream* 2.1.205–7) and Kate Hermia's 'I frown upon him, yet he loves me still. I give him curses, yet he gives me love. The more I hate, the more he follows me' (*G* 81; *A Midsummer Night's Dream* 1.1.194, 1.1.196, 1.1.198); Peter and Hannah echo Demetrius's words, though less precisely, when they say respectively 'it's as if our love has melted like snow and now the object and pleasure of my eye … is Kate' (*G* 93; *A Midsummer Night's Dream* 4.1.164–5, 4.1.169–70) and 'like in some sickness, I loathed this food, but … I've … come to my natural taste, and now

I do wish it, love it, long for it' (*G* 93; *A Midsummer Night's Dream* 4.1.172–4). Numerous though they are, these many resemblances and quotations do not engage spectators in anything more than a pleasant game of allusions, in line with the play's rhematic subtitle, *An Entertainment with Trumpet.*

Many audience members were facilitated in recognizing these references by the fact that a production of *A Midsummer Night's Dream* had opened about a month earlier and was still being performed as part of the same season, so that the Globe's most faithful patrons had recently heard those lines. This is not always the rule with Shakespearean quotations in the reconstructed theatre but it happens fairly often, especially when suggestions are based on less known plays or seldom repeated passages.

Something similar happened on a wider scale with *The Storm*, Peter Oswald's rewriting of Plautus' comedy *Rudens* that was billed alongside *The Tempest* and *Pericles, Prince of Tyre*. In this instance, the plays were linked not so much by quotations as by common themes and situations. The similarity between *The Storm* and *The Tempest* is made obvious in their titles, which are synonymous by choice, the most common translation for 'rudens' being 'the rope'. Yet Peter Oswald's decision has a possible source in the original Latin, because 'rudens' could be interpreted not as a noun but as the present participle of the verb 'rudo', 'to roar', 'to wail' or 'to shriek', thus leading to the English version's subtitle, *The Howler*, that can in turn be read as a synonym of *The Storm*. This rather complex train of thought goes to prove that the playwright's choice is not arbitrary, but not the expected one either. It clearly shows the intention to emphasize the parallel with *The Tempest*: both plays begin with a raging sea that causes a shipwreck, in consequence of which, in the end, a young woman is restored to the condition from which she was violently removed as a child.

From other points of view, though, a clear opposition emerges. In *The Tempest*, father and daughter have been living together, secluded from society, while in *The Storm* they have been separated and are reunited only in the course of the play. The prostitute Palaestra may well be considered the opposite of Miranda, who wonders at the existence of several men (*The Tempest* 5.1.184–7). Even more consequential for the two plots is the stark contrast between Prospero, who has carefully planned all the day's events (*The Tempest* 1.2.238–42, 3.3.83–93, 4.1.139–42, 5.1.1–6), even causing and managing, by means of Ariel, the storm itself (*The Tempest* 1.2.1–2, 1.2.15–16, 1.2.194–6), but in the final scene renounces his magic, and so his control over nature (*The Tempest* 5.1.33–57) and Daemones, who has decided 'I will never make another / Decision in my life' (*S* 73), and therefore maintains a passive attitude throughout most of the story, but gradually gets to the point of taking the initiative by freeing his slave Sceparnio the moment nobody is asking him to do so any more (*S* 91).

Besides the tempests, it is perhaps precisely some of the points on which *The Storm* and *The Tempest* diverge that bring the former nearer to *Pericles*: like Daemones, the protagonist is separated from his daughter Marina (*Pericles* 3.4), who is kidnapped (*Pericles* 4.2. 140–7) and sold to a brothel (*Pericles* 4.3), just like Palaestra (*S* 13, 29). Both plays also hint at incest, although in Shakespeare's it is consummated by two secondary characters (*Pericles* 1.Ch.), while in Oswald's it is a risk Daemones and Palaestra themselves run (*S* 66–70, 84–5, 87).

Most of these analogies would also be true of Plautus' *Rudens*, which was probably chosen as *The Storm*'s source for this reason, but Oswald's will to draw his play closer to the Shakespearean romances is evident in some changes he made. If the title points to *The Tempest*, an aspect of the ending is clearly reminiscent of *Pericles*: not in the Latin comedy, but only in its English re-writing, Daemones marries the priestess Ptolemocratia (*S* 76, 88, 89–90), thus somehow mirroring the king of Tyre's discovery that a vestal of Diana is his long-lost wife Thaisa (*Pericles* 5.3), to whom he is thus reunited.

So up to 2015 *The Storm* is probably the newly written text that is most closely associated with the Shakespearean works produced by the Globe in the same year, but a connection can almost always be found, and the season's title usually points it out. *The Golden Ass*, for instance, shared the 2002 stage with two other comedies exploring the multifarious mysteries and ultimate magic of love, *Twelfth Night* and *A Midsummer Night's Dream*, the latter featuring also another donkey-man, Bottom (*A Midsummer Night's Dream* 3.1.97–193, 3.2.6–34, 4.1.1–83). In 2011, 'The Word is God' celebrated 400 years of the King James Bible with *The Globe Mysteries*, the reflections and explorations of *Doctor Faustus* (Marlowe's), *Hamlet* and *Anne Boleyn*, and the complex intertwining of love and ethics that characterizes not only the story of Henry VIII and his second wife but also those of all the couples in *The God of Soho*, *Much Ado About Nothing* and *All's Well That Ends Well*. The 2014 season responded to the centenary of the First World War specifically, with *Doctor Scroggy's War*, and by means of a more general reflection on 'Arms and the Man' that evoked internecine as well as international conflicts, from antiquity to the present, not only in *Titus Andronicus*, *Antony and Cleopatra* and *Julius Caesar* but also in Simon Armitage's dramatization of *The Last Days of Troy*, David Eldridge's *Holy Warriors* and Richard Bean's mutineers on *Pitcairn*. In 2015 'Justice and Mercy' were discussed in Rory Mullarkey's version of *The Oresteia* as well as in *The Merchant of Venice*, *King John*, *Measure for Measure* and *Richard II*.

One way or another, Shakespeare's plays are never far from those written for the twenty-first-century Globe.

# Language centre-stage

When Peter Oswald became the first playwright to work for the reconstructed Globe, a strong accent was placed on the fact that his were verse plays. As a matter of fact, artistic director Mark Rylance's statement in the application for the Resident Dramatist Attachment Award begins with the assertion that 'Peter Oswald is an unusual playwright. He writes in verse, an activity that is far from fashionable' (p. 2).[13] Conversely, the writer said in the same context that 'before the building of the Globe, there wasn't a single theatre built for verse in Britain' (p. 5)[14], implying that the reconstructed playhouse was specifically meant for verse drama. Rylance explained that 'the original Globe plays are plays in which verse is always at the centre of the dramatic argument. The performance space demands this' (p. 2). Also Tim Carroll, who directed several productions for Shakespeare's Globe Theatre, among which those of Peter Oswald's three new plays – *Augustine's Oak*, *The Golden Ass* and *The Storm* – described *Augustine's Oak* as 'written mainly in verse for a space which was made for verse-speaking' (Neill 1999b: [5]).

Nevertheless, in the following years, new prose works too have been staged at Shakespeare's Globe Theatre. Writers have always considered words the means to supply the special effects the venue does not seem to allow, devoting a special care to the creation of appropriate, specific idioms, in the conviction, enucleated by Chris Hannan, that 'the audience has to enjoy the language. The space is an auditory space more than it is a visual space' (2014)[15] and 'the language reaches out to the audience; it draws them into a relationship with the stage' (ibid.). Other authors have shared their reflections on this theme and on the choices they made, e.g. Simon Bent (Woddis 2006: 8), Ché Walker (Neill 2008: 4; Neill 2013: 3–4), Frank McGuinness (Neill 2009: 4), or Nell Leyshon (2010), yet not all of them have felt it necessary to employ verse. Peter Oswald himself declares that he never thought 'the Globe was a theatre *only* for verse – just that it was designed with verse in mind, because the original on which it was modelled was designed with verse in mind' (private communication, 17 May 2017).[16] In other words, the Elizabethan architecture does not imply the rejection of prose; it just ensures the venue's suitability to verse, thus attracting authors interested in making this choice, which is anyway not unavoidable but due to an idiosyncratic preference or to the influence of the Shakespearean model.

Four plays entirely written in verse actually have still another motivation: Seamus Heaney's *The Burial at Thebes*, Frank McGuinness's *Helen*, Tony Harrison's *The Globe Mysteries* and Rory Mullarkey's *The Oresteia* are adaptations of verse dramas (respectively Sophocles's *Antigone*, Euripides's *Helen*, a selection of medieval mystery plays and Aeschylus's trilogy of the same title) and their form may therefore have been determined by these specific examples. The same observation is even more convincing in the case of *Man Falling Down*, a reflection on human destiny that starts with the Creation but then sees Adam and Eve, banished from the Garden of Eden, become modern-day refugees: its passages that come from Milton's and Blake's poems are obviously in verse, because Jack Shepherd and Oliver Cotton have simply reproduced the sources they had chosen, in these instances as well as when they have included prose excerpts from the Bible.[17]

*Liberty*, on the contrary, is entirely written in verse in spite of being the dramatization of a novel, Anatole France's *Les dieux ont soif* (The Gods Are Athirst). Glyn Maxwell, who had already conceived it in this form before it was destined for the Globe, asserts that

> verse on stage is nothing to do with lyrical uplift, or the past, or mystery. It … is a truer way of sounding the note of the passing

moment than prose is. Verse includes the ending of the breath
(in the life as well as the line), the pressure of silence, the gesture
towards memorability – like a plant towards light – and, in strict
craft terms, it deflects the author from simply following his usual
paths. (Robins 2008: 15)

When asked more specifically about the tradition he feels to
be a part of, he answers, 'my faith is based on Shakespeare, my
form on Robert Frost, my stories on old stories, and my characters
on the life I know' (ibid.). These statements are quite in harmony
with his play, in which verse implies a perceptible rhythm and a
pithy quality rather than a high-flown style, while its form is not
Shakespearean, constantly adopting as it does a flexible unrhyming
five-beat line. All in all, Maxwell's playwriting in verse does not
seem to be significantly influenced by the reconstructed theatre or
by its titular author.

More strongly reminiscent of the Bard's dramatic poetry are
those scripts that alternate verse and prose to specific effect. A small-
scale example can be found in the first playlet of *Gabriel*, 'When the
Trumpet Strikes', in which the very young Duke of Gloucester's
servants comment the action in rhyming couplets; after being 'called
to arms' by their six-year-old master, they finally explain: 'such epic
scenes of war we oft rehearse - / That's why our lines are in heroic
verse' (*G* 26). The same meaningful intermingling of different forms
can be found with wider extension and often deeper implications
in Peter Oswald's plays, which – it may be worth remarking –
were probably modelled on Shakespeare's works more than any
of the following, because this was explicitly Mark Rylance's initial
suggestion, as stated in the application for the Resident Dramatist
Attachment Award 1998/99 (p. 3).

In *The Golden Ass*, different metres and occasional passages
in prose are employed in accordance with the situation, without
foregrounding these variations, which are on the contrary exposed
and mocked, like almost all theatrical conventions, in *The Storm*.
Towards the end of the play, Sceparnio accidentally shoots himself
and although the bullet is said to have gone straight through his
head without hitting anything, his first words cause some alarm:

**Sceparnio**   Free. I am free. No wishes. I am empty.
                No fears. I am a sky with no horizon,

> A fish free-floating out of school, bound homewards,
> Into the air, a leaf in love with falling.

Daemones Oh no!

Ptolemocratia Has he lost his mind?

Daemones Much worse! I am afraid he's gone into verse. (S 86)[18]

This metatheatrically funny dialogue actually encloses a reflection on one of the main serious themes in the play, freedom. Sceparnio is a slave, and the other characters have never heard him speak in verse, although the audience has, in a soliloquy, when he first sees a woman emerging from the sea and hopes to be on his way to liberty (S 18–19). When his head is hurt, he feels free, and he abandons prose to say so, while for his master, Daemones, and the priestess Ptolemocratia this is a sign that he is out of himself, because according to a rooted theatrical convention, poetry is not at all appropriate for the character of a slave.

As a matter of fact, Ampelisca and Palaestra, who are in the pimps' possession, go through similar changes. The former always speaks prose in public, and adopts verse only twice: when she finds refuge in the temple of Venus, believing her owners to be dead or at least lost in the shipwreck (S 31–2) and then in a soliloquy on the same subject (S 39–40). Palaestra also switches to verse when she has apparently regained her liberty, either because Plesidippus has bought it or as a consequence of having found her father and proved she was born free (S 78, 83–4, 89–91).[19] Actually, she does not return to prose when she pretends to be voluntarily going back to her life as a prostitute (S 87), perhaps because she is presenting this as her own choice, or maybe unconsciously giving away the fact that she is lying in order to lead Charmides towards the 'weak spot' that will crumble under his weight. Finally, it is when she hears Sceparnio is 'back to prose again' (S 91) that Palaestra asks her father to free him, implicitly confirming the connection between verse and liberty.

If in *The Storm* 'the free speak freely with the free' (S 18–19), that is to say free characters can choose to employ verse, according to the tone and subject of the conversation, while slaves are expected to stick to prose, in *Augustine's Oak* the essential distinction is a linguistic one. Prose stands for Old English, pentameters for Latin and more ancient-sounding hexameters for the Celtic language of the Britons in this history set in the late sixth century, at a time when the three idioms represented competing cultures and powers in Britain. Furthermore, since Latin was the tongue of the Roman church and the Welsh believers were Celts, in Peter Oswald's first Globe play prose corresponds to paganism and verse to Christianity. Stylistic differences that stand for sharper linguistic contrasts therefore assume paramount importance for a plot centred on St Augustine of Canterbury's mission to Christianize Ethelbert, king of Kent, and to reinstate the pope's authority among the Welsh bishops.

There are no fixed rhyme schemes in the verse parts of *Augustine's Oak*, so it may not be easy for spectators to recognize the different forms, but dialogues in the three languages evidently have distinctive rhythms and sound altogether different. Moreover, as in *The Storm*, Oswald offers a key to this representation. In 1.3, the encounter between King Ethelbert and the monks from Rome is mediated by the few people present who know both languages, i.e. Queen Bertha, Princess Tata and the courtier Osbert, the only Latin-speaking pagan, who has been appointed to translate the words exchanged between his sovereign and Augustine (*AO* 25–9). The outcome is a funny scene, because the audience can obviously understand all characters, while most of them miss part of the conversation, but also a quite effective demonstration of the linguistic convention the playwright has adopted; what is more, this passage provides some food for thought concerning the impact of verbal incomprehension and translations. Having thus clearly established the rule, the writer can then take it for granted when Tata remarks that Edwin knows Latin and wonders if this means he is a Christian (*AO* 40–4), when the newly converted Ethelbert speaks Latin (*AO* 52–3) or when Romans and Britons converse in that language (*AO* 65–70).

All these are instances of people understanding each other; perhaps more interesting is the non-verbal dialogue, as it were, between Augustine and Ethelbert before the king accepts the monk's religion and his tongue (*AO* 46–8), a scene in which the inability to interpret each other's words is somehow bypassed by the interlocutors' will to overcome the barriers created by incomprehension and pride, so that in the end neither knows what the other means but they have prepared the ground for mutual acceptance. The audience, who can understand what both characters are saying, is thus in a position to be amused by their inconsistent sentences, but can also observe the positive effect of their humble and welcoming attitudes. Later on, spectators may notice that Paulinus, whose predication has better results than Augustine's mainly because he is not hampered by pride (*AO* 60–71, 83–4, 87, 91–2), uses prose, i.e. English, to address Edwin and his subjects (*AO* 83–7, 89–92), even though he reverts to pentameters when alone or in conversation with Tata (*AO* 87–9): this way, Oswald reinforces once again by means of the language distinction the theme of humble understanding and acceptance in contrast with incomprehension and pride.

Summing up these experiences of verse drama at the Globe, and on the other hand the wealth of new plays in prose that have been produced by the Elizabethan-like theatre, it seems fair to conclude that the playhouse is suited to poetic rhythms but does not necessarily require them. Its focus on sound, due to the fixed scenery as well as to the excellent acoustics, allows and even encourages experiments with words; the many distractions it offers may even ask for an 'extravagant' language, as Chris Hannan has defined it (2014), as a way to keep the audience's attention, yet these mechanisms can work just as well in prose. The connection with Shakespeare does not seem to be very strong from the point of view of metres and forms, which vary according to specific, autonomous concepts; nevertheless, the Bard appears to bear a sort of general, ideal influence on the choice to write in verse, because his name keeps coming up when this subject is discussed specifically (Neill 1999a; Gardner 2005; Robins 2008).

# Laughing matter

Just as in the case of language and verse, when it comes to comic features the Globe's twenty-first-century playwrights have a complex relationship with the theatre's first and foremost dramatist. Artistic director Dominic Dromgoole has referred more than once to 'cheap jokes' as one of the ingredients for successful new writing at the reconstructed playhouse (2007 EOSI; Logan 2009), but a comic turn is obviously an effective way to capture or regain the spectators' attention and put or keep them in a good mood, so it cannot be seen as something specifically handed down by Shakespeare to his successors. The idea to mix up funny characters and situations or irresistible one-liners with serious subject matter is not exclusive to this theatre either. The first example that comes to mind may be *Hamlet*'s 5.2, because Voltaire's disgusted bewilderment (1733) has crowned the gravediggers kings of tragic laughs, but Beckett's Vladimir and Estragon could claim the same title, and the authors that have followed these examples are innumerable. The Globe's writers themselves often employ light tones to treat weighty subjects elsewhere too: Howard Brenton, for instance, had written Conlag and Daui and the two cooks in *The Romans in Britain* ([1980] 1990)[20] for the National Theatre long before he created *In Extremis*'s Alberic and Lotholf, to keep quoting comic double-acts in dramatic situations.

With respect to humour, the new Globe plays seem to thrive, rather than on the imitation of Elizabethan characteristics, on the consciousness of what actually differentiates their audience from the theatregoers of four centuries earlier. This is most evident in the new shapes taken by such a typically Shakespearean figure as the fool and by the triumph of a comic device that would have been meaningless in the Bard's time, i.e. the laugh-provoking use of anachronisms.

# No fools

Even though, as Catriona Fallow has remarked, Shakespeare remains the unavoidable term of comparison for the reconstructed theatre's new playwrights (2014: 93), hardly any of them have followed in his footsteps as regards a comic figure which is almost symbolic of his theatre, the fool. In the twenty-seven plays examined here there is not one character defined as such. *Augustine's Oak*'s Lilla has been described as one with the authority of Peter Oswald himself: 'a richly comic, outspoken and earthy figure, a "fool" ', in the words of his interviewer Heather Neill (1999a: 15). The importance of his comic persona is highlighted by the fact that its development is one of the main points on which the writer decided to take some liberties with the facts chronicled by his source, Bede's *Historia ecclesiastica gentis Anglorum* (Ecclesiastical History of the English People). Yet Lilla has only some of the characteristics of Shakespearean fools. Being a faithful and sincere companion for the exiled Edwin, he can recall Lear's jester, but that is not his profession; he refers to himself as a warrior (*AO* 39) and he is employed twice as a messenger in very important situations (to ask King Ethelbert's protection for Prince Edwin against the usurper King Ethelfrith, *AO* 32–3, and to convey King Edwin's marriage proposal to Princess Tata, *AO* 78–81). So he appears to be far too active and high-status for a buffoon; his role may be closer to Kent's than to the Fool's in the context of *King Lear*. Furthermore, his comical aspects are not based on his ability with words but either on physicality, as when he turns into a sheep (*AO* 39–40), on his bewilderment facing religious problems (*AO* 39–40, 55) and questions of honour (*AO* 54, 57–8) or just on the way his anxieties and enthusiasms contrast with Edwin and Tata's calm (*AO* 54, 57–8, 73–5, 77, 79–81). Finally, he appears to be a troubled thinker (*AO* 39–40, 53–5, 91) rather than a witty commentator of the surrounding events.

*The Storm*'s Sceparnio plays a role that is in some ways nearer to that of the fool. He is Daemones's slave and his only companion; to a certain extent he entertains his master, although this function is mutual (*S* 10–12); he helps higher status characters realize their situation and their mistakes (e.g. *S* 15–16); he exhibits a knack for words and even performs a song (*S* 34). Yet he is still far from being a proper fool because, even more than Lilla, he is first of all an active character, constantly devising and carrying out plans to solve his and other people's problems. In this essential aspect he is still closer to the Plautine shrewd servant from which he derives than to Shakespeare's inspired and truthful but essentially passive jesters. He could even be identified as the text's protagonist. To begin with, he is on stage and speaks more than any other character, opening and closing the play proper (*S* 9 and 91).[21] Furthermore, his journey from lonely servitude to 'free love' (*S* 91) is arguably the main trigger of the whole plot. Finally, he is the 'hero' of numerous actantial models (as defined by Greimas 1966), while the other characters are the subject of at most one or two, because he embarks on the quests for his own freedom and for Ampelisca's love, to restore Palaestra to Plesidippus and to reunite her with her father, not to mention such minor undertakings as treasure-hunting or getting into the temple.

From the point of view of his role in (or rather out of) stage action, *The Lightning Child*'s Ladyboy Herald, a sort of narrator figure Ché Walker inserts in his rendering of Euripides's *Bacchae*, bears a better resemblance to the Shakespearean fool, as he does not participate but rather comments on events. Moreover, he is clearly subordinated to the powerful figure he accompanies, Dionysis, and his linguistic skills are obvious, even though in a far from classical style, e.g. in his presentation of the god (*LC* 16–17). He also dares stand up against his master to tell him the truth (*LC* 59–60). But he is far from the fool in two essential respects: he is hardly ever funny, and he is a herald, somebody who announces, so his speeches are not directed primarily to the person he serves but to other characters (in this case, Neil Armstrong) and to the spectators.

The role of jester as court entertainer whose ability mainly resides in the dexterous use of words is paradoxically played by Abelard at the court of King Louis (*IE* 26–32), where, after amusing the sovereign with his logical demonstrations (*IE* 26–7, 28–9), he also gives him a frank opinion (*IE* 32), thus carrying out another typical function of the fool. But all this happens only in one scene, while the rest of the play shows Abelard in very different attitudes and situations.

Doctor Scroggy, the title role of Howard Brenton's First World War script, is more constant in acting the fool, and more conspicuous too, in his red wig. Besides offering the injured soldiers champagne and oysters, he cheers them up with incessant word play, and like many Shakespearean jesters he employs irony, paradoxes and laughter to highlight essential truths (*DSW* 76–80, 105–6). His sanity is repeatedly questioned by Jack (*DSW* 70, 105). He even hints at the possibility of a professional career in show business for his patients and himself (*DSW* 69, 79). Yet, Scroggy is not a proper fool because he is illustrious physician Dr Gillies's *alter ego*. Even though he tends to keep separate his two functions, as surgeon and as wise entertainer ('Nothing to do with me. Fellow on my staff called Scroggy organised it', the doctor says, for instance, of the soldiers' show in honour of Queen Mary, *DSW* 92), the two are obviously the same person, who can speak as one or the other without needing to change 'costume' (*DSW* 82, 89). He even discusses the reasons of his double identity with such a constantly earnest person as Sister Catherine (*DSW* 83). He may accept the brusque replies of his patients (*DSW* 70, 77–9, 106), but he is ultimately a figure of authority, a major and a recognized medical genius (*DSW* 11), not a buffoon. Furthermore, in his case good-humour and fun are not only the means but also the goal of his actions: he wants to bring the mutilated soldiers back to life (*DSW* 80), and it is particularly to that end that 'glum just doesn't work' (*DSW* 70).

Another character written by Howard Brenton takes up this role even more unexpectedly, King James I. In his dealings with courtiers and religious leaders he exploits a mixture of humour, literary skills and eccentricity to dig up and sort out problems that tact and good manners would probably leave untouched (see in particular his first meeting with the divines, *AB* 73–9). Yet not only is he once again a far too central and active character to be considered a fool, but more relevantly his licence resides in a status that is the opposite of the jester's irrelevance: he can speak his mind freely because he wields the highest power, as he first states (*AB* 75) and then implies (*AB* 78–9) and as his main interlocutors point out too (*AB* 80).

A much riskier position in which to use wit and word skills to spell out uncomfortable truths is that of *A New World*'s protagonist, eighteenth-century revolutionary thinker and political activist Tom Paine. He almost performs the functions of a public conscience and he is repeatedly persecuted for his outspokenness; but he is too engaged in action and not enough funny to be a fool. Quite the opposite can be said of the Narrator Tom o'Bedlam. An ex-inmate of the asylum and thus obviously connected with madness, he is the character that comes closer to the typical Shakespearean fool in many ways: he is a professional entertainer, who sings for a living (*B* 13) and does not spare puns (see e.g. *B* 49); he reveals unpleasant truths (*B* 35, 49–50, 105); he is a commentator that does not take part in the action; because of his association with insanity he has no authority at all. The main thing that distinguishes Tom o'Bedlam from Shakespeare's inspired jesters is the fact that he does not work in a palace, for a monarch or some nobles, but on the streets, for the passers-by. So he is, even more than Tom Paine, a sort of 'people's fool', an interesting equivalent of the Shakespearean figure for our democratic age. The link with the audience's present, in which power is ultimately supposed to be equally shared by everyone rather than concentrated in the hands of one, is reinforced by the fact that those Tom o'Bedlam addresses are actually for the most part the Globe's spectators themselves.

The lack of proper fools in the new Globe scripts may perhaps be more generally connected with the political context in which they have been written: when public consciousness is deemed to be more effective than a single individual's awareness, hidden realities are best revealed through humour to the community. This function is usually carried out by whole plays, but at times it can also be fulfilled by single characters, like Tom o'Bedlam, or King James when he shows the ropes of religious power, or Sceparnio when he jokingly points out the luxuries of a freedom we usually enjoy carelessly.

## Anachronisms

The connection between fictional and real world on the one hand and the juxtaposition of past and present on the other are also at the heart of the kinds of comedy that seem to be more frequent on the Globe's stage than elsewhere. The irreverent portrayal of historical figures, making fun of national and international icons, is certainly one, and another is the light use of quotations from Shakespeare's works. These devices work particularly well in the context of a playhouse that constantly reminds spectators of what is considered a theatrical golden age and a period in which British and more generally Western culture and identity are deeply rooted. A third technique, often combined with these, is that of anachronism. As a matter of fact, since different time frames are inevitably combined in the spectacle of a performance at the Globe, it is not surprising that playwrights often choose to make the most of their overlapping.

Actually, there is a sort of anachronism that is almost inevitable in a history play: in order to be understood by spectators, characters are made to speak in a more or less historically inaccurate way, especially when the action is set in a rather remote past. This inconsistency usually goes unnoticed, though, or is accepted as a convention, together with the fact that events taking place in foreign countries are performed as a rule in the audience's language. If Abelard and Heloise converse in English, for instance, there is no reason why they should not use a twenty-first-century vocabulary. Writers usually avoid terms or phrases that will openly jar with their context,[22] but they can choose to do the opposite for specific effects. Both Seamus Heaney's *The Burial at Thebes* and Frank McGuinness's *Helen*, for instance, are written in a modern idiom that foregrounds their relevance to the present in spite of their ancient origin. Even more forceful linguistic anachronisms add to the bewildering unpredictability of Peter Oswald's *The Golden Ass*, featuring not only terms like 'flexisexual' (*GA* 12), which could be called a word of the future, since it is a neologism based on the only five-year-old 'metrosexual', but also references to things that did not exist in the play's fictional time (e.g. 'the clock struck one', *GA* 38).

Anachronisms are less noticeable when they are limited to a prologue- or epilogue-like frame; several examples can be found in the opening or closing lines of *Gabriel*'s playlets (e.g. *G* 22, 30, 94). In the case of Heloise producing from her habit a Penguin book (*IE* 90), the effect is stronger because the action is carried out by one of the protagonists still in character and because it involves a material object from the future, but it is mitigated by its position at the very end of the play, constituting almost a stepping stone for the spectators' return to their daily world.

*The Lightning Child* features anachronisms throughout its main narrative, a retelling of *The Bacchae*, which involves references to taxis (*LC* 12), the Pope (*LC* 13), McDonald's (*LC* 15), a Rubik cube (*LC* 36), an Alfa Romeo car (*LC* 53) and Mary Quant eyelashes (*LC* 54), to quote but a few. These elements stand out in stark contrast with the ancient Greek myth, but not as obtrusively as might be expected, because this whole episode is framed, together with the twentieth- and twenty-first-century ones, by the out-of-time reality of Dionysis and Ladyboy Herald, into which Neil Armstrong has momentarily stepped by reaching the Moon (*LC* 9).

A far more impressive breach in the play's time has been added by Tony Harrison to the Flood episode of *The Globe Mysteries* (see *M* 31–41).[23] His previous version of this text, first performed on the terraces of the National Theatre in 1977, already contained several anachronisms, mainly due to the fact that all his Old Testament characters, including Noah and his wife, speak like Christian believers, invoking the Trinity's blessing (*M* 36) and even using Mary's name as an interjection (*M* 35). But in his 2011 reworking of the script for the Globe Harrison goes beyond the medieval frame of reference that belongs to the mystery plays he is adapting and he introduces an element that reaches the audience's present: the patriarch's wife does not want to leave because she is knitting 'new Leeds scarves for the lads' in view of the fact that 'next week's FA Cup' (episode 4 of the prompt book, 'Noah's Ark').

An apparent anachronism opens *The Last Days of Troy*, Simon Armitage's dramatization of the *Iliad*, with Zeus selling souvenirs to the tourists at the archaeological site of what is supposed to have been the ancient Ilium (*LDT* 7–8). This initial image brings together the

present and the past in the spectators' eyes, but it does not impinge
on the chronological accuracy of the plot: the ancient gods being
immortal, it should be no surprise that they are still living. The only
liberty Armitage takes with the Homeric world view in this respect
is to suppose that with the advent of new deities the Olympians
have lost all power (*LDT* 130–1) and are consequently condemned
to a never-ending beggarly existence. By thus linking the classical
narrative with today's society, the dramatist is actually reconciling
their distant outlooks on the human condition and so finishing off his
plot with a paradoxical form of realism. Nevertheless, audiences are
likely to receive the impression that Zeus and Hera live in a bizarre
intermingling of past and present, which, combined with their striking
lack of majesty, provides some comic relief when the ancient tragedy
reaches its climax (in scenes 2.6 and 2.12, *LDT* 102–3, 128–31).

An even more complex and yet quite consistent chronological
structure characterizes *Holy Warriors*, significantly subtitled *A
fantasia on the Third Crusade and the history of violent struggle
in the Holy Lands*. In David Eldridge's history play, a realistic
depiction of Richard I's times in Acts 1–3 is followed by a fast-
paced overview of future conflicts in the Holy Land up to the
performance's present and then by the enactment of a stage in the
Lionheart's life in a twenty-first-century setting. These oddities find
their explanation in 4.1: after his death, the English king prays
that he may have his time again (*HW* 47, 51) and he is given a
second chance with the privilege of hindsight. First he is shown the
consequences of his actions and of other leaders making the same
mistakes, and then he is allowed to relive a crucial moment with
the benefit of the foreknowledge he has thus acquired, represented
by the fact that his decisions are now set in the third millennium,
after all the historical events he has just witnessed. So the second
half of the play actually takes place in the afterlife, out of time, and
even Richard's final meeting with George W. Bush is not properly
anachronistic. Yet spectators are bound to perceive it as such, and
to be impressed by a medieval monarch who points out that 'it
takes about ten seconds to send me a text' (*HW* 64). Such apparent
inconsistencies are mainly aimed at stressing the similarity between
past and present and thus fostering some very serious reflections
on what can be learnt from history in order to avoid repeating the
same mistakes over and over again, but Eldridge does not neglect
their comic potential. At the end of his centuries-spanning visions,

for instance, an understandably puzzled Richard asks the spirit of Eleanor of Aquitaine, 'what are these Kingdoms of Syria and America? What is the Soviet Union, mother?' (*HW* 61).

If *Holy Warriors* stretches the spectators' capacity to move through different epochs and recognize their interconnections, the new Globe playwrights' taste for anachronisms probably culminated with *The Storm*. Peter Oswald's comedy incorporates in its ancient Greek setting anything from scientifically correct observations on the composition of planets Venus and Pluto (*S* 9) to guns (*S* 48, 50–6, 85–7), from a reference to Bakewell tarts (*S* 33) to considerations on the 1995 film *The Usual Suspects* (*S* 79), with a consistently up-to-date language. The presence of anachronisms in the play is so wide and deep that the author has one of the characters justify it, early on in the script, with an appropriately paradoxical monologue that makes fun of the *vexata quaestio* of the Globe's period aesthetics:

> Look – relax about the anachronisms. We've got permission. The playwright actually phoned up Plautus and said, Titus Maccius, is it alright if we're not strictly period? And Plautus answered, 'Look Pete, I wouldn't be talking to you now if it wasn't for anachronisms. You go ahead and use them'. So that's the way it is. If fictional characters can't be free of historical constraints, who can? We've got our rights. (*S* 18)

Daemones's arguing that the text's anachronisms are legitimate is certainly yet another expression of *The Storm*'s playfulness and an opportunity for more logic-defying fun, but it constitutes also the most explicit form of prevention against a serious problem, to wit, the risk, that every anachronism runs, of being taken for a mistake. For this kind of humour to work, two essential conditions must be fulfilled: the inconsistency in dramatic time must be apparent and unquestionably voluntary. Both criteria are much easier to meet when the comic effect is based on the collision of very distant periods; guns in Antiquity or Penguin books in the Middle Ages, for instance, are so obviously out of place that they cannot go unnoticed and they are very unlikely to be laid at the door of an author's carelessness. It is therefore probably not by chance that the explanation quoted above follows a less patently 'wrong' reference to Christmas, a celebration the origins of which are not far from the play's time setting.[24] By having a character state once and for all that there are anachronisms in *The Storm*, Oswald makes sure that even the subtler ones will trigger laughs rather than scholarly disputations.

Undeclared slight discrepancies may on the contrary irritate spectators. Some have felt Simon Bent was cheating, for instance, by setting Long John Silver's early piratical adventures in the mid-seventeenth century – so that he would have been over 100 years old in Robert Louis Stevenson's *Treasure Island* (Billington 2006a; Thaxter 2006). Since artworks have always been free to move their characters to different places and ages, and that is nowhere more evident than in the theatre, where revivals of classic texts often assign them new settings, the specific cause of these perplexities is probably to be found in the suspect that such a limited inconsistency might have been meant to escape the audience's notice. Actually, Bent's moving a well-loved popular figure to the context he wished to explore, Cromwell's Commonwealth, was part of his aiming at a very difficult achievement in this buccaneering history play, that is, the combination of light entertainment with accurate details and deep reflections. In his linguistic choices, too, he mixed contrasting elements, taking the King James Bible and seventeenth-century pamphlets as his main sources, but weaving in more modern material, especially in the pirate's patois (Woddis 2006: 8). The result is overall fascinating, but may occasionally annoy some spectators with unfunny anachronisms, such as the use of 'albatross' as a synonym of 'Jonah' to taunt the man whose presence onboard is supposed to be hindering the ship's departure (*UBF* 108): the seabird metaphor sounds appropriately old-fashioned and nautical, and coupling it with the unassailable reference to the prophet lends it further authority, but the outcome is an even more jarring perception that this usage of the word only makes sense in relation to *The Rime of the Ancient Mariner*, which was written some 150 years later.

At any rate, all of these examples illustrate the same mechanism, whether with fully successful or somewhat questionable results. Historical inconsistencies are paradoxically innate in the heterochronia constituted by the Globe, an authentic reconstruction that brings together Elizabethan architecture and twenty-first-century audiences, so rather than allowing them to disturb the performance, playwrights often choose to parade them and put them to use either as thought-provoking references to the spectators' reality or simply as sources of entertainment.

## Paradoxical topicality

Real or apparent anachronisms, especially in the more thought-provoking instances, are also a clue to how mindful the Globe playwrights are of the present. This attention may surprise those who see the reconstructed theatre as solely devoted to the celebration and the study of the past, but it is actually quite consistent with the playhouse's peculiar structure, which gives as much visibility to the spectators' reality as to the characters'. What is more, topical themes are something dramatists can depend upon to catch their varied audience's attention; they are actually considered attractive for prospective punters too, so that the plays' relevance to the concerns of the day is consistently remarked in announcements, interviews and promotional material. As can be expected, the two new scripts set in contemporary London – *The Frontline* and *The God of Soho* – are full of what residents and visitors are likely to have seen and heard discussed shortly before the performance, from the war on drugs to celebrity culture, from racism to homelessness, from the politics of the Mayor of London (a more local reference, but one that in recent years even tourists are bound to have met due to Boris Johnson's iconic fame) to those of the US President.

Much less predictably, period pieces are often topical too. Sometimes new texts are commissioned with an eye to anniversaries. This kind of programming has been most conspicuous in the 2014 season, responding to the First World War centenary both in its overall theme 'Arms and the Man' and more specifically in the piece depicting that conflict, *Doctor Scroggy's War*. A similar occasion was the 400th anniversary of the King James Bible in 2011, that was celebrated with the bill entitled 'The Word is God', including a staged reading of the whole Authorised Version itself and Howard Brenton's *Anne Boleyn*, in which the origin of that translation is dramatized in connection with the earlier English Gospel by William Tyndale, probably read by Henry VIII's second queen. In the Globe's 1998 application for the Resident Dramatist Attachment Award there is also evidence of a similar plan for 2000 that did not reach completion, a scenario by Peter Oswald on the life of Saint Paul that could have chimed with the opening of the Millennium Bridge between Bankside and St Paul's Cathedral (p. 1).

Certain themes or figures may also be the talk of the day without any specific historical reason and constitute an attractive feature nevertheless. *Under the Black Flag* was produced, for instance, in the midst of a pirate frenzy sparked by the first *Pirates of the Caribbean* film, *The Curse of the Black Pearl* (2003), and it opened on 9 July 2006, only three days after the second movie of the franchise, *Dead Man's Chest*, was released. Similarly, *Anne Boleyn* first appeared in 2010, at a time when the Tudor epoch, and particularly Henry VIII's second queen, were enjoying a burst of success in popular culture with Philippa Gregory's novel *The Other Boleyn Girl* (2001), its sequels and prequels (five, published between 2003 and 2008) and the film version starring Scarlett Johansson and Natalie Portman (2008), Hilary Mantel's Man-Booker-Prize–winning *Wolf Hall* (2009) and *Bring Up the Bodies* (2012), and Michael Hirst's television series *The Tudors* (2007–2010).

Period pieces and stories set out of time can also address contemporary political and social concerns, though maybe indirectly. Both *We the People* and *A New World* discuss racism, albeit in the context of the dawning United States of America. The gin craze portrayed in *Bedlam* has been compared by dramatist and reviewers to twenty-first-century binge drinking (Akbar 2010; Allum 2010; Neill 2010: 2; Marlowe 2010b). *Augustine's Oak* ends with a hymn to the British Isles' diversity as the core of their true identity (*AO* 96). In *Man Falling Down*, Adam and Eve become asylum-seekers after being chased from Paradise, and the play ends with God, Saints and Angels as refugees too. Eric Schloesser saw his *We the People*, which stages the birth of the American constitution, as part of the debate on the opportunity to draw up a written constitution for the UK and as depicting a process of democratization other countries were experiencing at the time the play was produced, most notably Iraq (Matthew and Sharpe 2007: 1). A similar focus on human and civil rights characterized in the same year Jack Shepherd's *Holding Fire*, which combines the ill-fated love story of a maid and a boot boy, Lizzie and Will, with the historical depiction of the Chartist movement's struggles. Its public scenes include current-sounding protests against the inequalities of the economic system (*HF* 25–6), a discussion of the basic principles and problems of communism featuring a young Engels (*HF* 71–76) and an extensive debate on the pros and cons of violent action and reformism (*HF* 84–9). Several of the Globe's new plays – *Under the Black Flag, In Extremis, A New World, Anne Boleyn, Holy Warriors, Pitcairn* – focus on the relationship between different faiths and on the way politics are connected to religion, a theme which has been constantly kept at the centre of public debate by the 'war on terror' following the 9/11 attack, while *The Last Days of Troy* evokes a clash between East and West that is, in Armitage's own words, 'a blueprint for a conflict that rages to this day' (2014: vii).

Sometimes the links can be more specific, as in the case of *Gabriel* dramatizing the story of Arabella Hunt and Amy Poulter in the year same-sex marriage became legal in England and Wales (2013) or of *Blue Stockings* portraying a group of young women's struggle for their right to graduate at the same time as British students protested against the consequences of soaring university fees (when Jessica Swale recalls hearing the same slogans repeated inside and outside the rehearsal room, Amer 2013; Swale 2013) and only a few months after Malala Yousafzai was shot because of her activism for female education.

When the play is the re-writing of a classical text, its topicality is very often enhanced by the adaptation, be it just in the language, as in *The Burial at Thebes*, with its Hiberno-English expressions evoking Irish conflicts, or by means of added characters and episodes. In *The Lightning Child*, for instance, gender issues are repeatedly brought to the fore, most conspicuously in the figure of Ladyboy Herald, that has no precedent in Euripides's *Bacchae*. Peter Oswald developed the theme of prostitution and treated it more explicitly in *The Storm* than Plautus did in the play's model, *Rudens* (Oswald 2005; Woddis 2005),[25] and gave very current nuances to Daemones's past as a businessman (see e.g. *S* 20, 56–7). Frank McGuinness's success in making *Helen* relevant to the years of the war in Iraq is palpable in the sheer number of reviewers that quote the Greek veteran's outraged astonishment ('The war was for nothing?/We endured all we endured –/We fought for something that never was?', *H* 30) and refer it to the weapons of mass destruction that were supposed to be the reason why the conflict began in 2003 (see e.g. Billington 2009; Carpenter 2009b; Clapp 2009; Elkin 2009; Fricker 2009; Hemming 2009; Hitchings 2009; Nightingale 2009). Similarly, although with less praise, several critics stressed Captain Mission's 'war on terror' speech in *Under the Black Flag* (*UBF* 117–18; Shore 2006a; Spencer 2006; Taylor 2006a).

Some scripts contain references to the audience's present that are even more explicit than these phrases echoing contemporary statements or sounding appropriate in the frame of twenty-first-century debates. There are assertions concerning the future (in the characters' perspective) and anticipating developments, problems and struggles of our times, sometimes with a touch of irony, when centuries later the proposed goals have not been achieved yet. Such is the effect of *Augustine's Oak*'s ending wish that one day the British Isles will be united and proud of their diversity (*AO* 96). Mixed feelings are likely to be aroused by Dr Maynard's suppositions on the future of what is now called psychiatry: it is true we 'look back upon the [then] current asylums and express horror at our brutal treatment of the ill' (*B* 72) in the eighteenth century, but we are still far from understanding the reasons that cause madness (*B* 26), and the idea voiced by Annabel that 'the more opulent our lives, the more we suffer greed and vanity, and the madder we get' (*B* 124) is rather food for thought than a hypothesis our society has found to be true or false. *Holding Fire* also offers predictions that call for the spectators' consideration, such as the presence of well-informed working-class leaders (*HF* 6) or the end of poverty (*HF* 81) or Chartist Lovett's more general concluding speech on the sunny future of Britain (*HF* 114). On a quite lighter note, in *Gabriel*, a character announces that the score of *The Fairy Queen*, that went missing shortly after Purcell's death, has been found again in 1901 (*G* 94).

Some of these allusions are likely to trigger deeper thoughts on the spectators' present, others will only recall it, but all establish a connection between the fictional time and our own. Similar links can also be more explicit at the expense of the scenic illusion, as when Howard Brenton wraps up the discussion on how the lives of Abelard, Heloise and Bernard will be known in the future by having the twelfth-century abbess produce a Penguin edition of her lover's letters and hers (*IE* 90); even more openly, Anne Boleyn explains to the audience that 'you're strange to me, as I must be strange to you' (*AB* 115), and Sceparnio concludes his free-wheeling monologue with a reference to 'the free world, as it used to be called, in the past of your present, which is my future, if I have one' (*S* 34).

Finally, some plays give a strong sense that characters and spectators ultimately share the same reality by having the former say to the latter things that fit both their epochs; this way, they break the fourth wall with their direct address, but they do not trespass the borders of the story's time. This effect is particularly forceful when it touches on a sensitive issue, as in the case of Tom o'Bedlam's pleading:

> When in the future you meet us Tom o'Bedlams, think on us. I may be filthy, reeking of the street. I may talk to myself, my clothes be peeling themselves off my skin.
>
> But if we meet one day, I want you to think on this.
>
> Think what embroidered waistcoat once embraced my chest.
>
> What perfumed breath once crept out of my mouth. What soft hands I once used to hold my children. (*B* 105)[26]

But the same mechanism also works well with less evidently problematic questions, like the Republican nature of the American constitution, stressed by Benjamin Franklin's answer to an actress among the groundlings ('So what kind of government have we got, then?/A republic, m'am, if you can keep it', final lines of *We the People*, *WP* 99).[27]

Some playwrights seem to have chosen this topicality of the past as a way to tackle hot issues of the present in an effective way; Howard Brenton certainly does so, but also Trevor Griffiths's Tom Paine appears to embody a very contemporary ideal, for instance, and David Eldridge's *Holy Warriors* significantly live in the twenty-first as well as in the twelfth centuries. Other writers aim less specifically at raising the public conscience regarding social problems such as binge drinking and mental illness (Nell Leyshon in *Bedlam*) or education rights (Jessica Swale in *Blue Stockings*). There are also references to the twenty-first century that seem to be less deeply concerned, like Samuel Adamson's depiction of a same-sex marriage (*G* 37–9), that quickly gives way to other themes. However, whether moved by strong feelings or just enjoying a shared allusion, whether by breaking the fourth wall or by representing a separate world that mirrors the audience's, all these dramaturgical devices make the fictional reality evidently relevant to the spectators and thus build on the overlapping of time frames the reconstructed theatre evokes.

# Founding narratives

A quick look at the list of the twenty-seven new plays produced by the reconstructed Globe in its first twenty years is enough to notice the striking prevalence of the historical genre, and the presence of a significant group of texts based on classical myths. As a matter of fact, more than half of the scripts can be ascribed to the former group. The latter contains five works (*The Golden Ass*, *The Burial at Thebes*, *Helen*, *The Lightning Child* and *The Oresteia*), but it may be combined with the two Bible-based pieces (*Man Falling Down* and *The Globe Mysteries*) to form a category of plays dealing with some founding narratives of Western culture, whether nowadays confined to the realms of fictions and symbols or still believed, at least in part, to be actually true. Somewhere in between history and myth lies the siege of Troy, since the Homeric epic is usually read as a poetic and symbolic account of an actual war or at least of a turning point for the economy of the ancient world, and the same may therefore be said of Simon Armitage's dramatic rendition.

It may even be argued that the remaining three titles strive to adhere to one of these two groups. *The God of Soho* depicts a possible modern myth,[28] addressing as it does essential aspects of human life such as love and identity by means of a plot in which divinities descend to earth and interact with men and women. In *The Frontline*, which portrays the multifaceted society that inhabits the area of a North London tube station nowadays, Ché Walker inserts, sometimes a little forcibly, several fragments of local and international history: Mordechai Thurrock tells part of the story of his historical drama *Sickert* (F 10, 24–5, 47–8); Miruts and Salim fight over the sixty-year-long Ethiopian–Somali conflict (F 14–18); Ragdale drops a hint at his having escaped from a Second World War prison camp (F 34); Miruts upholds the tradition of Ethiopian Christianity (F 36); Violet denounces British colonialism (F 37–8) and gives an unusual account of English history (F 38–9); Erkenwald recalls the remains of prehistoric animals found in the London area (F 41); Jayson chronicles the life of a nineteenth-century boxing champion (F 51); Donna takes pride in the tradition of the London underground (F 57, 59), prompting Miruts to comment on the Victorian era (F 58–9), and then conjures up ghosts from Camden's past (F 60–1); Babydoll asks Ragdale if he is going to give her 'a

World War Two liquorice' (*F* 85); Mahmoud evokes the fights of the Dhulbahante Dervish (*F* 96–8). While Plautus's *Rudens* is a comedy without any historical references, presumably set in the author's time (third–second century BC) or in that of his Greek model Diphilus (fourth–third century BC), Peter Oswald situates it in the fifth century AD and explains Charmides's return after having been arrested with the fall of the Roman empire (*S* 80). This event and its consequences are then variously commented upon by the characters (*S* 80–1, 88–9), so that this comedy full of anachronisms turns out to have, paradoxically, a historical ending, resulting in what the epilogue defines 'a bewildering history lesson' (*S* 92).

A further reflection shows that the two categories outlined above, that comprise nearly all of the plays written for the reconstructed Globe, are in turn united by their common focus on the origins of the society in which they have been created. This comprehensive genre can thus be seen to appeal to the many kinds of spectators that visit Shakespeare's Globe: if there is one thing they presumably all share, it is the interest in the past and in the roots of British culture that they have shown by coming to the reconstructed theatre. Moreover, foundational narratives, whether ostensibly fictional, upheld by religion or based on historical research, usually address essential issues of human life, such as freedom, power, personal and social relationships, equality, illness or death. As Jessica Swale put it, 'every single one of the new plays that's been chosen has raised an important question or issue' because 'if you've got seventeen hundred people watching a play, there's a lot of plays which would really fascinate three hundred people in that audience, but the other fourteen hundred wouldn't find it interesting. So … [Dominic Dromgoole] always chooses plays with big ideas, that should be interesting to everybody' (2014).

## Myths and religious narrations

The plays that deal with ancient myths all have a classical precedent. *The Burial at Thebes* and *Helen* follow their model rather closely: Seamus Heaney and Frank McGuinness mainly use linguistic choices to emphasize the plays' relevance to the audience's present, and introduce fairly small changes, such as the identification of the servant who stands up to stop Theoclymenes's murderous rage (*H* 59–61) with the gatekeeper that speaks to Menelaus (*H* 18–21) and the decision to make it a female character. Even *The Golden Ass*, which dramatizes a very complex narrative work, full of diverse episodes and stories-within-the-story, is relatively faithful to its source, in its exuberant spirit when not exactly to the letter. Tony Harrison's *Globe Mysteries* is similarly near to the medieval mystery plays they adapt. In translating *The Oresteia*, Rory Mullarkey compressed the action of Aeschylus's trilogy into a single play, but he strived to keep intact not only its ethos and themes but also its structure, by maintaining all the characters' entrances and exits and even preserving at least 'a sense' of nearly all the choral passages (the exception being the Furies' first one, which he decided to sacrifice in order to get the plot going faster, Mullarkey 2015: [5]).

Simon Armitage's approach to the *Iliad* was bound to be less faithful, since he was turning an epic poem into a play. Indeed, he introduced episodes related in the *Odyssey* and in Virgil's *Aeneid*, added four scenes set in contemporary Turkey (1.1, 2.2, 2.6 and 2.12) and even changed relevant aspects of the story. The twenty-first-century scenes constitute a sort of frame for the drama and establish the impoverished Zeus as a knowledgeable narrator, at the same detached from human destinies and wounded by the loss of power he has suffered perhaps because of that war's outcome (*LDT* 130), whose descriptions and commentaries clarify and complement the action without modifying its meaning. Where the script really differs from its classical sources is in Andromache's fate: instead of being carried away as a slave, she remains on the shore near Troy thanks to Helen, who hides her in the tapestry she has woven and then makes sure that her work is left behind (*LDT* 135–7). This episode concludes a series of dialogues between the two princesses which characterizes Armitage's take on the well-known story. During these confrontations, the 'face that launched a thousand ships' proves to be something more than an exceptional beauty, when, though maintaining a sort of mysterious aloofness, she rejects the accusations of Hector's wife but also shows a deep understanding of their reasons (*LDT* 16–19, 112, 116–17, 134–5). The change is quite consistent with the dramatist's choice to give Helen a more important role (Armitage 2014: vii) and its meaningfulness is highlighted by its unquestionably strong position at the very end of the play, but it is also emblematic of how *The*

*Last Days of Troy* does not overturn the Homeric representation of the female condition: another woman's intervention may enable Andromache to escape slavery, but only in the shape of an object that is abandoned instead of loaded on the ship.

Ché Walker is the author that most conspicuously modifies the tragedy he rewrites, by adding the Neil Armstrong frame plot and several inserts presented as almost autonomous playlets with their own titles: 'Drax and Shug and a pitbull called Cleopatra' (*LC* 19–21, 30–2, 46–7, announced on p. 18), 'Limbic Resonance' (*LC* 26–8, 34–5, 47–50, 61), 'Atalanta getting Frantic' (*LC* 41–4), 'Presidential Pardon' (*LC* 56–9). In spite of Ladyboy Herald's suggestion that spectators 'don't try and make sense a this night' (*LC* 30) and rather 'figure it out on the train home' (*LC* 30), the function of these adjuncts is rather clear; it is even expressed by Dionysis himself, after the end of the last one: 'Use me, don't abuse me … or you'll end up limbless voiceless everything-else-less like you see all from these li'l stories we been landing on' (*LC* 59).

In other words, the supplementary episodes are meant to elucidate the sense of the main plot derived from Euripides. As for the overarching situation, it provides the occasion for these examples to be shown and offers some commentary that can further guide the spectators' interpretation. As Ladyboy Herald says at the beginning of the text, 'one thing the Gods gotta keep teaching you humans is to respect your own limits … And we're gonna show you a story that proves this very position' (*LC* 10).

The core messages enucleated by the two characters do not exactly coincide, but this is almost necessary to prevent *The Lightning Child* from becoming a philosophical argument instead of an artwork. What remains, on the contrary, quite clear, is the intention to illustrate the tragedy's possible meaning for a twenty-first-century audience.

Drawing an ancient narrative nearer to the spectators' daily reality is also what Jack Shepherd and Oliver Cotton did by associating in *Man Falling Down* a first part relating the story of Adam and Eve, from the Creation to their banishment from the Garden of Eden, and a second act set in the theatregoers' present, in which the two become refugees struggling to start a new life. In the absence of a written script for this play, which is the issue of a workshop on the use of masks in performance, it is not possible to analyse in detail its structure and the way it employs several sources (among others, besides the Bible, extracts from Milton's and Blake's poems), combining them with newly composed material and improvised segments. It is anyway clear that *Man Falling Down* shares with all the other texts investigated in the present section the intent to show how relevant to the present their ancient stories can be.

# Histories

Compared to these mythical and religious scripts, the history plays written for the reconstructed Globe offer a wider range of approaches and structures, in part simply because they are twice as many and they are not necessarily based on well-known precedents.

Since contemporary scripts rarely adhere completely to the canons of a single genre, to begin with, they might be reasonably expected to fall also into other categories. They all display traits typical of adventure story, comedy and musical theatre, but history is decidedly their focus, with three exceptions: *Under the Black Flag*, in which the unrealistic tragic aspects and more conspicuously the tropes of pirate fiction prevail over the nonetheless relevant depiction of the Commonwealth period;[29] *Bedlam*, combining a portrayal of eighteenth-century London with the structure of a comedy, particularly evident in the ending characterized by poetical justice (*B* 93–4, 112–25) and marked by a wedding (*B* 127); the 'entertainment with trumpet' *Gabriel*, dedicated to a musical instrument, although in a very specific epoch, because the natural trumpet is typical of baroque music.

Furthermore, nearly all of these texts feature specific recognizable figures that contribute to make their belonging to the historical genre immediately evident: only two – *Bedlam* and *Liberty* – do not have any such characters, and the latter contains several references to Evariste's and Louise's interaction with Marat (*L* 29–30, 32, 33, 37, 52, 82, 86). Oliver Cromwell appears only in two scenes of *Under the Black Flag* (*UBF* 25–7, 70–5),[30] and so does Dr Maudsley in *Blue Stockings* (*BS* 14–15, 30–3), which also presents in a more central role the less known Elizabeth Welsh, mistress of Girton College between 1885 and 1903; all the other plays have historical personages among their protagonists.

The majority of these texts (eleven out of sixteen) are concerned with British history,[31] even though they may have a foreign setting and wider concerns, as in the case of *Holy Warriors* or *Pitcairn*. Thomas Paine is English-born but Trevor Griffiths concentrates *A New World* on his contribution to the creation of the USA and to the French revolution. These two events, which have evidently conditioned the evolution of the UK too, are the subject respectively of *We the People*, centred on the composition of the US Constitution, and *Liberty*, focusing on the Reign of Terror. *In Extremis* is set in France and shows how some advanced medieval philosophers anticipated aspects of modern thought and even the Mexican characters of *The Heresy of Love* are representative of religious phenomena that were born in the old continent. All in all, the events depicted appear to be nearly always relevant both to the specific fates of Britain and to the history of Europe and the West in general and therefore likely to appeal to the Globe's varied audience. Dromgoole's last two seasons as artistic director have displayed a wider geographical scope than the previous, with histories set in the Near East (*Holy Warriors* and to a certain extent *The Last Days of Troy*), the Pacific island of *Pitcairn* and Mexico (*The Heresy of Love*), in what may be a significant move towards new and more varied perspectives but could also be an effect of the casual circumstances that influence the timing of productions.

From the point of view of their structure, these plays may seem generally speaking rather traditional. Except for *Anne Boleyn*, *Holy Warriors* and *Pitcairn* (which simply starts with the arrival of another British ship on the island twenty-five years after the mutiny on HMS *Bounty* and then goes back to tell the story from the beginning), they follow the chronological order of events, and the time they represent is not longer than a human life, often concentrating on a rather short, specific period, like the French Reign of Terror in *Liberty*, the Federal Constitutional Convention of the United States in *We the People*, or the protagonists' university years in *Blue Stockings*. They mostly seem to adhere to an old-fashioned model of history too, centred on the actions of powerful or talented individuals; only a minority – *Liberty*, *Bedlam*, *Blue Stockings*, part of *Gabriel* and *Pitcairn* – focus on ordinary people.

These traits bring the reconstructed Globe's history plays very close to the biographical genre, but this aspect may not be particularly relevant in defining them. As a matter of fact, as Richard Palmer points out, 'historians may deal in abstractions, but the allure of drama depends fundamentally on the personal appeal of characters vividly and engagingly created by actors' (1998: 54) and 'the persistent presence of a biographical bias in history plays may, therefore, reflect as much the perceived demands for successful theatre as it does attitudes about history itself' (ibid.: 55). It is hardly surprising that a huge unsubsidized playhouse in which performances have to fight physical discomfort and multifarious disturbances for the spectators' attention should be mindful of the advantage extraordinary individuals have in engaging their interest.

What is more, most of these plays differ from traditional biographies, whether fictional or fact-based, in one fundamental respect: with the exceptions of *Under the Black Flag, A New World, Holy Warriors, The Heresy of Love* and *Nell Gwynn*, which are centred on one protagonist, they have several main characters.[32] These can be imaginary unrecorded people (in *Bedlam, Liberty, Blue Stockings*), well-known personages (in *Augustine's Oak, In Extremis, We the People, Anne Boleyn*) or a mixture of the two (in *Holding Fire, Gabriel, Doctor Scroggy's War, Pitcairn*), but they invariably represent a plurality of foregrounded voices.

In *Gabriel* this multiplicity corresponds to an episodic structure, so that most playlets focus on different protagonists, although groups of characters can share the central position even within a single scene (e.g. the four artists in the *Fairy Queen* sequences, *G* 55–9 and 83–94, or the two brothers in 'Three Trumpeters', *G* 61–8).[33] All the other plays have several main roles, which are connected to each other, usually directly (even in the case of Anne Boleyn and King James, in spite of the time gap between them). *Holding Fire* presents the only example of principal characters that do not interact in person: Lizzie becomes involved with the Chartist movement of which Lovett is a leader, so they work for the same cause, but they never meet face to face. The other relationships are more intimate: the central figures of *Augustine's Oak* are two generations of the same family; *In Extremis*'s Abelard and Heloise are lovers and Bernard is their main philosophical opponent; *We the People* chronicles the Federal Constitutional Convention, following some of its participants; the main characters of *Liberty* are the six participants of the initial picnic; those of *Bedlam* are all closely connected with the asylum; King James conjures up Anne Boleyn after finding her copy of Tyndale's *The Obedience of a Christian Man*; the Girton students and teachers are at the heart of *Blue Stockings*; Jack Twigg becomes a patient of Dr Scroggy; the population of Pitcairn is a small and tightly knit group.

The majority of these plural subjects tend to evoke a community; they are not just a number of people, they represent a collective entity, albeit a heterogeneous and sometimes even conflicted one, such as the workers fighting for their rights (*Holding Fire*), the Parisians living under the Reign of Terror (*Liberty*), the American Founding Fathers (*We the People*), eighteenth- and late seventeenth-century Londoners (*Bedlam* and *Gabriel* respectively) or the first female Cambridge students and their teachers (*Blue Stockings*).

Their closeness notwithstanding, the presence of several protagonists entails a multiplicity of perspectives, making plots more complex, not necessarily on the plane of the events they include, but on that of their interpretation. When Edwin avows he has broken his promise and he actually believes in something (*AO* 92–4), for instance, spectators see it both as a liberation for him and as a terrible blow Tata must face; throughout *Liberty* theatregoers are invited to wonder how will each of the six picnickers adapt to the growing tension and survive the Reign of Terror.

In these conditions, the linear presentation of scenes in their chronological order and the comparatively short span of time covered may be read as the simpler aspects of a narrative that is inherently elaborate. As a matter of fact, among the history plays with a single protagonist are the ones which display the widest range of contexts and happenings, *Under the Black Flag*, *A New World* and *Holy Warriors*, relying on the central figure to provide a sense of continuity and help the audience follow the plot in spite of the many possible disturbances around them. In conclusion, traditional and simple elements are balanced with others that tend to make both the stories told and the interpretation of historical events they imply fairly complex.

Focusing on a plural subject is a significant recurring choice in these plays. At Shakespeare's Globe, spectators, standing or sitting in close proximity with a heterogeneous multitude of strangers who are sharing the same experience, though often reacting in strikingly different ways,[34] are necessarily, at times painfully, aware to be part of a group, however ephemeral; therefore, a community that has to face occasional divisions and constant frictions is something they can immediately relate to, with the double consequence of boosting their interest in the action on stage and fostering an understanding attitude towards their fellow audience members (which is the premise of a more relaxed atmosphere and a better enjoyment of the performance).

Moreover, the group portrayal establishes a situation that chimes with the prevalent choice of myth and history as subject matter in that both tend to create a sense of community. This mechanism works especially well for those spectators that recognize themselves in the civilization of which a defining moment is depicted, because the play's events remind them of what they share, while the characters' different perspectives make it easier to find someone they can identify with and show that a lack of homogeneity – like the one they are probably witnessing at the moment – is just natural in any society. But those who do not feel part of this group can experience a sense of community too: they can get to know something of the culture they are interested in (as they have proved by choosing to visit the reconstructed theatre) and at the same time visibly take part in one of its expressions; for them, too, the multiple protagonists offer both a better chance to find one they can empathize with and a reassuring example of diversity. The prevalence of basic, universal themes, like religion, liberty or social justice, and the variety of main characters also avoid creating a clear-cut division, such as British/foreigner, and the plot being set in the past (history) or out of time (myth) makes sure that no theatregoer really belongs to the society depicted in the play, so that each audience member is likely to feel more or less close to the identity represented on stage from time to time, while constantly sensing to be part of the temporary community in the auditorium.

In conclusion, both the choice to present foundational narratives and the features displayed by most of the Globe's new history plays are strongly connected with the specificity of the reconstructed theatre, the exterior appearance of which immediately evokes a meaningful past, as well as with the playhouse's peculiar structure, that foregrounds the presence and the role of the audience.

# Come all ye ...

The unique relationship between past and present Shakespeare's Globe Theatre tends to create and the way skilful playwrights have woven it into their works can be effectively exemplified by the case study of how ballads are employed in three scripts – *Holding Fire*, *A New World* and *Bedlam* – in significantly different forms but always with a double effect of involvement on the one hand and historicization on the other.

It may best be said explicitly that although the term is here used in a rather wide sense, including both 'traditional' and 'street' ballads (de Sola Pinto and Rodway [1957] 1965; Bold 1979), it is still restricted to its historical meaning, excluding twentieth- and twenty-first-century jazz, pop and rock ballads, which constitute quite another musical genre, characterized by slow rhythms and sentimental or romantic themes.

Although in various forms, the popular narrative songs generally called ballads have enjoyed a wide success for quite a long time, from the Middle Ages to the Victorian era, so they would not seem particularly useful in period recreations. Yet, since the genre fell out of use more than 100 years ago, it is apt to evoke the past, albeit in rather vague terms, and with this function it is used in these three plays set between the eighteenth and the mid-nineteenth centuries.

In the published version of Nell Leyshon's *Bedlam*, the accurate research underlying its songs is foregrounded by a detailed list of their sources (*B* 128). Three of the six pieces are so-called traditional ballads, i.e. popular narrative songs that were presumably composed, certainly spread and preserved orally before being collected and published by scholars: *Four Drunken Nights* (*B* 50–2), an adaptation of number 274 of Francis James Child's *English and Scottish Popular Ballads* (1882–98); 'Oyster Nan' (*B* 69–70), from Thomas Dufrey's *Pills to Purge Melancholy* (1719); 'Loving Mad Tom' (*B* 104–5), from Thomas Evans's *Old Ballads* (1810). All could have been performed in the streets of London in the eighteenth century; even the changes made to the first one are quite in line with the adjustments this sort of pieces underwent almost every time they were performed. The precision of these references may very likely be lost on most spectators, but the verse structure (ballad stanzas or quatrains of four-stress lines, though mostly rhyming *abab* instead of the typical *abcb*, see Bold 1979: 20–1), together with the narrative rhythms and simple, repetitive melodies are bound to evoke the popular songs of a time long past. Some listeners may even recognize 'Four Drunken Nights' (entitled 'Our Goodman' in Child's collection and known also as 'The Merry Cuckold and Kind Wife' or with a different number of nights the inebriated subject recalls, up to seven), because it is sometimes still sung today as a traditional piece, especially in Irish contexts.

The connection between the ballads' words and *Bedlam* is a rather loose thematic one: like the play they tell stories of excessive drink, sex and madness. In the case of 'Loving Mad Tom' the link is stronger, because its ending anticipates Tom o'Bedlam's immediately following monologue asking the audience to consider the human being beyond a street-dweller's rugged appearance:

> My silver cups are turned to earth,
> I'm jeered by every clown;
> I was a better man by birth,
> Till fortune cast me down.
> > To picking straws now must I go,
> > My time in Bedlam spending.
> > Good folks like you your beginning know,
> > But do not know your ending.

This passage highlights what may be considered the main idea on which Leyshon's text is focused, i.e. the flimsiness of any distinction between 'mad' and 'sane' people (as wise Dr Maynard puts it, 'the human mind is so delicately balanced that it is a miracle any one of us is deemed to be sane', *B* 124), here explicitly extending the reflection to the performance's spectators. The other two ballads have an almost opposite function from the point of view of their contents, their light-hearted bawdy narratives providing some comic relief; more precisely, 'Four Drunken Nights' enlivens the atmosphere just after Gardenia has discovered the tragic situation of Stella, imprisoned in the asylum although no longer insane and denied help from her former lover (*B* 47–9), while 'Oyster Nan' helps the spectators return from the interval to the play's world just before Tom o'Bedlam and Dr Maynard present their perspectives on mental illness in two forceful interlaced monologues (*B* 70–2).

As for the way they are introduced in the script, all three ballads interrupt the plot, they are not part of the story but they definitely belong to its environment, sung as they are by the Bedlamites, a group of former inmates of the mental hospital, now street musicians, and Phyllis, the gin-seller. Since both the vendor and Tom o'Bedlam, voice of the Bedlamites, interact with the audience as well as with the play's main characters, treating the ones and the others as potential customers (see *B* 9, 11, 13, 49, 53, 69, 70), their songs create a sort of intermediate reality, halfway between the fictional world and the theatregoers'. When listening to their music and laughing at their jokes, in particular, the spectators, like unpaid extras in the role of passers-by, become part of the picture traced by Leyshon of a carefree, fun-loving society, apparently unaware of its tragic dark corners.

'The Ballad of Thomas Paine' presents a situation that is almost opposite to that of *Bedlam*'s researched materials, since it has been written by Trevor Griffiths expressly for the stage version of his biographical script. Here is how it appears in the prompt book:

> So it's off with the old and it's on with the new
> And it's up with the many and down with the few
> It's goodbye to the lion, it's hello to the dove
> For we're sailing to the city of brotherly love
> Philadelphia's the place, '74 the year,
> Thomas Paine's is the story and yours is the ear ...
>> They carried him off on a stretcher of flax
>> And they pushed him away in a cart
>> And the lass paid his diggings the while he was ill
>> For he'd won his way into her heart
>> Ma Downey's the place, winter the season,
>> Paine on his back in a struggle for reason ...
> Whores, sailors, deckmen, rogues, pimps, and drunks
> Defrocked lawyers and derelicts all stinking like skunks
> Find refuge in Race Street at the bottom of the pit
> And drink themselves daft as they sink in the shit.
> Race Street's the place, '75 the year,
> Common Sense is the issue, the crisis is near ...
>> Now it's off with the new and it's back to the old
>> One story completed, one more to be told,
>> To England we journey and trouble ahead
>> the country in turmoil, the people in dread,
>> The French up in arms in old Liberty's name
>> Revolution the flag, the sword and the flame[35]

Its model is obviously not the 'traditional' ballad but rather the later 'street' or 'broadside' ballad, another kind of popular narrative song, composed to be sold in print, even though mainly spread orally, 'more leisurely and circumstantial in the narrative' (de Sola Pinto and Rodway [1957] 1965: 21) and 'less wedded to one dramatic incident' (ibid.). As a matter of fact, its verses give more or less detailed directions as to where and when an episode takes place instead of relating the event itself, and with this function they were sung separately, setting the scene for respectively Paine's departure towards the United States, his arrival while very ill, his meeting with publisher Bell in an infamous neighbourhood and his return to Europe. The song's words are obviously meant to help the listeners understand what is going on, stating the time and place and, in the case of the second verse, explaining some contemporaneous pieces of stage business. It thus makes clear some passages of a narrative that unfolds over more than thirty years of wars and revolutions in three countries.

As in *Bedlam*, the status of the ballad's performers blurs the distinction between fictional and real world, since the Mongrel Folk appear to be a group of street musicians belonging to Paine's time and space, but their words, describing the protagonist's whereabouts and sometimes even foreshadowing his future, cannot be reasonably interpreted as the lyrics of a piece he hears. So the singers are visually part of the hero's environment, but their ballad is evidently meant for the Globe audience's ears. Like Phyllis and Tom o'Bedlam, the Mongrel Folk stand somewhere between two worlds, but unlike them, they interact neither with the spectators nor with the main characters of the play.

*Holding Fire*'s 'Ballad of William and Lizzie and The Welshman' displays the same ambiguity in still another fashion. Jack Shepherd's (*HF* 69–70, 93, 106–7) is, like Griffiths's, an original composition based on the model of broadside ballads; as a matter of fact, it seems to fall into a specific subgenre, that of the 'sorrowful lamentation', relating the sensational story of a condemned man or woman and often sold in print on the day of the protagonist's execution (Bold 1979: 76–8): 'Oh he was just a serving lad,/And she a kitchen maid,/I'll tell the tale of their young love,/And how a man was slayed' (*HF* 69).

Compared to the typical sorrowful lamentation, this ballad shows two main differences: it is not written from the point of view of the condemned criminal and instead of closing on the execution, it has an open ending; even in the printed version, that goes on to tell of how William is wounded, arrested and sentenced to death

(*HF* 106–7), Lizzie's future remains uncertain, but in the prompt book's script, the text is reticent about the boy's capture too.[36] Both peculiarities are quite consistent with the song's theatrical context: within an already fictional reality, a street singer relating the lovers' story in the first person would run the risk of uselessly puzzling the audience, while anticipating the protagonists' fate would spoil the suspense of their flight.

Other features of 'The Ballad of William and Lizzie and The Welshman' are on the contrary in keeping with the broadsides' style. The mix of sentimental and sensational elements, for instance, is apt to capture the attention of spectators at Shakespeare's Globe just like that of nineteenth-century passers-by with a story that the prompt book version effectively summarizes as 'the fondness of their hearts/Through price of murder paid'.[37] The abundance of specific details, like the name, profession and provenance of nearly all its characters, was meant to bear evidence to the truthfulness of street ballads, while within *Holding Fire* its main function is to make the audience realize immediately and beyond doubt that the song's protagonists are the same Will and Lizzie whose adventures are being acted on the stage.

Nearly all these traits, those that take Shepherd's creation nearer to the traditional broadside ballad as well as those that mark their distance, appear to be strengthened in the final version of the play, compared to the printed one: the focus on sentimental and sensational aspects of the plot is sharper, both protagonists' names are given in the first lines of the second stanza, and the boy's fate is omitted. The coherence of these changes suggests the importance of the features the playwright consistently decided to enhance, so as to recreate the street ballad model as effectively as possible while adjusting it to a theatrical context.

In the script, this piece is performed twice, first without the last verse by a ballad singer (*HF* 69–70), then in its entirety by a prisoner in Warwick Gaol (*HF* 92–3). The former appears to be plying his trade in a tavern where Lizzie's father, Mr Bains, is soon joined by her sister, Beth; their reactions to the ballad are meaningful: the man is so drunk he does not realize he is listening to a sensational rendition of his elder daughter's painful vicissitudes, not even when the younger tells him she does not like that song (*HF* 70). The musical piece thus indirectly informs the spectators of Mr Bains's intoxication and of Beth's getting to know the world and its harshness, but also of the notoriety Will and Lizzie have acquired. Later on, its last verse carries the news that its heroine is still on the run (*HF* 93).

Once again, the people who perform the ballad belong to the fictional world of the play, but their audience is made up of the Globe's theatregoers as well as of other characters, the ones and the others invited to recognize Lizzie and Will as its subjects and to use the song as a source of information. Beth's reaction and Mr Bains's indifference may give this metatheatrical situation a further edge by leading attentive spectators to reflect on the similarity between the morbid curiosity elicited by the sorrowful lamentations and their own interest for the sensational aspects of the young lovers' story; while the drunken man appears to lack any understanding of the situation, the girl, who takes her sister's experiences to heart, epitomizes the compassionate refusal of such an exploitation of misery, passion, violence and murder for the purposes of commercial entertainment.

In conclusion, in spite of belonging to quite different subgenres, the ballads in *Holding Fire*, *A New World* and *Bedlam* share a tendency to create a duplicitous effect: on the one hand, they highlight the distance between the fictional reality and the outside world by contributing to the depiction of a historical setting, by interrupting the plot and by presenting a *mise en abyme* of the play's themes and episodes, but on the other hand they foster the theatregoers' involvement by enlivening the atmosphere, by providing useful information and most of all by creating a situation of communal spectatorship that blurs the distinction between characters and audience members. From this point of view, they can be considered a model of how musical pieces work in the context of drama in general and of the new Globe plays in particular, engaging spectators as much as possible while almost flaunting the artificial nature of their reality. Still, these ballads also carry out a specific function with respect to the script's and the performance's time frames, which they both differentiate and bring together, just like the reconstructed theatre's architecture does.

# 3

# The Spectacle of Spectators

An aerial photograph or a plan of Shakespeare's Globe Theatre may strike the viewer for its peculiar geometry, with twenty sides approximating to a circle, or for its eerie void-centred shape, resembling a doughnut or an atoll rather than a building, but these characteristics almost disappear when the venue is seen or experienced in use: far from being a hollow polygon, it is obviously full of people. As with most theatres, the majority of its inhabitants are spectators; unlike the punters of other playhouses, though, the Globe's audience members dominate the place not only for their number but also for their position. The groundlings fill the centre of the space and the gallery dwellers encircle it, so that actors appear to be upstaged, confined as they are to a comparatively small and peripheral section of the structure.

A somewhat cynical interpretation of this image may see it as a fitting metaphor of the way power is actually distributed by the theatre's financial status: a huge unsubsidized venue, it is compelled to be acutely mindful of its customers' desires. The performers' actions in the Globe must constantly adhere to the demands of the audience that faces and surrounds them, because should the spectators desert the venue, they would leave a threatening void at its heart, in more ways than one. What is more, the auditorium can be painfully emptied not only in the long run, if its productions are unsuccessful, but also during each performance. Punters are free to go at any time and the groundlings find it especially easy to do so, since they are already standing and they have invested only five pounds in their ticket.

From the point of view of the playwrights, these conditions entail the necessity to attract audiences with appropriate subjects and themes and, more characteristically, to keep their interest constantly alive throughout the work. These needs are common to all commercial theatres, but they gain unique force from the Globe's specificities. To begin with, the temptation to leave is fuelled by the physical discomfort of standing or sitting on a wooden bench for hours, as well as strengthened by the ease with which it could be yielded to. Moreover, the spectators' visibility makes their moods obvious both to the performers and to their fellow viewers, so by going away, moving restlessly or even just fidgeting, they constitute a potentially contagious distraction. As a result, the gradual failing that can plague any production may become a much faster process in the reconstructed Elizabethan playhouse, where it can catch and spread even more readily than a fire in its thatched roof. Dramatists are therefore called to exert an especially continuous attractive force on their audience, in the knowledge that even a short hiatus in the connection between stage and auditorium can quickly degenerate into an unmendable rupture.

The Globe is therefore undoubtedly a difficult theatre in this respect, but it offers some promising opportunities too. Spectators are always in sight, their collocation making sure that nowhere in the building can the stage be watched without seeing some punters too, and in the open air the sun (or a set of lanterns that simulate its effect when missing) sheds light on them as much as on the actors: in a word, they are part of the spectacle. Instead of trying to ignore their presence, artists can put it to use, employing them as a mass of supernumeraries that spontaneously represents the community each production is meant to address.

The present chapter will outline and discuss the implications for the playwrights and their work of the prominent role spectators play at the Globe. Its starting point will be a brief analysis of the reconstructed theatre's audience itself and of how it has been perceived by dramatists. The devices they consequently employ to capture and hold the attention of viewers and listeners will then be examined. Finally, three different ways in which the patrons' visibility can become an asset in the writers' hands will be the object of specific discussions.

## Spectators as participants

Since it was first conceived, Shakespeare's Globe was meant to be a working theatre, but in order to keep it open the project team's commitment was not enough: the collaboration of punters was needed. Although Sam Wanamaker saw the Elizabethan playhouse as a possible answer to the requests of contemporary stage movements, and specifically to the desire for a closer relationship between performers and spectators, there was no guarantee that the plan would be successful. Moreover, its issue came to life several decades after it was devised, maybe too late. Finally, even though Wanamaker's enthusiasm was shared by younger talented theatre practitioners, such as Mark Rylance, it might not be matched by non-professional audience members. As Andrew Gurr later recollected, 'we did sometimes discuss whether the end-product of our labours would work as a modern theatre. None of us seriously believed that it might attract big crowds' (Gurr 2008: xvii).

So the team's labour was unexpectedly rewarded by the audience, that proved to be eager to join in the 'theatrical experiment' and growingly interested in its developments, reaching an attendance rate of 97 per cent (and even 99 per cent in the case of the £5 standing places) for the 2012 regular season (*Annual Report* 2012: 6). Furthermore, the spectators' contribution was surprising not only for its quantity but also for its quality. In Gurr's words, 'the effect on actors and audience of open-air playing, where large crowds make themselves into visible and active participants in the event, has been the biggest revelation of the whole project so far' (Gurr 2008: xviii), and it has attracted widespread attention. Researchers and artists at Shakespeare's Globe have been constantly observing this phenomenon, as the EOSIs show: one or more questions on the audience have always been asked, and the answers testify to the food for thought this subject provides. Journalists and reviewers, who usually disregard the spectators' role, never fail to mention it when describing a performance at the Globe. Recent scholarly studies on audiences, such as Dennis Kennedy's *The Spectator and the Spectacle* (2009), have sections centred on this unique case.[1] Quite appropriately, one of the first PhD theses written at Shakespeare's Globe is Penelope Woods's insightful 'Globe Audiences' (2012).

All these analyses show a double focus of interest: how the audience works and who the spectators are. The two questions are related, of course, because different reactions can be expected from regular or occasional playgoers, younger or older patrons, Shakespearean aficionados or first-timers, British people or foreigners. An even more complex but not less important aspect of this issue is what the Globe punters are perceived to be, by the artists who face them – either directly as performers or in a mediated way as components of the creative team – and by their fellow onlookers too. The importance of these 'readings', of which spectators are the object rather than the subject, is apparent in the light of Susan Bennett's foundational *Theatre Audiences* (1997), which extensively deals with the predicament of community or constituency companies facing the challenge of addressing the wider public of mainstream theatre (see e.g. Bennett 1997: 160–3), and places the interaction between spectators on the same level of prominence as that between stage and auditorium (ibid.: 139).

It is difficult to obtain a complete set of data concerning the composition of an audience,[2] especially in the case of a theatre that 'seats' 1,700, of which 700 actually stand, and where all ticket-holders are welcome to enter and exit the auditorium at any time during the performance. Therefore, it may be wise to avoid shakily based estimations of the extent reached by phenomena, but it is nevertheless possible to observe and assert their existence.

The presence of tourists is, for instance, a rather indisputable fact (at least because it characterizes all the main theatres in London), but its rate a highly debatable one. As Penelope Woods has pointed out, the spectators she interviewed assumed there was a considerable number of tourists around them, but seemed to base their identification on apparel (comfortable walking shoes, light waterproof jackets, backpacks, etc.) that was likely to be worn or carried by anybody planning to stand for a couple of hours in the open air (Woods 2012: 101). Woods suggests that what is possibly perceived as 'touristic' is an attitude, the fact of considering the building an attraction in itself, something to be observed and/ or photographed irrespective of the performance (ibid.: 100–1). Looking around oneself in eager curiosity, with or without the assistance of a camera, is certainly a typical behaviour of tourists, but it is also the one generally required by landmarks – a category into which the Globe is usually considered to fit,[3] thus sanctioning this avid gaze as more appropriate than a blasé indifference and undermining its specificity.

Sometimes all foreign spectators are labelled as tourists, an assumption that is better grounded than the outfit-based one, but not exempt from counterexamples. There are at least two other significant categories of audience members that come from abroad: the Globe's cultural status and cheap standing tickets attract the international student population of London universities, and long-distance habitués keep coming back from all over the world to attend performances and special events. Although it is once again difficult to ascertain their number, their knowledgeable enthusiasm can be easily recognized and distinguished from the inexperienced excitement of newcomers, so they may fit a broader definition of 'tourist', as a person who travels in order to attain a pleasurable experience,[4] but they do not embody the cliché of unprepared sight-seers.

This distinction is relevant to the reason why tourists are not just one of the many possible examples in the context of this study. Penelope Woods appropriately points out that visitors of this kind 'are suspected of not understanding, not knowing how to behave, and of not belonging' (Woods 2012: 268).[5] Critics, artists and – paradoxically – other spectators that stress their presence therefore display the negative perception of audiences that Helen Freshwater has shown to be widespread in almost all ages and environments (Freshwater 2009: 38–55). Tourist spectators are expected to respond inappropriately to a production of which they ignore the premises, the context and maybe even the language: they are supposed to be passive, silently puzzled at best, and to disturb the performance at worst. Actually, Front of House reports[6] have occasionally registered noisy school groups and punters that repeatedly tried to photograph or film the actors, but these episodes are remarked as exceptions, not common instances of audience behaviour.

On the contrary, both critics and practitioners often observe that spectators, and especially groundlings,[7] are exceptionally knowledgeable and responsive, that they laugh at difficult literature- or history-based jokes[8] and their attention overcomes noise, fatigue and downpours.[9] Such remarks might have been prompted by the discovery that the auditorium's reality did not match the speakers' negative expectations, but they are too specific and strong to be dismissed as mere surprised reactions. Both the examples quoted in the notes, for instance, draw a comparison with other spectators, in one case contrasting the attentive groundlings with the critic himself, feeling restless in spite of his more comfortable position, in the other supposing that another audience would not react as smartly as the Globe's.

Moreover, these impressions can be easily and effectively backed up by a short reflection on the 'groundlings' queue' that lines the theatre's Bankside wall a couple of hours before every performance. These spectators display their knowledge of Shakespeare's Globe and their commitment to the viewing experience by arriving so early in order to choose their place in the yard. Furthermore, while waiting they tend to create a sort of community, similar to the one Susan Bennett describes outside the Theatre Development Fund/TKTS booth in Times Square (Bennett 2005: 416), exchanging advice and anecdotes, but with one significant difference: critical analysis of the productions is one of the main subjects among the groundlings, discussed with varying degrees of competence but constant passion. These theatregoers really seem to fit the definition of 'an elite of Shakespeare mavens', even though many could also be classified as 'tourists' in that they are not Londoners, thus blurring the distinction outlined elsewhere by Bennett (2008: 494).

It is once again difficult to quantify them, so as to define the percentage of devotees in the pit, but their relevance can nevertheless be affirmed on the basis of their position: since they usually favour the area near the stage, they are likely to be the most conspicuous both for the players and for the rest of the audience, and consequently to influence the performance through feedback and example. Thus they constitute the core of the specific 'Globe audience' outlined by composer Claire van Kampen as an active participant in the experiment of the reconstructed playhouse, having 'become a theatre practitioner, and thus truly able to "play" with the company, responding to the many different aspects of new evidence from the play-texts, and from the Elizabethan stage, to contribute to the discoveries coming out of this exciting space' (van Kampen 2008a: 88).

The spectators' role at Shakespeare's Globe has actually been at the centre of a theoretical debate that is possibly destined never to find a fully satisfying conclusion: as several scholars have pointed out with varying degrees of perplexity,[10] 'original practices'[11] will never be able to reach the field of reception, because the audiences' background will always be that of twenty-first-century people. The presence of interested and knowledgeable spectators that keep coming back and learning may answer Gordon McMullan's misgivings that the audience will necessarily lack the Elizabethans' familiarity with their stage conventions (McMullan 2008: 231). Anyway, besides the obvious differences in the extra-theatrical world, the experiences and notions of today's theatregoers that were unavailable to Shakespeare's contemporaries cannot be bypassed. Long-lost connections and interpretations may perhaps be recovered, but newly acquired ones cannot be erased.[12]

Claire van Kampen has hypothesized a seemingly absurd way to recover the sense of contemporaneity and topicality that Elizabethan drama certainly had in its time:

> One way of addressing the issue of 'authenticity' could perhaps be achieved by having the actors playing in twenty-first-century dress to their modern audience, with music played on modern instruments; but we then have the issue of Shakespeare's text, which is now very far from our contemporary speech and includes many period references. (van Kampen 2008b: 183)

The easiest way to overcome this remaining barrier between the fictional world and its spectators' is, obviously, to stage present-day drama: the question of the audience is thus connected to that of new writing in a paradoxical kind of 'original practice', because by combining two elements firmly grounded in the twenty-first century the Globe can reconstruct the relationship between author and spectators that its antecedent usually housed.

The lack of information concerning audience composition that characterizes the theatre's Shakespearean productions and almost any other large-scale venue can be observed in the case of its new plays too. The only dependable statistics are the overall attendance rates, which outline a smaller but still consistent participation: the 71 per cent capacity registered in 2013 (Annual Report 2013: 5) amounts to approximately a thousand spectators per performance, which would mean a full house in an average-size playhouse. It seems fair to suppose that these are not exactly the same people that usually crowd the Globe, because school groups, Shakespeare purists and tourists who want to experience Elizabethan theatre are unlikely to choose these productions. Some playwrights have also actively tried to attract different kinds of punters; Ché Walker is probably the one who set himself this goal more explicitly: by focusing *The Frontline* on contemporary Camden, he hoped to 'bring a new, younger audience to the Globe, ... a blacker audience' (Curtis 2008), and according to several critics he did (e.g. Davis 2008; Fisher 2008; Hallissey 2009; Williams 2009).

These differences notwithstanding, both artists and reviewers seem to assume the existence of some core characteristics in the reconstructed theatre's audiences, presumably due to the playhouse's architectural specificities. As a consequence, playwrights working there keep a certain kind of auditorium in mind while writing. Moreover, they consider this aspect of their commission quite important, because Shakespeare's Globe is generally perceived to be 'very much a theatre for audiences' (Leyshon 2010 EOSI) just as other playhouses have a repute for being especially designer- or director-friendly. It is therefore useful to this study to sketch the main expectations of the authors concerning their perspective spectators.

At first sight, they are not an easy body of people to address: 'I think they're just unruly' (Walker 2007 EOSI) was Ché Walker's comment after having performed on the Globe stage as an actor. Nell Leyshon has specified the playwright's point of view: 'a lot of the time there is a lot of movement in the groundlings and around the benches where people are restless and I think one of the challenges is to keep them still, to keep people engaged' (2010 EOSI). Howard Brenton has added the aural dimension to this portrait by stating that 'they are also much more vocal: laughs are quicker, responses seem sharper' (2007). This impression is partly due to the fact that proximity and light make reactions much more apparent than they would be in the dark beyond a proscenium arch, but there is also an objective basis for the audience behaving differently than elsewhere, as Brenton points out: 'they can see each other. They can easily move about' (2014a).[13] Not only groundlings can change positions and attitudes much more than they would in a traditional seat, but all reactions tend to spread across the house because they are perfectly visible and audible. Moreover, as Leyshon put it, spectators 'will vote with their feet' (2010 EOSI): knowing they can come and go whenever they like, and maybe feeling less committed to the viewing if they bought a cheap standing ticket, spectators are very likely to leave if they are not satisfied with the show. What is more, they can easily stop following the performance even without exiting the venue, because at any time 'they've got other things to look at' (Walker 2007 EOSI), be it the Elizabethan architecture and décor or other theatregoers. All in all, 'the audience in the Globe is very relaxed and therefore very powerful' (Brenton

2014a). Having to face them, Nell Leyshon feels writers must 'buy ourselves quiet scenes' (2010 EOSI) and that 'we need an element of fun ... to get the audience in' (ibid.), but Howard Brenton offers a more complex view of the Globe's possibilities:

> The theatre has something of Joan Littlewood's dream of a fun palace: it encourages laughter, big waves of it, which can be glorious. But over the years we who have worked there have discovered that it is far more than a venue for knockabout. (Brenton 2014b)

Jessica Swale sums up her description by saying that 'the Globe audience is vocal and generous and they like to be involved but they're also "trainable"' (2014), i.e. capable of adjusting their reactions to the tone set by the production. Ché Walker has also pointed out the positive effect of the spectators being particularly willing to have fun: 'the Globe audience are by far the most open-minded, adventurous and supportive audience I've ever worked for' (2009). In other words, they can easily forsake a performance, but they would much rather appreciate it. As Chris Hannan put it, 'being outdoors and in daylight gives you a sense of connection, a real sharing of space with other people' (Woddis 2011), creating a sense of community that has a potential for 'making no division between the people who watch and the people who take part' (ibid.). In particular, Howard Brenton has emphasized that 'eye contact between performers and spectators builds a sense of shared undertaking' (2007), so that the audience feels like participating in a communal experience rather than judging somebody else's work. The playwrights' impression may therefore be summed up by Glyn Maxwell's reflection on the eve of his Globe debut: 'I wonder if the noisiest crowd in London theatre may not also be the most attentive, or at least the crowd who know best what they're doing there' (Robins 2008: 15).

Notwithstanding the impossibility to trace a detailed picture of the audience at Shakespeare's Globe, in conclusion, practitioners may perceive it as being characterized by an interested and reactive attitude, and this stance, together with an imposing mass and a striking variety of spectators, is probably what they envisage in working for this theatre.

# Spectators as a challenge

Either standing or sitting on wooden, mostly backless benches and exposed to all sorts of inclement weather, the Globe's spectators are doomed to be physically uncomfortable. What is more, they are subject to innumerable distractions coming from the skies – in the form of gliding birds or hovering helicopters – or from their fellow theatregoers, perfectly visible and audible all around, not to mention the curiosity aroused by the Elizabethan architecture itself. On top of that, they are far from sharing the same knowledge base and interests: a motley crew of 1,700 people, including school groups and tourists, connoisseurs and first-timers, foreigners and Southwark-dwellers, they bring all sorts of different backgrounds and needs to every performance. They also have all imaginable chances to express their dissatisfaction effectively by fidgeting, moving, grimacing and yawning in full view of the actors or even by leaving the building at any time, so that attracting and holding their attention is a goal theatre artists cannot afford to overlook. Writing a good piece is obviously the playwrights' main way to win spectators, but some features that recur in the new Globe scripts seem to outline the traits of a typical crowd-pleaser.

A very conspicuous tool playwrights can employ to captivate the audience's attention is certainly the plot: sudden twists are likely to rekindle everybody's interest and suspense can keep it keen, regardless of tastes, expectations and knowledge. As Table 3.1 shows, adventurous elements are considerably present in the new plays produced by Shakespeare's Globe. Only Simon Bent's *Under the Black Flag* fits into a recognizable genre – that of pirate tales – but perhaps just *The Burial at Thebes* and *The Globe Mysteries* are never tinged with the thrilling mood of daring deeds and surprising incidents. These choices are even more meaningful because they are uncommon in contemporary drama: hidden treasures, courageous feats, disguises and last-minute escapes feature more likely in pantomime, comedy or children's theatre, while in these texts they are mostly combined with decidedly serious themes and lofty references.

In order to elicit the auditorium's feelings, conflict is an almost unavoidable ingredient, and in such huge canvases as those outlined here it is very likely to take the shape of a war. Battles take place in or around (offstage or just before the action) half of the plays

*Table 3.1  Recurring plot features that help catch and hold the audience's attention in the new plays written for Shakespeare's Globe Theatre*

| Feature | Number of plays | Plays |
|---|---|---|
| Wars and revolutions | 13 | *AO, UBF, HF, WP, L, BT, H, NW, G, LDT, HW, DSW, O* |
| Other fights and battles | 8 | *MFD, IE, F, AB, GM, BS, P, HL* |
| Flights and pursuits | 10 | *AO, GA, UBF, IE, HF, F, L, H, NW, O* |
| Surveillance to be avoided | 13 | *S, UBF, IE, BT, H, NW, B, AB, BS, LDT, DSW, O, HL* |
| Disguises | 12 | *S, UBF, IE, H, B, GM, G, BS, LC, P, O, HL* |
| Treasure hunts | 5 | *S, UBF, F, GS, G* |
| Coups de théâtre | 23 | *AO, GA, S, MFD, UBF, IE, HF, F, L, H, NW, B, AB, GS, G, BS, LC, LDT, HW, DSW, P, HL, NG* |
| Comic traits | 23 | *AO, GA, S, MFD, UBF, IE, HF, WP, F, L, NW, B, AB, GS, GM, G, BS, LC, LDT, HW, DSW, P, NG* |
| Topicality | 20 | *AO, S, MFD, UBF, IE, HF, WP, F, BT, H, NW, B, AB, GS, G, BS, LC, LDT, HW, DSW* |
| Shakespearean references | 10 | *GA, S, UBF, F, NW, B, GS, G, BS, NG* |
| Supernatural elements | 15 | *AO, GA, S, MFD, UBF, BT, H, AB, GS, GM, G, LC, LDT, HW, O* |

*Table 3.1  (Continued)*

| Feature | Number of plays | Plays |
|---|---|---|
| Musical moments | 27 | *AO, GA, S, MFD, UBF, IE, HF, WP, F, L, BT, H, NW, B, AB, GS, GM, G, BS, LC, LDT, HW, DSW, P, O, HL, NG* (all) |
| Love stories | 15 | *AO, S, IE, HF, F, L, H, NW, B, AB, GS, G, BS, DSW, NG* |
| 'Outrageous' elements | 22 | *AO, GA, S, MFD, UBF, IE, HF, WP, F, H, NW, B, AB, GS, GM, G, LC, LDT, HW, P, O, NG* |

and many of the other texts feature some kind of shared fight or siege or are based on extensive and fierce ideological clashes. Some tropes of suspense recur, either within the context of material wars and revolutions or in relation to more abstract contrasts or even as a result of private problems: protagonists are often pursued; several characters must avoid some kind of surveillance also in other situations; disguises can be assumed by people who need to escape or to hide, or for other reasons too, but the thrill of the question whether they will be recognized or not remains; there are even several treasure hunts, although their objects as well as the tones of their representations differ widely.

Both within adventurous plots and in other kinds of drama, a very effective way to excite the spectators' interest is to surprise them with what is not by chance called a coup de théâtre. Like the ones presented above, this device is by no means exclusive to the Globe, but the texts under scrutiny here employ it with a frequency that cannot be overlooked. Not only do most of them feature the traditional narrative twist that turns the tables in the middle of the play or near its end, but many do so multiple times and even the smallest occasions for similar effects are fully exploited to surprise the audience with a revelation rather than just providing the necessary information.

Adventures are obviously not the only kind of plot strand that can be effectively employed to capture theatregoers' attention: regardless of genre, a conflicted love is probably the most universally effective means to grant continuity of drive and feeling to a story. It is used pretty often at the Globe, but perhaps less than might be expected: nearly half of the new plays – *The Golden Ass, Man Falling Down, Under the Black Flag, We the People, The Burial at Thebes, The Globe Mysteries, The Lightning Child, The Last Days of Troy, Holy Warriors, Pitcairn, The Oresteia, The Heresy of Love* – do *not* give it a prominent position. What seems to be more characteristic is the way lovers often embody ideas, especially in the religious field. The first instance that comes to mind is probably Chris Hannan's *The God of Soho*, in which the Love Goddess Clem and the New God face a crisis and then a renewal of their relationship that give warmth and add a narrative dimension to a philosophical reflection on the actually very human presumption to be in control of everything. Religious and personal motivations intermingle in *Anne Boleyn*: the strong-minded eponymous heroine asserts that God 'works His purpose, His way, through our [her and Henry VIII's] love' (*AB* 96). A love story is also the apparent subject of Brenton's first play for the Globe, *In Extremis. The Story of Abelard and Heloise*, yet once again its protagonists' peripeties are mainly caused by ideological contrasts. In Peter Oswald's *Augustine's Oak*, Bertha and Ethelbert seem to embody the clash between Christianity and Paganism, while Tata and Edwin represent the opposition between atheism and religious revelation; both couples are examples of happy attachments hampered by divergent beliefs.

There are two love stories in Trevor Griffiths's *A New World* too, though this time they belong to different moments in the life of the same man. In the first part of the text, Tom Paine has a difficult relationship with Marthe, while in the second he finds a more like-minded companion in Carnet. So the audience can follow a pretty traditional story in which a problematic and ultimately disappointing attachment is followed by one that grows constantly deeper and stronger, but at the same time the two female characters embody a contrast of ideas that is at the heart of the age depicted in the play. Obligations imposed by religion and society cause Marthe and Paine to suffer, while Carnet's straightforward attitude towards love and sex chimes with the thinker's libertarian humanistic stands, so that what could be a sentimental plot is once again employed to make historical and philosophical conflicts more palatable and easier to apprehend.

On the whole, love stories may not be especially abundant on the Globe stage, but these conspicuous examples show that they are often employed to maintain the spectators' attention focused on what might otherwise be hastily dismissed as 'boring' themes.

Other traits of these plays that attract theatregoers and keep them engaged have already been discussed in the previous chapter: comic moments, topical references and Shakespearean quotations are all likely to capture the interest of punters. It may be remarked that while the opportunity for a laugh or a hint to current affairs work equally well in almost any context, allusions to the Bard and his times are especially effective in 'his' theatre. Their considerable presence can therefore be read as a sign that the Globe's new dramatists generally seek to harness the playhouse's specificities as means to deal with its difficulties. An instance of this connection may be seen in the way they implement another device to catch the audience's attention, the use of supernatural elements. The presence of otherworldly events and creatures may seem to be in stark contrast with the Globe's open-air, short-distance, unplugged kind of theatre. Ghosts, spirits and magic were quite often presented on similar stages in Shakespeare's time, of course, but in the age of CGI apparitions and miracles are usually associated with technologically advanced devices. Nevertheless, more than a half of the plays analysed here include something of the sort.

Shakespeare's Globe usually represents the supernatural in ways that do not require any special effects besides words, acting and more often than not a little atmospheric music. Most of the superhuman gifts or curses represented do not actually call for any visible breach in the laws of nature. The truthfulness of a prediction is realized the moment stage action confirms it, for instance; the main enrichment from which it can benefit is an eerie or majestic literary quality, and it is worth noting the four characters established as prophets – Olwen in *Augustine's Oak*, Tiresias in *The Burial at Thebes*, Theonoe in *Helen* and Cassandra in *The Oresteia* – all speak in verse. Likewise, people can appear to be conditioned by magic or by a divine intervention without needing anything more than good timing in the performance and possibly some peculiar acting or an appropriate musical accompaniment; this is what happens when Severus is maddened by Woden in the woods and then healed by

Tata's singing (*AO* 53–7, 60), or when both Peter and Hannah change the object of their affections after a magic flower's juice has been squeezed into their eyes (*G* 92–4).

In other plays, divinities and their messengers appear to the audience too: Woden, Freya and Loki (*AO* 36); an angel (*AO* 76–7); Isis (*GA* 11, 99–101); Venus (*S* 88) and her envoys (*S* 53); the Dioscuri (*H* 61–2); Dionysis and his Herald (*LC*); Zeus, Hera, Athene and Thetis (*LDT*); Apollo, Athena and the Furies (*O*); not to mention God, Satan, angels and demons in the Bible-based plays *Man Falling Down* and *The Globe Mysteries*.[14] Once again, they do not necessarily need any particular machinery; the effectiveness of their words and actions and the human characters' response to their presence vouch for their nature, and an out-of-the-ordinary aspect may add to their appeal, but is not compulsory. In the case of ghosts, the fact that they reappear after their death (as the very appropriately named Hamlet demanding to be avenged, *UBF* 103–20) is enough to mark them as such, although their being incorporeal is emphasized when, like the above-mentioned Hamlet, they can be seen only by some of the people on stage.

Similarly, Richard the Lionheart's awakening after his funeral and the dialogue between Eleanor of Aquitaine and him establish the setting of *Holy Warriors*'s fourth act as a sort of Purgatory (*HW* 50–1). What follows is an extended prophecy; its tone is set by the Troubadours' sung verses (*HW* 51–2), while its correctness can be witnessed by the spectators' memory, since the events foretold here for the benefit of the play's protagonist are historical facts that belong to the past in the audience's timeframe (*HW* 52–61).

Elsewhere, some of the Globe's new plays seem to call for very traditional stage magic, usually emphasizing its sleight-of-hand basis. *The Golden Ass* is full of transformations so obviously impossible to be realized in a naturalistic way (to mention only one, perhaps the most impressive, according to the stage direction Pamphale 'turns into an owl and flies off', *GA* 43) that they become the visual equivalent of an unbelievable tall tale; not by chance, Tim Carroll's direction and Laura Hopkins's design connected the play with all sorts of naïve popular entertainment, most notably fun fair 'monsters' pavilions. The miracle *The Lightning Child* explicitly requires Dionysis to perform almost by way of self-introduction sounds rather like a conjuror's trick: he 'magically produces a bottle of wine and a glass, which he pours without touching' (*LC* 22).[15]

This kind of spectacle possibly climaxes in the 'Creation' episode of *The Globe Mysteries* (*M* 14–17). For Deborah Bruce's production, a professional magician, Richard Pinner, was called in to help with such effects as Adam and Eve being extracted from a box (*M* 16).[16] While in *Man Falling Down* the solemnity and powerfulness of God's actions were conveyed by means of an imposing golden mask and coherently majestic gestures and movements, Tony Harrison's poetry was spoken by an ordinary-looking white-bearded man and accompanied by simple effects based on the performers' ability and such immediate metaphors as fluorescent tennis balls representing stars and planets. In both situations, the text offered the fascinating force of words – taken from the Bible and from Milton's *Paradise Lost* by Shepherd and Cotton, written expressly by Harrison – and called for the traditional poor but fascinating magic of the stage. The choice to highlight what is specific to the theatre was further underscored by the metatheatrical aspect of this scene in *The Globe Mysteries*, which saw the world spring to life from the contents of a cart-load of boxes.

All in all, in dealing with the supernatural, the new plays written for Shakespeare's Globe seem to trust the possibility to weave an enchantment with the basic elements of the performance – actors, words and essential props – depending on the apparent paucity of its means as a factor that enhances rather than weakens the charm of the result.

The choice to rely on the playhouse's strong points in order to counteract its disadvantages is even more apparent in the new texts' use of music. The rich décor and audience-surrounded acting area of Shakespeare's Globe do not allow for much in the way of scenery, so the aural dimension is certainly valuable as a means to establish the time and place of the action, but this use of sound and melody does not account for their being put centre stage. While incidental music is generally used to set the scene, all the new Globe plays feature at least one moment in which song, dance or an instrumental piece is foregrounded, not to mention the musical entertainment spectators usually enjoy before the performance begins and the jig that closes most of the shows. From the point of view of their function, these passages are probably better explained by the fact that they are almost universally understandable and engaging. Since audiences at the reconstructed playhouse always comprise people from very different backgrounds, including some who do not habitually speak

English and may find it hard to follow a fast-paced drama they are not familiar with, music can be extremely useful to express feelings and outline situations in a language that is accessible to all.

Furthermore, rhythm and melody can attract and engage spectators even bypassing their rational thought: theatregoers can enjoy a musical number or a dance piece within a drama production just like they would in the context of a concert or a ballet. Of capital importance in this sense is the fact that at the Globe all music is performed live and in view of the audience. This choice is due to the prevailing Elizabethan style of staging, which obviously excludes all sort of electrical equipment, but not only. As a matter of fact, microphones and other 'forbidden' appliances have been occasionally – though very seldom – employed to achieve an appropriately up-to-date sound, e.g. for King Porter Stomp's contribution to *The God of Soho*, while recorded pieces have never been accepted. So the accent falls on the importance of audience and performers sharing the same time and space rather than on the kind of technology involved. The force of this presence, strengthened by the short distance, the shared light and the lack of barriers between players and theatregoers, gives all vocal and instrumental pieces a specific charm that is very likely to enthral listeners regardless of their understanding of the words' import or references.

Besides the close connection it establishes between stage and auditorium, another feature of Shakespeare's Globe gives an essential contribution to the success of musical performances: its outstanding acoustics. Reviewers have observed that the Elizabethan-style playhouse is an excellent venue for opera and musical theatre (e.g. Morrison 2008; Woolf 2009). Perhaps more significantly, professional musicians have proved to hold the same belief by working on projects that would enable their harmonies to reverberate in its 'wooden O': conductor Peter Manning and composer Dominique LeGendre have selected it for the debut of their operatic collaboration *The Burial at Thebes* (Bredin 2008; Tait 2008), while *Gabriel* was created expressly to fulfil star trumpeter Alison Balsom's desire to perform in this space (Robins 2013).

In conclusion, Shakespeare's Globe has all it takes to make the most of musical performances within its new plays, and productions can certainly benefit from vocal or instrumental pieces not only to establish a scene's setting but also, more interestingly, to involve spectators from all backgrounds and help ease the text's comprehension for those that find its language challenging. So by devising such moments and embedding them in their plots, dramatists respond effectively to the theatre's peculiarities.

The new playwrights' ability to harness the Elizabethan structure's potential and counterbalance its ostensible shortcomings is perhaps most evident in the fact that their works have absolutely no restriction of setting in space and time and they consequently revel in exotic ambiences that tickle the audience's imagination, as shown in Table 3.2. Out of twenty-seven plays, only one is entirely set in contemporary Britain, Ché Walker's *The Frontline*, and its focus is precisely on the variety of people that make Camden an ever-surprising world in itself. The others range from before Creation (*Man Falling Down, The Globe Mysteries*) to the present (*The God of Soho, The Lightning Child*), with Antiquity (*The Golden Ass, The Storm, Helen, The Last Days of Troy, The Oresteia*, in a sense *The Burial at Thebes*) and the eighteenth century (*We the People, Liberty, A New World, Bedlam*) two frequently recurring choices. Though mostly rooted in British soil, they touch the Mediterranean (*The Golden Ass, The Storm, Helen, The Last Days of Troy, The Oresteia*), the Middle East (*Man Falling Down, The Globe Mysteries, Holy Warriors*), France (*In Extremis, Liberty, A New World, Anne Boleyn, Holy Warriors, Doctor Scroggy's War*), the United States (*We the People, A New World, The Lightning Child*), an unspecified Caribbean country (*The Burial at Thebes*), the island of *Pitcairn*, Mexico (*The Heresy of Love*), North Africa and the mouth of the Amazon (*Under the Black Flag*), venturing also on a trip to the Moon (*The Lightning Child*), a spell in Purgatory (*Holy Warriors*) and four visits to Heaven (*Man Falling Down, The Globe Mysteries, The God of Soho, The Last Days of Troy*).

*The Burial at Thebes* actually presents a rather complex situation because it is the opera version of Sophocles's *Antigone* as translated by Seamus Heaney. The poet's earlier well-known rendering of the classical tragedy already endowed it with a new layer of meaning by means of Hiberno-English terms that evoked analogies with the conflicts in twentieth-century Ireland (Cotta Ramusino 2009). While retaining this text almost unchanged, with all its implicit references, the Globe version sets the action in the Caribbean, so that three different contexts overlap in the performance. Although the West Indian environment is not inherent in the script, I think it must be taken into account because it is unquestionable not

*Table 3.2  Setting in time and space of each new play produced by Shakespeare's Globe Theatre*

| Play | Setting | |
|------|---------|---|
| | **Place** | **Time** |
| *Augustine's Oak* | Britain | Sixth–seventh centuries |
| *The Golden Ass* | Roman Empire | Second century |
| *The Storm* | Greece | Fifth century |
| *Man Falling Down* | Heaven; Eden; Britain | World's beginning; present |
| *Under the Black Flag* | England; North Africa; South America | 1649–1660 |
| *In Extremis* | France | Twelfth century |
| *Holding Fire* | Britain | 1837–1869 |
| *We the People* | United States of America | 1786–1787 |
| *The Frontline* | Camden | Present |
| *Liberty* | Paris | 1793–1794 |
| *The Burial at Thebes* | Greece/Ireland/the Caribbean | Antiquity/twentieth century |
| *Helen* | Egypt | Antiquity |
| *A New World* | England; United States of America; France | 1774–1809 |
| *Bedlam* | London | Eighteenth century |
| *Anne Boleyn* | England; Calais | 1527–1536; 1603–1604 |
| *The God of Soho* | Heaven; Soho; Essex | Present |

*Table 3.2 (Continued)*

| Play | Setting | |
|------|---------|---|
| | **Place** | **Time** |
| *The Globe Mysteries* | Heaven; Eden; Palestine | World's beginning–first century |
| *Gabriel* | London | 1690–1695 |
| *Blue Stockings* | Cambridge | 1896 |
| *The Lightning Child* | United States of America; Moon; Greece; London; South Africa | 1969; Antiquity; 2013; 2009; 1956 |
| *The Last Days of Troy* | Troy, then Hisarlik, Turkey | Antiquity; present |
| *Holy Warriors* | Holy Lands; Rome; Sicily; France; Purgatory; United States of America; England | Twelfth century–present |
| *Doctor Scroggy's War* | England; France | 1915–1917 approximately |
| *Pitcairn* | Pitcairn | 1789–1814 |
| *The Oresteia* | Greece | Antiquity |
| *The Heresy of Love* | Mexico | Seventeenth century |
| *Nell Gwynn* | London | Seventeenth century |

only in St Lucian Derek Walcott's design and direction but also in Trinidadian Dominique LeGendre's music, and if the former pertain to the production, the latter's Rapso rhythms and sounds must certainly be considered part of the opera's text.

In any case, the variety of places and even more of epochs represented on a stage that is apparently devoted to Elizabethan England is impressive and cannot be disregarded as a mere chance.

Both Howard Brenton and Jessica Swale have described the way the Globe can conjure up places as one of its main virtues:

> the big Globe space allows the writer to dictate the character ... you can say you're anywhere and the space allows that. Because it's a sort of blank canvas. (Swale 2014)

> It may have something to do with the powerful presence of the building itself; you can dress the stage but not change it; there are no sets, no projections, no lighting effects, just the collective imagination of the audience to awaken with words. (Brenton 2014b)

Equally telling is Dominic Dromgoole's proud answer to the people who were seeking new plays to be filmed for HBO: 'we're absolutely no use to you here because the sort of plays we are doing are, you know, two-hundred-million-dollar studio films, I mean we're doing blockbusters' (2006 EOSI).[17]

This grand, lavish quality is not restricted to the mostly imaginary design of the productions: an even more remarkable figure is the number of characters that take part in the action – and consequently of actors taking them on. In a time when most dramas are two- or three-handers or even monologues, the smallest cast required by these scripts is *Liberty*'s eight players, the average sixteen, while the characters range from *The Burial at Thebes*'s ten to *Holding Fire*'s seventy-nine, with an average of twenty-nine (see Table 3.3).

Just as in a musical – the kind of show that usually sports similar quantities of performers, and of spectators too – variety is instrumental in striking the audience's imagination and keeping it engaged. Since the visibility of fellow theatregoers and the unavoidable fixed scenery of Elizabethan architecture and décor make realism unattainable, playwrights are encouraged to exploit what Brenton aptly calls 'word painting' (2007) to create ever-changing, surprising environments and atmospheres. Music is of paramount importance in helping build stark contrasts or smooth transitions, but so are performers and costumes. A new situation can be promptly evoked by the entrance of one or more figures, their attitudes and apparel suggesting provenance, status, context or activity even before they start to speak,[22] but in order to make such changes swift, there must always be actors ready to take the

*Table 3.3  Number of characters and of actors for each new play produced by Shakespeare's Globe Theatre*

| Play | Characters[18] | Performers in the Globe production[19] |
|------|------------|----------------------------------|
| Augustine's Oak | 24 | 15 |
| The Golden Ass | 57 | 28 |
| The Storm | 12 | 9 |
| Man Falling Down | 54 | 9 |
| Under the Black Flag | 30 | 17 |
| In Extremis | 19 | 18 |
| Holding Fire | 79 | 18 |
| We the People | 33 | 25 |
| The Frontline | 23 | 23 |
| Liberty | 18 | 8 |
| The Burial at Thebes | 10 | 10 |
| Helen[20] | 11 | 16 |
| A New World | 37 | 20 |
| Bedlam | 17 | 17 |
| Anne Boleyn | 20 | 15 |
| The God of Soho | 21 | 11 |
| The Globe Mysteries | 34 | 13 |
| Gabriel | 54 | 18 |
| Blue Stockings | 21 | 17 |
| The Lightning Child | 26 | 17 |
| The Last Days of Troy | 16 | 12 |

*Table 3.3  (Continued)*

| Play | Characters[18] | Performers in the Globe production[19] |
|---|---|---|
| *Holy Warriors* | 62 | 20 |
| *Doctor Scroggy's War* | 39 | 16 |
| *Pitcairn* | 15 | 15 |
| *The Oresteia*[21] | 17 | 15 |
| *The Heresy of Love* | 12 | 12 |
| *Nell Gwynn* | 19 | 12 |
| Average | 29 | 16 |

stage even before their colleagues have left it, so that the piece's pace depends on the number of its players too.

The importance of this mechanism notwithstanding, the characters' number and diversity are even more relevant in presenting the varied audience with a symmetrically wide deployment of personalities, relationships and predicaments, so that any spectator can easily find someone to empathize with and that the frequent shifts between different plot strands can avert the perils of boredom and fatigue.

A more complex connection between the need to catch and hold the audience's interest and the uniqueness of Shakespeare's Globe can be recognized in the way some of its twenty-first-century authors have not only used but also represented the attractive potential of scandal. Even a very mild shock can reclaim the spectators' waning attention. Such is the function of many irreverent portrayals of divinities (Isis in *The Golden Ass*, Venus in *The Storm*, Dionysis in *The Lightning Child*, a whole pantheon in *The God of Soho*, the ancient deities in *The Last Days of Troy* and even the Christian God in some passages of *Man Falling Down* and *The Globe Mysteries*), sovereigns (Louis VI of France in *In Extremis*, Princess Victoria and Prince Albert in *Holding Fire*, Henry VIII, James I and the eponymous heroine in *Anne Boleyn*, Mary II in *Gabriel*, occasionally Richard III and Philip II of France in *Holy Warriors* and Charles II in *Nell*

*Gwynn*) or other authoritative people (e.g. Benjamin Franklin in *We the People* and *A New World* or John Dryden in *Nell Gwynn*). A similar effect can also be attained by the unexpected and funny use of four-letter words in contrast with a play's overall restrained and high-flown language and in the mouth of otherwise very dignified and almost solemn characters, like Mother Helene, abbess of Ste Marie Argenteuil (*IE* 68), or pious queen Bertha, whose 'oh bugger the monks!' (*AO* 49) turned out to be among the lines most quoted by reviewers (see e.g. Meeke 1999; Nightingale 1999).

These opportunities and their frequent usage notwithstanding, both the new playwrights and the management of Shakespeare's Globe often resort to the presence, or at least the promise, of stronger outrageous content.

The reconstructed playhouse's advertising leaflets have frequently teased theatregoers with such threats as 'a riotous erotic comedy of love and desire' (*The Golden Ass*), 'bare flesh and filthy language' (*Under the Black Flag*), 'beer, ballads, bad language and bloodshed' (*Holding Fire*), 'really bad language and really strong content' (*The Frontline*), or 'scenes of lust, violence, absurd comedy and unexpected romance' (*Bedlam*). Nothing unacceptable, but plenty of titillation and thrills. 'Health warnings' have also been humorously used this way, and many reviews comment on the notices Shakespeare's Globe publishes and on their alluring tone (e.g. Hart 2006a; Shore 2006a; Spencer 2006; Carpenter 2009a; Brown 2011; Coveney 2011; Mountford 2013).

> 'Contains dirty language, filthy content, nudity, violence and scenes of a highly sexual nature.' So reads the sign outside The Globe, warning audiences what to expect before they commit to Chris Hannan's new play.
>
> If such warnings don't make a sell-out, what will? (Cooper 2011)

Courting scandal is, at least to a certain extent, a way to court potential patrons too, and the reconstructed Elizabethan theatre has rather constantly built on the ill repute playhouses enjoyed in the sixteenth and seventeenth centuries in order to attract attention and customers. Some titles already seem to announce a sensation: people expect to find violence *Under the Black Flag*, sex in (*The God of*) *Soho* and all sorts of misbehaviour in *Bedlam*; *Helen* and

*Anne Boleyn* are famous femmes fatales; *The Story of Abelard and Heloise* (which is the subtitle of *In Extremis*) is a well-known love affair with a gory twist.

These promises are not always quite honoured. The nakedness in *Under the Black Flag* 'turns out to be a brief flash by the oldest member of the cast' (Irvine 2006; see *UBF* 25), and *Gabriel*'s bare man (*G* 36) is evidently meant to be funny rather than enticing, while only *The God of Soho* featured a young attractive actress in the nude (although the playwright expressly writes that he does not 'mind if her nakedness is done by non-realistic means', *GS* 83).

From the point of view of sensuality, too, some plays fulfil expectations but others do not.[23] Author Chris Hannan explains that sex in *The God of Soho* was carefully handled by director Raz Shaw and himself so as to make it funny rather than salacious (Hannan 2014), and the majority of reviewers thought they succeeded (e.g. Coveney 2011; Evans 2011; Nathan 2011).[24] The same can be said even more forcefully of Peter Oswald's take on Apuleius's sexually explicit *The Golden Ass*, in which several couples, not all human, copulate (or try to) in a quite comic and unrealistic atmosphere. *Bedlam* repeatedly suggests both that drunkenness leads to casual intercourse and that madwomen are frequently exposed to sexual assault, but scenes are written so that they may actually take place off stage or be immediately interrupted (as in the case of Laurence's attempt to rape May, *B* 100). Sexuality is much talked about but never performed in *The Lightning Child*. Spectators who thought *Helen*'s story to be 'hot' were in for disappointment: the main point of Euripides's and Frank McGuinness's play is precisely that Menelaus's wife has been waiting faithfully for him more than ten years, and after a short expression of their enthusiasm at recognizing each other (*H* 28–30) the focus shifts to their flight from Egypt, so the famed ancient beauty has at most a few occasions to flirt with her husband. Similarly, Howard Brenton offers very little in the way of enticement in either *In Extremis* or *Anne Boleyn*, since both plays contain several dialogues on the subject of sex (*IE* 10–12, 17–18, 37–40, 41–5, 46, 49–50, 54–7, 60–1, 61–2, 63–4, 67–8, 74, 86; *AB* 15, 18, 25, 29, 30–2, 40–1, 51, 53, 68–9, 70, 95–6, 107, 109, 109–10), but hardly any nudity or intercourse in the former and none in the latter.

*Anne Boleyn* is an example of another unfulfilled implied promise too: while contemporary literary and cinematic accounts of Tudor times often dwell on fierce acts, Brenton's script contains threats (*AB* 43–6, 53–4, 55–7, 109–10) and a witness's horrific account of torture (*AB* 51–2), besides the protagonist's memories of her beheading (*AB* 11, 113–14), but on the plane of action it is hardly violent. Words and bullying behaviour build up a stiflingly menacing atmosphere but give no satisfaction to an audience's morbid curiosity. This forceful indirect representation of violence had a partial precedent in II.4 of *In Extremis*, in which Abelard is emasculated. More than one critic protested the scene was too tame,[25] probably because the action is very fast and almost invisible: after a page of threatening dialogue (*IE* 63), the victim is pulled down and thus hidden by his attackers (*IE* 63); among further menacing allusions a knife is raised out of the scrum (*IE* 64); Abelard screams and is left bleeding on the ground, while one of the aggressors gives Fulbert something gory that fills him with horror (*IE* 64).[26]

These choices are in contrast with those of many Globe plays, that rather dwell on gruesome spectacles. Besides innumerable fisticuffs and beatings and a handful of hangings, although sometimes incomplete, there are several gory images in these plays, from the comparatively peaceful blood-letting and leeches of *Bedlam* (*B* 20–1) to Natty's literally spectacular marital violence (*GS* 52–4).

These scenes, just like the sexually charged ones, are particularly affecting for the spectators because the actors' bodies are but a few feet – sometimes inches – away. In the programme for *The Globe Mysteries* Richard Beadle explains the original and possibly current goal of such a frightening close-up presentation in the case of the Passion:

> The mysteries portrayed the terrible sufferings of his last days and his cruel death by crucifixion, at length and in unswerving detail, in some of the most violent and affecting scenes ever seen on the English stage. It was held to be the moment of humanity's redemption from sin and death, holding out to believers the promise of an everlasting life hereafter, and it was the dramatists' aim to ensure that their audiences were made to feel personally and deeply implicated in what they saw on stage. (Beadle 2011: 3)

This may still be true for some spectators, but certainly not for all, so the display of violence must have another sense. A possible interpretation is that it is meant precisely to stress the current lack of compassion, portrayed in the 'professional' attitude Tony Harrison gives to the knights that torture and crucify Jesus (see *M* 124–7, 134–48). This aspect of the Passion scenes was emphasized in Deborah Bruce's production by a silent piece of stage business which added a still more disturbingly morbid dimension to the executioners' indifference for their victim's suffering: after raising and securing the cross, they took a picture of themselves smiling proudly beside the result of their 'good job'.[27]

A critique of the widespread voyeuristic attitude towards cruelty and gore can be hypothesized also in *The God of Soho*'s bloodthirsty tabloids (*GS* 17, 35–6, 53–4) and in the mix of gruesome details and cheap sentimentality with which Antonia describes at length the field dressing of a deer for a hypothetical cooking TV programme at the end of *The Lightning Child* (*LC* 61).[28] A similar, though more oblique, criticism may perhaps be recognized in the treatment of *Holding Fire*'s scene 2.14, in which the blood-soaked Lizzie and Will quarrel literally over Eli's corpse (*HF* 66–8). The sensational nature of this scene seems to be later commented on by the play itself when the murderous lovers become the object of a street ballad (*HF* 69–70, 106–7),[29] thus exposing the way both representations cater for a popular morbid taste.

No specific reflection seems to underlie the numerous gory images of *Under the Black Flag*, on the contrary: several people are killed in various but constantly gruesome ways (*UBF* 28, 38, 51, 52, 59, 67, 108–10, 122, 137, 138, 143) and sometimes tortured at length (*UBF* 91–2, 92–5, 99), limbs are severed (*UBF* 98, 141–42) and eyes blinded (*UBF* 69), so that a flogging (*UBF* 30) almost appears to be irrelevant; an episode of cannibalism is kept off stage (*UBF* 73), either because considered excessive or due to the technical difficulties of its representation, and its repetition is announced but prevented (by killing the potential cannibal, *UBF* 142–3). They certainly convey the idea of an endless cycle of revenge, but they do not comment specifically on the spectacle of violence.

Whatever the messages they purport, these plays certainly do so by means of considerable quantities of stage blood. They thus exploit the morbid curiosity Hannan, Shepherd and Walker seem to expose. In the case of these three playwrights, the choice to show the kind of gruesomely appealing images they denounce can be a double-edged sword: on the one hand it involves the spectators very effectively in a reflection on how they respond to such scenes, but on the other it feeds and maybe even exploits that same taste for the detailed depiction of atrocities. The desensitization they highlight seems to have reached theatre critics too, since they hardly ever mention this aspect of *Holding Fire*, *The God of Soho* or *The Lightning Child*. Chris Hannan himself (2014), when asked about the risk of pandering to the morbidity he exposed with graphic representations of sex and violence, answered with an account of how he collaborated with director Raz Shaw to make the couple's love-making (*GS* 67–9) funny and then sad, not salacious at all, but did not even mention Natty's beating Baz so savagely that his bleeding face leaves a red pool on the stage (*GS* 53–4).

It is interesting to notice that on the contrary Ché Walker felt the need to justify the violence of *The Frontline* (Smith 2008), though just by saying that Gloucester's blinding in *King Lear* (3.7) is far worse. Yet his Camden-based play is much less gory than the others discussed here: there are several fights of different kinds (*F* 20, 39, 39–40, 107, 109, 110), but only one weapon actually gets to be used, the gun that kills Miruts with a single shot (*F* 109). What makes both critics and author react more in this case is probably the combination of contemporary setting and realistic presentation, not so much of the scene as of the whole play: the grotesque and symbolic tones of *The God of Soho* or *The Lightning Child* and the distance in time that marks all the other texts seem to make them feel less real, although the atrocities they portray are represented with gruesome precision.

All these recurring features, and the specific ways in which they are used by the Globe's twenty-first-century dramatists, manifest the preoccupation to attract and hold the audience's attention with uninterrupted tenacity. At the same time, they often display the will and the ability to capitalize on the reconstructed playhouse's peculiarities – the obvious historical and cultural connections, the impressive acoustics, the paradoxical versatility of its fixed scenery, the proximity of spectators and performers or even the punters' visibility itself – in order to address the issue of potentially catastrophic distractions.

# Spectators as interlocutors

The spectators' visibility and audibility is certainly one of the main sources of distraction for their fellow theatregoers at Shakespeare's Globe, but it is also something shows can play on, including the punters in the spectacle, acquiring a metatheatrical edge and engaging the patrons directly. Like participants in a jam session, theatregoers are invited to contribute so as to make each performance lively and unique. Strategies of involvement are implemented when plays are staged, but their origins can often be traced back to the scripts, which can allow, suggest, plan or even prescribe them. Playwrights can thus assign several kinds of roles to audience members. Their importance as creative agents is attested by what has become a tradition: at the end of the last night of each production, the actors throw roses into the auditorium, thus reversing the custom of showering stage stars with flowers and inviting the spectators to take a bow and enjoy a success that is attributed to them too.

As director Tim Carroll put it, at the Globe 'an actor cannot go out on that stage and give a soliloquy without speaking directly to the audience. It would be perverse: they are clearly in the same place as the actor' (Carroll 2008: 40). So every time playwrights write a soliloquy for this space, the situation they are creating is that of a performer 'holding a conversation with the audience' (Chahidi 2008: 204), in the words of experienced Globe actor Paul Chahidi. This kind of direct relationship between people on stage and in the auditorium is pretty frequent (e.g. *AO* 73, *GA* 95–7, *S* 34, *UBF* 70, *AB* 41, *GS* 33, *DSW* 47), and it seems to form a connection stronger than the one it entailed in Elizabethan and Jacobean times. In the late sixteenth and early seventeenth centuries, as Anne Righter pointed out (1962: 55–6), it established an intentionally indeterminate relationship, while nowadays stage practice at the Globe tends to consolidate the conviction expressed by these and many other artists that soliloquies put character and spectator firmly in the same reality. This different attitude may clash with the desire to bring back to life the theatre world for which Shakespeare wrote, but it is very likely a consequence precisely of that drive. More specifically, the two diverging perspectives derive from reaching the same crucial point from opposite directions. Elizabethan playwrights could sense in the actor talking to the audience a vestige of the Mysteries' framework (ibid.: 20–2), which was likely to grate with the progressive separation of performers and patrons. Twenty-first-century artists, on the contrary, experience the shared space and light of the Globe theatre as part of a movement that aims at challenging and perhaps destroying the fourth wall centuries of proscenium-arch stages have solidly established. It is therefore natural that in dealing with the same ambiguous situation of a single character potentially bonding with the spectators the former authors would play it down, the latter embrace it with enthusiasm.

A peculiar kind of soliloquy is, from the theatrical point of view, the prayer (e.g. *UBF* 76), in which characters address other-worldly beings that do not appear on stage and may thus turn out to be the 'gods' in the upper gallery; this possibly brings such supplications nearer to the passages in which audience members are given a specific role in the play rather than to a proper soliloquy, because it implies the presence of other characters, not in the performance area but in the auditorium.

A canonical use of the device can be recognized on the contrary in the solitary speeches of Bishop Santa Cruz (*HL* 10–11, 46, 67, 96), the ambitious clergyman who will ultimately bring about the fall of sister Juana de la Cruz in Helen Edmundson's *The Heresy of Love*, based on the historical figure of the seventeenth-century Mexican nun who wrote philosophical, sacred and secular poems, drama and prose works. In the play, Santa Cruz recognizes, like everybody else, her intelligence and talent, he feels attracted to her, but he is ready to sacrifice her in his pursuit of power, especially after he is made to believe she has betrayed him. A deceiver and a schemer whose plans largely determine the piece's plot, the bishop explains his projects and their motivations in several soliloquies. In doing so, he has an obvious precedent in Shakespearean figures such as Richard III and Iago. Just as those characters referred back to the Moralities' Vice (Righter 1962: 86–8), Edmundson's creation builds on the audience's ability to recognize this parentage in order to be not only understood as a convention but also appreciated as part of a successful tradition. Yet the main function of all these villains' confessions remains that of alerting the audience of their lies and thus making the subsequent scenes easier to follow. From this point of view, their speeches are close to the very practical ones that often mark the opening of a script.

An audience-directed monologue towards the beginning of a play or section thereof often provides spectators with some useful information concerning the setting or the premises of what will follow (see e.g. *S* 9, *UBF* 29, *H* 3–5, *AB* 14, *GS* 13, *O* 5); more seldom, the same sort of monologue may wrap up the plot towards its end (as in *GA* 103). This function can also be performed by a more traditional prologue, spoken by a character that does not belong to the story (the Weather, *S* 7–9) or plays a minor and often passive role (Aneirin, *AO* 11).

This sort of introductory part is rather common in drama, and its liminal position, bridging the gap between the theatregoers' reality and the fictional world, allows it to trespass the fourth wall without breaking it, so to speak. But several of the new plays written for Shakespeare's Globe (*We the People, The Frontline, A New World, Gabriel, The Lightning Child, The Last Days of Troy, Pitcairn*)[30] feature a sort of narrator that intervenes also in the middle of the action to offer further information or comments. The classical chorus may interpret the situation and form opinions on it for the benefit of the spectators without addressing them directly and rather giving the impression to be just expressing their feelings or sharing remarks among themselves (see e.g. *BT* 8–9, *H* 44 or *O* 20–2). The narrator figures, on the contrary, undertake rather explicitly the task to guide the audience through the play, although sometimes their words may not be incongruous with their fictional context, especially when their role is confined to certain scenes; in *We the People*, for instance, Timothy Matlack behaves as if he were talking to other patrons of the Indian Queen Tavern when he introduces some of the delegates as they arrive (*WP* 15).

The twenty-first-century Zeus of *The Last Days of Troy* is a sort of busker and pedlar based near the archaeological site of ancient Troy. Beside selling *Iliad*-themed souvenirs and posing as a statue of his ancient almighty self, he recites the story of the well-known siege and thus takes on the role of narrator in a realistic context at the beginning of the play (*LDT* 7). In the second half of scene 1 this situation already veers towards a traditional soliloquy as he abandons the professional stance but perseveres in the narrative as an old man might dwell on the recollection of momentous events (*LDT* 8). His following interventions have no such context; on the contrary, he details situations almost like a voice-over commentator during the ancient characters' speechless actions (*LDT* 32–4) or dialogues

(*LDT* 59–62) and introduces episodes in a historical present (*LDT* 49–50, 83–4, 102, 131) that may sound like a journalist's chronicle ('We'd been expecting resolution here today, a killer blow to bring this great war to an end, but instead … confusion reigns', *LDT* 49). Even though he never addresses the audience in the second person, his position in a non-theatrical context is only initially established, but then abandoned in favour of explicitly direct communication with the spectators. A suggestion on the part of present-day Hera that he is all the time talking to himself like a slightly deranged person might do (*LDT* 103) is not strong enough to counterbalance his recurring presence on the margins of Homeric scenes and can easily be dismissed as a nagging wife's generic grumbling.

Simon Armitage makes Zeus an obviously double character, acting as the king of gods in antiquity and narrating as a poor old man in twenty-first-century Turkey. Other playwrights assign the two roles of participant in the action and commentator for the benefit of the audience to the same figure, but make the distinction less clear. Hiti and Mata, for instance, who take turns to explain situations on Pitcairn, do so simply by addressing spectators directly, without any change in their aspect, behaviour or perspective as the two youngest inhabitants of the island. Their knowledge is apparently based on hindsight and thus enables them to anticipate what is to come (e.g. 'The next history day is the day we launched the boat', *P* 95). Yet it is limited to what they will experience directly, a condition which explains the need for two different narrator figures. 'I do not know what happens next so I will sit and watch the next history day with you' (*P* 87), Hiti himself declares at the end of the scene in which he has died. The supposition could be advanced that even though they do not undergo any visible change and switch seamlessly from one mode to the other, the two young Tahitians inhabit two different time frames: the fictional one, in which they live day by day like all other characters, and the one of their listeners, to whom they present events on the island like memories. The distinction is blurred, though, since Hiti seems to share with the audience immediately the realization that his love for Mata is requited (*P* 53). All in all, their status appears to be deliberately ambivalent.

In *A New World*, Trevor Griffiths makes Franklin's narrator status explicit by having him relate Tom Paine's life retrospectively, from what can be described as the point of view of a ghost, though one that plays the role that was his, when his presence is required.

This complex situation first shows in Franklin's initial monologue, when he concludes: 'trouble is, I can't recall if I'm here to meet him or to send him off. Never mind, he'll know' (*NW* 1). As a matter of fact, there will be several scenes in which Paine arrives at or leaves from a port's docks throughout his story (*TAT* 2–4; 8–9; 102–4; 106–7; 147–150; 150–1; 182–3; 183–4), so it is humorously true that it is easier to tell his bearings for the character, who lives in the moment, than for the narrator, who keeps all these greetings and farewells in his mind. It is interesting to remark that this uncertainty was not in the screenplay. In a film, costumes and make-up, titles and effects make situations easier to recognize, and the narration is mainly carried out in voice-over, so that Franklin would appear only as a character, just like Paine, while on stage his double status may cause in the audience the little confusion he is made to share here. Actually, the production's creative team discussed 'whether "Franklin" is dead throughout' and having determined that 'he is alive for two scenes' but 'when he is narrating he is dead', went on to consider how could this difference be shown by means of make-up and costume changes.[31]

Another couple of lines the playwright added at the end of the first act are meant to help spectators understand the situation again with a metatheatrical joke:

The Author in the Sky determined long ago I should quit this role on the 17th April 1790. The Author here below has perhaps opportunistically decided to ignore that determination. Thus is it that – the length of the line for the Necessary permitting – we'll meet again, resume the journey, shall we say 20 minutes ... (*NW* 92–3)

In the course of the play, Griffiths also exploits the ambiguous temporal coordinates of his Franklin to give him a particularly rich and varied language, abounding in metaphors (like the euphemistic periphrasis for God that originates the joke quoted here), indicating aspects of the audience's world with eighteenth-century terms (e.g. the 'Necessary' above) and anachronistically quoting authors of the future,[32] while as a realistic character in the film he was necessarily limited to the lexicon and references of his time.

These narrator figures' ambiguous relationship with the audience, which they in turn ignore, draw into the fictional world or address as such, may once again recall the passage from medieval to modern drama. Anne Righter has described sundry solutions adopted by sixteenth-century dramatists to negotiate the coexistence of an increasingly self-contained fictional reality and the still unavoidably visible and audible crowd of theatregoers (Righter 1962: 31–78, *passim*), the majority of which involve a character addressing spectators in a somewhat ambivalent fashion. A significant difference between this transitional phase and the Globe experiment seems to be, as in the specific case of soliloquies, the opposite feelings their inherent volatility excites: embarrassment and concern in Tudor and Elizabethan times, enthusiasm and enjoyment in the third millennium, in accordance with the symmetrical movements away from and towards a stronger participation of the audience. A reversed distribution of relax and preoccupation can be observed with regard to the playgoers' need for explanations: while in the first permanent London theatres dramatists could find more competent and concentrated spectators than those who crowded church squares, inn yards and banqueting halls (ibid.: 55), the reconstructed Globe's playwrights have to cater for an especially diverse array of patrons unaccustomed to the distractions of an open-air, fully lit venue. From this point of view, a situation which is basically the same is perceived and experienced by artists and punters alike in antithetical ways depending on the previous and contemporary customs which have formed their expectations.

As for the features direct address usually displays in the new plays produced by Shakespeare's Globe Theatre, both in soliloquies and in the narrators' words, it gains strength from all aspects of speech that actually summon the audience. The most immediate one is the use of the second person pronoun 'you' referring to the spectators (e.g. in *B* 105 or *GS* 60). Its effect can be reinforced by the presence of something that points specifically to the theatregoers' reality as opposed to the fictional one, such as Ladyboy Herald's 'crowd-a-people' when there is no mob on stage (*LC* 16, 26) and his suggestion to interpret the play 'on the train home' (*LC* 30) or Sceparnio's contrasting 'your present' with 'my future' (*S* 34).

Another way to highlight the relationship between a character and the audience is to have him or her give information regarding the performance, such as the initial announcements (*S* 7), the interval's beginning and its duration (*NW* 92–3, *AB* 69), sometimes even hinting at the refreshments on sale (*S* 59, *F* 65) or, on one occasion, the warning that there will be a gunshot (S 86). A weaker version of this use can be recognized in Aristomenus's granting Clytus a fifteen-minute break (GA 46) and later offering him a cup of tea (GA 75):[33] the characters give the necessary information, but without addressing the spectators. Since Peter Oswald went from *Augustine's Oak*, that has no such announcement, through this compromise, to *The Storm*'s Sun and Rain explicitly forecasting snacks and stating that 'the Storm will resume in fifteen minutes' (S 59), it is possible to suppose that the virtues of direct address emerged in the course of his experience as resident playwright at the Globe, and this specific device was later appreciated and appropriated by other authors too.[34]

Finally, an effective way to stress the presence of the audience in the characters' words is by suggesting they expect a reaction, most commonly by asking a question, or respond to a supposed input from the spectators. This is a less widely employed device, because it is somewhat risky: the scene may be spoiled, if theatregoers give the wrong answer, whether they voice it or just think it and feel dissatisfied with what follows, apparently showing that the character does not understand them. On the other hand, if spectators do react as expected, the dialogue that ensues, however short and superficial, creates a strong bond between stage and auditorium. The mildest effect of this kind can be obtained by asking little more than a rhetorical question. A slightly stronger commitment is required when the character seems to be answering a predictable request from the audience (e.g. GA 103).

In *The Storm* Oswald goes further by having Sceparnio express the wish for a mobile phone, until a groundling offers his or hers, then wonder at it, seek instructions and eventually declare that it is quite useless, because he does not have the number of the person he wants to call (S 50).[35] This monologue requires at least one audience member to take part in the action as anticipated by the script, but it is written so as to make the spectators' collaboration probable and easy, and it even provides for a way out in case the interaction does not unfold according to plan. If no one reacts promptly, the actor, alone on stage, can improvise a little on the subject of the amazing technological device he is dreaming of, so as to give people the time to get the hint and decide to play along;[36] since he is surrounded by dozens of theatregoers, it would be very odd if none of them produced the desired cell phone, and the answer to Sceparnio's 'how does it [work?]' is bound to mention pretty soon the need to dial the number; in the very unlikely event that nobody cooperates, all the performer has to do is give up the gag and skip to the conclusion that he must needs search for Plesidippus in person ('I'll have to go and look for him myself, using my classical eyes and my ancient Greek feet! At the end of the day you can only rely on yourself', *S* 50), because the following action is not based on the assumption that he makes a phone call but on this renunciation.

Although in this passage Peter Oswald expects an audience member to perform some actions, he can rely on the fact that handing a telephone to a person who needs it and explaining its use are rather usual gestures; moreover, it is enough for the scene to work if only one groundling towards the front complies. In other passages, a more generalized and less predictable consent is required. Again in *The Storm*, Daemones's out-of-character speech regarding anachronisms interrupts his reflections on suffering as in response to the audience's attitude:

And as for Happy Christmas,
It's just a happy slappy mishmash –
What? I've never heard of Christmas?
*He goes downstage.*
Look – relax about the anachronisms. We've got permission.
  (*S* 18)

For his reaction to be reasonable, no explicit comment from the audience is necessary, nor do all spectators have to be silently puzzled or annoyed by the reference to Christmas. Each theatregoer can easily believe that somebody else's expression cued the explanation. If, that is, they can see the problem; otherwise, Daemones's sudden change of tone and subject will be quite meaningless. But it is fair to presume that a vast majority of the audience will immediately realize what is supposed to have happened, and that some are probably perplexed by the anachronisms themselves.

Richard Bean has the two *Pitcairn* narrators interact with spectators repeatedly and even includes their responses in the text, either as part of the character's speech ('Do you have this in England? Performers who don't work in the fields, and the workers have an obligation to feed them if they do performances? You do?', *P* 45) or in stage directions that somewhat paradoxically describe behaviours they cannot prescribe (e.g. 'Girls, hand up, who would sleep with a sailor for a nail? Two nails? *(There's always one.)*', *P* 16). These scripted audience reactions may recall those conceived by Piscator (see Bennett 1997: 24–6) and like them they are mostly based on a sort of reflex on the part of the theatregoers, who are very likely to repeat the answers they have just been taught, for instance (*P* 7). Bean takes a little risk when he asks the actor to address a single patron ('You, I'm talking to you', *P* 16, and 'You! Raise your arm', *P* 16); in these cases, he possibly counts on the performer's ability to spot the right person from their reaction to the previous general questions as well as on the fact that in such a peculiar venue as Shakespeare's Globe playgoers who stand near the stage are usually conscious they may be engaged directly and willing to cooperate. However, none of the responses Hiti and Mata are drawn to expect is actually necessary to the action's developments, they rather entail a little clowning on the verge of improvisation, so in case the audience should not comply, the actors can either change or skip the gag rather easily, without jeopardizing the overall success of the performance.

The beginning of *Anne Boleyn* will be analysed more in detail in the context of the play as a whole. Nevertheless, it may be appropriate to anticipate here that it involves a considerable piece of audience interaction (*AB* 11), because the heroine, alone on stage, repeatedly asks the audience not only rhetorical questions ('see?' or 'ready?') and interrogatives that could be directed to herself ('would it be a scandal?'), but proper questions, requiring an explicit answer ('do you want to see it? Who wants to see it? Do you?') and then she acts consequently. If theatregoers should answer that they do not want to see anything or guess that the promised scandalous spectacle is her Bible, the scene would not work, because her following words would be meaningless. Now, while the first condition for this dialogue to be consistent is easily met – theatregoers are there precisely because they want to see something and have no reason to deny it – the second is not as predictable: it is based on the assumption that the object or image everybody immediately connects to Anne Boleyn is not a book. Actually, for this soliloquy to realize its full potential, the audience's expectation must be, ideally, to be shown the severed head she will produce from the bag successively, or at least something as sensational, so that their disappointed looks at the Bible may prompt her exclamation ('don't you realise? This killed me!') and then her guessing at what they are after. Since this passage is based on a rather morbid curiosity on the part of the audience, which it highlights, it places a high bet on the spectators' attitude; it thus runs the risk of weakening the scene considerably, but when it succeeds it achieves the realization of a funny and pithy critique of the public's voyeurism.[37]

## Spectators as supernumeraries

The spectators' contribution to a performance at Shakespeare's Globe is not limited to their inner reactions or to the answers they may occasionally voice. They often act as more or less conscious spear-carriers. *The Storm* features a gag in which a voluntary from the audience is taken backstage, put in a basic costume and actually given a line to speak (*S* 57–8), but this is not the point. More significantly, the crowd of theatregoers, perfectly visible and in full light, is constantly part of the spectacle. In such passages as those discussed in the previous paragraph, their presence is acknowledged, but they are considered to be acting as themselves; elsewhere, they are cast in different, specific roles. An intermediate situation can be recognized in the final episode of *The Globe Mysteries*, 'Doomsday', when God addresses the multitude of good and bad souls (see *M* 224–7) that almost inevitably coincides with the spectators, but since the Judgement is set in the present and concerns every human being, audience members can still be considered to star in the show as themselves.[38]

In a sense, both situations are actually rooted in medieval Mystery plays (see Righter 1962: 20–4). The protagonist of those cycles was mankind, and the spectators were, without the need for any pretence, its natural representatives in the performance. Their inevitable involvement in the drama of Salvation could then at times become the basis for their identification with more specific collective characters, such as the addressees of a king's orders or of a prophet's warnings. They were the community who was reliving biblical history in the first person, the obvious partners and interlocutors of their fellow citizens, non-professional actors, who performed the main roles on the stage.

In the twenty-first century, *The Globe Mysteries* did not have the same ritual, religious value, that could only be based on the shared belief that the events dramatized were really at the core of each participant's existence. The representation of Tony Harrison's text was generally intended to be fictional rather than truthful. Nevertheless, as the 'Doomsday' episode shows, it aimed at engaging the audience directly, indicating them as the hypothetical, if not actual, addressees and ultimate beneficiaries of the staged action. Furthermore, by referring to a dramatic tradition as well as to a faith that characterized most of the spectators' heritage, it implicitly portrayed them as a community, at least from a historical point of view. Pointing out a shared past is, as shown in the previous chapter, a continuous and almost unavoidable effect of the reconstructed Elizabethan theatre, very often enhanced by its productions. So the community-building aspect of speeches that address the spectators as a specific – even though fictional – collective body chimes not only with the audience-centred architecture but also with the overall meaning of its cultural references.

Once again, as with soliloquies and audience address in general, passages that cast the patrons in the role of a specific crowd acquire in the twenty-first century a connotation that is almost antithetical to the one they could have for Shakespeare's contemporaries. Even though in both contexts they can remind listeners of the earlier medieval drama rooted in a community of citizens-believers-participants, nowadays they constitute not so much the repurposed survival of a previous convention (Righter 1962: 77–8) as rather an expression of the newly regained possibility of experiencing the performance collectively instead of individually, isolated by the allocated spaces and selective lighting of proscenium-arch theatres. Since this attitude is at the core of the Globe project, and the themes of history and identity recur in the new works produced by the reconstructed playhouse, it is not surprising that their audience should be repeatedly called to perform a role, not only in the context of a third-millennium mystery play.

Playgoers can easily be cast as almost themselves when they are presented with a performance within the performance. An instance of this minimal shift from their actual identity can be recognized in the beginning of *The Last Days of Troy*, when the present-day Zeus starts his narrative as if he were offering it to the archaeological site's visitors (*LDT* 7). It is almost predictable that this relationship should then gradually slip into a plain narrator-audience rapport, as described in the previous subchapter. Jessica Swale's *Nell Gwynn*, portraying the story of one of the first British actresses, features several passages in which spectators are implicitly asked to play their seventeenth-century equivalents (*NG* 16–19, 52–4, 60–1, 102–3, 131–2). In this case, the identification can be more forceful, because the scenes are set in a theatre, and they can even spill out of the traditional acting area into other parts of the auditorium: in 1.1 Nell is selling oranges in the yard and from there she talks to Ned, who is delivering a prologue on the stage, and to the Hecklers, whose shouts can come from anywhere in the galleries or among the groundlings, thus emphasizing the punters' involvement in the play (*NG* 16–18); 1.9 and 2.3 require King Charles II to attend a performance and interact with the actors from the royal box (*NG* 102–3), which is very likely to be represented by the lords' rooms (i.e. the parts of the upper gallery directly above the stage) in the Globe.[39]

Just as in some of the first plays that employed this feature to experiment with the changing relationship between stage and auditorium in secularized drama (Righter 1962: 34–5), theatregoers are often more generally typecast, so to speak, as punters, customers or targets for street vendors. In *Bedlam*, for instance, they are offered gin (*B* 11, 12, 49, 53, 69), invited to bet on the outcome of a bare knuckle contest (*B* 11) or of a cock fight (*B* 12) and asked to remunerate the Bedlamites for their singing (*B* 13, 70), while near the tube station of *The Frontline* salvation is among the goods being hawked (*F* 8–9, 19–20), together with food (*F* 5–7, 108), drugs (*F* 9–12) and lap dances (*F* 5, 11, 13).[40] In *Under the Black Flag*, too, it is religious beliefs Ebenezer, John Silver and Tom try to sell (*UBF* 16–17, 21–4); the published script assumes the mob they address to be represented in part by a few actors (a Digger, *UBF* 16, and at least four Citizens), but the prompt book's version goes even further, cutting these roles and thus assigning exclusively to the audience the role of the crowd whom the agitators incite and the soldiers disperse.[41]

This trope can become disquieting because of the merchandise on offer. The spectators must feel at least uncomfortable when, in *A New World*, a trader shows them a pair of slaves, plainly extolling their merits and suggesting how to use them. This situation is only hinted at in the screenplay (*TAT* 11, 12), but Griffiths developed it into a full monologue for the stage:

Ladies and Gentlemen, like the Good Lord himself at the marriage feast of Canaa, the best has been left for the last, Parcel

No 12, the Last Parcel, friends, a father and son the papers say,
step up an' tek a closer look if ye will, touch 'em if ye like, they're
perfectly housetrained, what 'm I bid for this un, or this un, or
the pair together? ... Look at this un. Perfect for drawin'. Perfect
for pullin'. Study the hams. The hocks. Perfect for breedin' too,
study the loin, study the groin, I'll tek fifty, I'll tek fifty five,
this 'n'll give ye peekynins for a new dawn, so he will ... Good
English, this 'n, smart, up from the Carolinas ... (NW 6)

Although this speech is delivered at the same time as a short
dialogue, it is bound to attract the audience's attention, both for the
way it is voiced by the 'Barker' and because it necessarily hurts the
listeners' sensibility by describing people as if they were animals,
even quoting the Gospels in the process. Spectators cannot help
playing the part of perspective buyers, and are thus compelled to
ask themselves how would they react in that situation – and what
to do in the present one, actually, because they must decide whether
to look at the slave characters or not, and how.

A similar scene was initially written by Peter Oswald for the
beginning of *Augustine's Oak*: in a Roman market, a trader would
have presented to the theatregoers various people on sale, until Pope
Gregory came by and bought them their freedom. On the one hand,
this episode would have been stronger than the one in *A New World*
due to its position at the opening of the play, to its longer duration
and to the absence of any other contemporaneous action on stage;
on the other hand, its words sound less outrageous because there is
no quotation from the Scriptures, there are less specific references
to the slaves' bodies, and observations on their various nationalities
tend to give it a generally lighter, almost playful tone. Unfortunately
this scene, which is present from the second to the sixth drafts (dated,
respectively, 9 December 1998 and 14 April 1999), disappears from
the seventh (7 June 1999), presumably because of the choice to cut
the Roman setting and the character of Pope Gregory.

The audience may feel uneasy in a different way when cast as
spectators of objectionable shows; if the implied accusation is less
grievous, they may not feel as sure of their innocence: after all, they
have come to see a performance that was likely to feature those
scenes. Self-examination is thus prompted in *Bedlam* when the
Narrator addresses some theatregoers as if they were the Sunday
visitors who come to watch the asylum's patients for entertainment

(*B* 35). Similarly, the Ringmaster presents the third part of *The Golden Ass* as if it were a variety show characterized by all sorts of violence (*GA* 76, 77, 91, 95). In this section of the play, Lucius, still a donkey, is appalled by the careless lust and insensitive cruelty of the people around him, that 'are all beasts' (*GA* 89). He refuses to rape a woman, shouting, 'I shall not do this! I am not human!' (*GA* 95) and then starts to harangue those watching him, who 'are turning into worse than vermin' (*GA* 95). Those 'human lions,/Vultures with hands,/Rats with ambitions' (*GA* 94–5) are none other but the spectators of the play, who have been presumably laughing at its many funnily depicted horrors.

In an earlier episode of the same text, the audience had already been standing in for its fictional counterpart, when Lucius was tried for the murder of three Thessalians (*GA* 34–40), not in the courtroom but in the amphitheatre, ostensibly by reason of the interest his case attracted (*GA* 36), actually because it was a huge joke the whole city played on him (*GA* 40). Then, too, a connection was drawn between a gruesome spectacle and the fierceness of its spectators: the culprit was ordered to remove the cover and show the corpses of his victims before the method of his execution was chosen, so that all could 'be beasts' as he had been (*GA* 38–9). So both scenes make the spectators feel part of a desensitized audience and urge them to consider their attitude and responsibility in relation to the spectacle of violence.

Theatregoers are cast as jurors of sorts in *Liberty* too. In the course of the play, every time characters must face an interrogation or plead their case in a court of law, they speak, alone on stage, directly to the audience (*L* 89–90, 97–8, 112). This choice is important because it compels spectators to identify themselves momentarily with the people responsible for the Reign of Terror, its trials and its executions, and not only with the victims represented by most of the protagonists. The sequence of these scenes is structured so as to develop the listeners' compassion towards the characters' faults. First comes the magistrate Renaudin, a secondary and clearly unsympathetic character, who makes fun of Evariste when he is a newcomer (*L* 47–8) and then becomes more and more sheepishly ready to repeat his every word when his colleague's authority grows (*L* 84–6); more importantly, in his judicial work he aims at condemning as many of the accused as possible (*L* 47–9) and he makes arbitrary decisions (*L* 84), so when he falls victim of a hasty trial himself the audience may be tempted to think that justice is done; they are compelled to reconsider the harshness of this judgement when he asks for mercy stressing that he has a wife and they expect a child (L 89–90). Next, it is Louise who answers the questions that are supposed to come from the magistrates among the spectators (L 97–8); self-important and sharp-tongued (see e.g. L 51–3), she is arrested in consequence of her insisting to meet Marat (L 86), but when after trying to explain her position (L 97–8) she finally bursts in anger and contempt, her aristocratic dignity becomes evident (L 98) and shows the dramatic aspect of her attempts to adapt to the new revolutionary order. The third character to be interrogated is Philippe (L 112), whom the audience knows to be very likely guilty, as his first dialogue with Evariste contains a sort of unspoken confession (L 15). Nevertheless, his speech is probably the most affecting, not only because since the first scene he has been a pleasant figure, wittily criticizing his friend's excesses (see e.g. L 61), but also due to the fact that his final assertion, 'I agree with everything you want me to!' puts his judges, i.e. the spectators, in the position of brainwashers imposing their views on one of the most critical and independent-minded characters in the play (although the rest of the act will show that Philippe has only superficially capitulated, but is still quite himself).

Finally, not in a trial but on his way to the guillotine, Evariste himself harangues the audience as if people were laughing at him for his conviction that the Terror as well as the Revolution is instrumental to the achievement of future liberties (L 123). Once again, he appears to be a victim of the system he has supported and implemented, and he is unquestionably guilty of witnessing his friends' ruin in cold blood (L 61–2, 68, 81, 86, 98–102, 115–22), but he appears just as willing to accept his own execution for the same cause, and the spectators must recognize that they do enjoy the rights he has been fighting for. In conclusion, all of these four scenes challenge the audience to judge characters whom poetic justice seems to condemn, but whose monologues reveal another side of their story, so as to make the listeners reconsider their assent to the sentences implied by the script.[42] Theatregoers are thus placed in the position of the Terror's magistrates, in the sense not only that they are addressed as such but also that they are led to feel they share the guilt of having hastily given sentence against

Renaudin, Louise, Evariste and possibly Philippe on the basis of rather superficial considerations.

The audience stars as the notorious assembly that passed arguably the worst judgement ever in *The Globe Mysteries*, when Pilate asks whom should he pardon and what should he do with Jesus (*M* 127–8). In Deborah Bruce's production, Caiphas held signs similar to the 'applause' board of old TV studios, encouraging spectators to answer 'Barabbas' and 'Crucify', but in the recorded performance I have seen nobody complied, so the only voices to be heard were those of the actors involved; the result effectively portrayed a few people deciding on behalf of a silent crowd, and this is probably the scene Tony Harrison envisaged, since it is difficult to imagine a twenty-first-century audience either joining in those cries or venturing to shout against them. The spectators' silence is, however, enough to make them appear responsible, in the fictional world, for what ensues.

At Shakespeare's Globe, theatregoers are often addressed as a political body. As such they can be placed at the receiving end of proclamations and official speeches: Charles II's dismissal of Parliament (*NG* 113–14), Saladin's triumphal discourse (*HW* 23–6), the launch of the third crusade (*HW* 28), the declaration of the establishment of the State of Israel (*HW* 58), Blair's allocution to the US Congress (*HW* 60–1) and so on. In these instances, audience members are simply supposed to accept more or less gracefully the decisions announced, but in other situations they seem to be presented with some very consequential choices to be made. They are called to interpret several roles of this kind in *A New World* (the people assembled in the Senate House Yard, *TAT* 26–32; Sam Adams's listeners, *TAT* 36–7; the Cordeliers, *TAT* 116–19; the crowd at the Bastille Day Celebration, *TAT* 144–5; the French National Convention, *TAT* 154–8 and in a scene absent from the screenplay, in which the protagonist delivers a speech against the new constitution after he has been released from prison, *NW* 155–6; the protesters awaiting Paine in New York harbour, *TAT* 183–4) and in *Holding Fire* (the London Working Men's Association, *HF* 5–7; a group of Nottingham frame-knitters, *HF* 25–8; an assembly of working men, *HF* 47–50; the crowd attending the Chartist meeting at Kersal Moor, *HF* 76–83; the People's Parliament, *HF* 84–9; the menacing mob in Newport, *HF* 99–106; the London Working Men's Association thirty years later, *HF* 113–14).

While Griffiths casts the audience in very different, sometimes opposite roles – in favour of or against the protagonist, American, French and English, protesters, elected representatives and ordinary people – Shepherd has them interpret various aspects of the same social group, the working class whom the Chartists wish to advance. Yet *Holding Fire* represents diversity from another point of view, i.e. within a single crowd, while each of those in *A New World* are indirectly represented (by means of the characters' reactions and occasionally of some performers that appear to speak on their behalf) as rather homogeneous. The scene of the People's Parliament (2.17, *HF* 84–9) features an actual debate, with leaders of different factions arguing forcefully for contrasting strategies, so that spectators may feel the need to take sides, at least until Lovett's proposal (*HF* 88–9) appears to satisfy, for the moment, all the delegates, and therefore presumably all their supporters in the auditorium too.

This sort of situation engages the audience on a deep and rational level; an analogous involvement is reached on the plane of immediate feelings and thrills when the crowd represented by the spectators is targeted by a military repression, as in *Holding Fire*'s scene 2.21, in which the Red Coats fire on the mob demanding the release of Henry Vincent (*HF* 99–106), or at the beginning of *We the People*, when Shay's rebellion is crushed by Major General Sheppard's army (*WP* 1–4). Both episodes are based on the image of weapons aimed at the theatregoers, which is particularly effective in Shakespeare's Globe, where up to 700 people can be seen standing close together all around the stage. Schlosser relies on this engrossing situation to make his play start literally with a bang, while Shepherd, as his title suggests, builds up the suspense leading to the shooting, in particular by means of a previous scene during which two cannons are threateningly placed downstage, trained at the audience (*HF* 76), and their devastating potential is explained in detail (*HF* 78–9), but although tension rises (*HF* 80–2), the massacre is eventually averted (*HF* 82–3).

The importance Shepherd attached to this scene is clearly displayed by the detailed notes he includes in the prompt book's stage directions, pointing out the desired effect. He clearly states he wants spectators to become part of the protesting crowd (p. 99) and even suggests some stylistic choices that may help overcome the safety issue of guns being shot in the direction of the theatregoers (p. 104).

The audience's emotional engagement is likely to be less thorough, even though the context is still that of an armed conflict, when they are cast in turns as Greek or Trojan warriors who hear Agamemnon's rallying speech (*LDT* 31–2), Paris's and Hector's proclamation of the duel that should end the war (*LDT* 38, 42) or Hector's battle cry (*LDT* 62).

Quite far from the chaos and din of these scenes is the composed dignity Jessica Swale evokes by having Mrs Welsh deliver a speech to the spectators as to the Cambridge University Senators who must decide whether the graduation of women will be the subject of a vote, and how (*BS* 67–8). The playwright considers this scene one of the best suited for the Globe theatre (Swale 2014), together with another moment characterized by direct address, the initial lecture by Dr Maudsley (*BS* 14–15).

As a matter of fact, the opening of the play initially caused some worries in a way that can actually be interpreted as evidence of its effectiveness: women in the audience started to hiss and boo the monologue massively, so that the artists involved feared the drama might be turned into a pantomime, marked by continuous uncontrolled interventions on the part of spectators. This drift was promptly checked since the second performance by having actor Edward Peel voice the speech without any pause, so that listeners were compelled to keep silent in order to hear the rest of his words (Swale 2014). The gravity thus achieved by the first scene was certainly instrumental to a more serious reception of the whole play, but possibly those initial reactions were not prompted by an amused, light-hearted attitude; on the contrary, they may prove that part of the audience felt directly touched by the discourse they were witnessing. Swale remarks that it was the female members of the audience who became noisy; this difference in the spectators' response shows that the speech had succeeded in tracing a division in the auditorium. Its shock value, it may be argued, lay not so much in the ideas Dr Maudsley exposes, explaining that women are biologically not fit for higher education, as in the fact that he repeatedly addresses the whole audience as 'gentlemen', as if there were no ladies in the house. Some female spectators' reaction was, in a sense, the same Tess has in the play when the same illustrious personage similarly ignores her (and the other girls') presence at his lesson: she compels him to acknowledge her existence by speaking out of turn (*BS* 27–33).

The fact that evidence of the productions and performances is often valuable material for the analysis of these passages may lead to think that the spectators' involvement is ultimately due to certain aspects of staging and acting rather than inherent in the script. Of course, it is only during the show that theatregoers can actually be affected, and it is up to the creative team and cast to engage them, but in the instances illustrated here the premises for this process are in the text. The fact that playwrights have prepared these situations is evident when there are such notes as Shepherd's quoted above, or even just the indication 'to the audience' in the stage directions, which can be found in the majority of these examples.

The structure of the reconstructed theatre encourages performers to cast the audience almost continuously in one role or another, and especially in the course of soliloquies actors find it very useful to do so without needing the writers' suggestion or even their assent (see Carroll 2008: 41–2; Rylance 2008: 107, as well as several EOSIs, such as Colin Hurley's from 2010). But symmetrically, it is possible to detect in the Globe's productions at least two examples of scenes in which a similar opportunity was offered by the text but not realized in the staging.

In both cases, it is useful to remember that while behind a proscenium arch characters mostly enter from the wings and face each other, presenting their profile to the spectators, an apron stage compels them to either use the doors and face the audience or enter from the yard, emerging from the groundlings, so that the prevailing confrontation, especially at the beginning of a scene, is the one between stage and auditorium rather than the one among performers whom theatregoers observe from the point of view of an outsider. So when Anne Boleyn meets William Tyndale and his followers (*AB* 41–2, 46–50, 92–7), either the heroine or her interlocutors must come from the yard. Since in these scenes the country people often express the view of Anne that is still prevalent in popular culture ('the King's … thing', *AB* 47, 'strumpet', 'concubine of Babylon', 'whore', 'witch', *AB* 95, 'stewing in an adulterous bed', *AB* 96), Brenton's script offers the chance to have them come from the audience as from the thick of the forest, where other people like them remain silent and possibly hidden, and confront her on behalf of the general public. John Dove chose on the contrary to foster the spectators' identification with Anne by having her enter from the yard and face the other characters on the stage.

Structurally different, but similar at heart, is an opportunity Raz Shaw's staging of *The God of Soho* did not exploit: near the end of scenes 1.9 and 2.2 (*GS* 54 and 59) characters exit towards a crowd of excited paparazzi. While in other moments the actor playing Baz, Edward Hogg, posed for the audience (e.g. when he referred to being 'in full view of my fan base', *GS* 38), in these two situations, the movement towards the public eye was directed to the tiring house, not to the yard, so that the celebrity-watching crowd did not coincide with the theatregoers in the auditorium.

These two examples, together with the playwrights' conscious reflections, illustrate the fact that using the audience as a huge ensemble of supernumeraries is not only a technique that productions can employ but also a dramatic device that playtexts can envisage and prepare. At Shakespeare's Globe, actors, directors and writers all seem to agree that the spectators' visibility makes it exceptionally powerful and thus consistently try to make the most of it.

# Spectators as subject matter

As some of the scenes discussed in the previous subchapter already show, the new plays written for Shakespeare's Globe feature a considerable number of metatheatrical moments. The fully lit space tends to keep spectators constantly aware that they are watching a fictional representation, so that even the slightest reference to somebody 'playing a part' does not go amiss. Moreover, the recurring allusions to Shakespeare and his world evidently entail at least a hint in that direction. Many passages of this kind, such as Te Lahu's two performances (*P* 46–60) or the entertainment Dr Gillies's patients present to the Queen (*DSW* 97), do not give a particular prominence to the spectators' role.

Even in *Nell Gwynn*, which portrays some protagonists of Restoration drama and includes several show-within-the-show scenes, theatregoers do not occupy a central position. Three anonymous punters disturb the performance in 1.1 (*NG* 16–17) and so does, in a different way, the appearance of King Charles II, to whom the protagonist tends to address her acting, either directly (in 1.9, *NG* 60–1) or by satirizing his companion (in 2.3, *NG* 102–3), but also in these situations the accent falls on the actors' rather than on the playgoers' behaviour. It is no surprise that the same focus on the artists and not on their audience should characterize the many witty backstage dialogues in which company members discuss their work (*NG* 27–30, 67–9, 91–6, 118–19); the punters' taste for female nudity and for gossip (*NG* 28–9 and 96, respectively) is just stated, the argument immediately moving to whether and how should productions consider and accommodate such demands. The visibility of the Globe's patrons is, on the contrary, instrumental to the punch line that concludes a romantic scene when Nell asks Charles Hart to kiss her and reassures him, 'It's all right. No one's watching' (*NG* 35). The joke would be funny in any theatre, but it is particularly effective where the two lovers are bound to see clearly the onlookers that surround them. So Jessica Swale avoids exploiting the theme in the most predictable occasions and chooses to take it up when less expected instead.

Generally speaking, the conspicuous and nowadays unusual situation of the audience in Shakespeare's Globe appears to highlight the implications of spectating. As Bernard Beckerman remarks, 'throughout Shakespeare's plays … we find numerous instances of eavesdropping, or concealed observation. This device also occurs in the plays of Shakespeare's colleagues and so may be considered a typical dramatic activity of the period' (Beckerman 1979: 25). 'Since Shakespeare introduced such scenes in more than half the plays he wrote', he goes on to argue, 'he must have found them an extremely useful means of enriching the dramatic appeal of his works' (ibid.: 26). The structure of Elizabethan playhouses suggests this may have been not only because this trope could rely on an accepted artistic tradition (ibid.), but also for the way it mirrored what spectators could clearly see and hear all around them: people watching and commenting the action on stage, usually without their presence being acknowledged by the performers. This doubling of the eavesdropping situation both reinforces its credibility and lends it all the thought-provoking force and dizzying delight of a mise en abyme. Such a direct connection with the theatre's architecture may explain why the observer image is a frequent feature of the plays written for the reconstructed Globe too, in an age when the tradition evoked by Beckerman no longer continues.

The trope of one or more characters that observe what is going on, either silently or adding their comments, can be found in most of the scripts analysed in the present study (e.g. *UBF* 85–6, *BS* 90–2, *LDT* 68–9, *O* 54–9, *HL* 49 and 55), although not all of them are properly eavesdroppers. The ass Lucius, for instance, watches the actions of the humans around him and draws his conclusions; being ostensibly an animal, he can do so without anybody noticing, even though he is not hiding (*GA* 70–3, 84–9).

Simon Bent goes so far as to have two groups of people spying on others at the same time, a visual equivalent to the web of betrayals that binds them (Isabelle and the English Ambassador observe Hamlet and Silver's meeting with Sula, while Kees, Frederick and Edward are looking on, ready to surprise all of them, *UBF* 86–90). All of these situations are apt to focus the audience's attention on their own condition and attitude, and generally speaking to guide their reactions, either as a model to which they can conform or as an example from which they will recede.

In *The Frontline* the onlooker figure can be interpreted as one of the pillars of the play's structure, although with a significant difference from all the other instances considered here: everybody is, or at least could and should be, aware of being seen and heard by other people. The piece's setting, a bustling public area outside a tube station, entails the constant presence of several unrelated individuals or groups of people, and, while all follow their own pursuits, they cannot help noticing each other too, at least occasionally. The result is as if there were, in the words of one character, a sort of 'ghetto Sky News' (*F* 107); almost everybody knows about everyone else, so it is not surprising that when a person goes missing their friends should ask around (*F* 73, 95) nor that Carlton on finding Mordechai Thurrock in 'his' phone booth should complain 'did no one stop you?' (*F* 43).

The main observer in *The Frontline* is, predictably, the narrator figure, Erkenwald, who comments on the action for the benefit of the audience (*F* 17, 20–1, 65, 109); his friend and rival Mahmoud occasionally takes on a similar role (*F* 36, 109), but most of the characters sooner or later prove to be eavesdropping on each other. Actually, the play's plot is largely based on people intervening in the big and small events they witness: Donna talks to Seamus about Benny (*F* 20–1) and goes to help Kurt (*F* 27); Miruts offers to vouch for Elliot (*F* 36); Violet chides Cockburn for manhandling the boy (*F* 37); Erkenwald and Mahmoud interrupt the drug dealer's assault on the woman (which, by the way, aims at compelling her to tell who stole the cocaine packet, thus assuming once more that everyone on the street knows about everything that happens there,

*F* 40); Marcus tries to stop Cockburn's flight after Miruts's murder (*F* 100).[43]

These interferences give evidence to the constant mutual vigilance of the characters, but they also highlight the essential difference between them and the audience, who cannot step in and change the course of events. The dramatis personae really act as spectators, on the contrary, when they only comment what they hear and see, either individually chipping in (like Seamus, *F* 38) or sharing their views in pairs (e.g. Erkenwald and Marcus, *F* 91–2; Carlton and Erkenwald, *F* 99). The most interesting example of this situation makes its metatheatrical aspect explicit:

**Seamus** This place is insane.
**Donna** Cheaper than the movies.
**Mordechai Thurrock** There really is some extraordinary theatre happening down here.
**Seamus** Y'not wrong. (*F* 24)

Besides voicing the spectacle metaphor, this short dialogue presents a double eavesdropping effect, because Mordechai Thurrock's remark actually refers to his own dramatic achievements, which he is extolling to a theatre agent on the telephone; Seamus catches his statement and answers as if it were part of his conversation with Donna regarding the happenings around them as a form of entertainment, so he proves to be both listening to the actor's call and watching the overall scene as a spectator.[44]

The spectators are directly or implicitly evoked by the innumerable metatheatrical aspects or moments in these texts, the most audience-centred instance of which is the performance of *Hamlet* in *Under the Black Flag* (*UBF* 49–53). In this passage, while playing with Shakespearean quotations, Bent also makes fun of questions pertaining to the theory and history of drama by means of the remarks uttered by the fictional spectators. Even before the beginning, the French Ambassador taunts his English colleague by pointing out that 'plays are not against the law for the Frenchman' (*UBF* 50); the answer, 'a slave market' (*UBF* 50), indicates the context in which the show is taking place, but also expresses the disgust of a representative of the Puritan Commonwealth. The borders between fiction and reality are blurred a first time when Silver starts the revolt back stage (by killing a pirate with what should be a prop, i.e. something that is 'not real', *UBF* 51) while Hamlet is waiting for the ghost to appear. The English Ambassador asserts that the action must have stopped because of 'some argument in the plot no doubt' (*UBF* 51), thus attributing the fight he cannot see to the play, while Isabelle ambiguously remarks that Hamlet 'doesn't know what to do' (*UBF* 51), apparently prompting him to switch from his own doubts to his character's and start the monologue 'to be or not to be' (*UBF* 51).

As the fight increasingly interferes with the action, the French Ambassador only wonders 'what is Tom' (*UBF* 52). His question could be interpreted as regarding the name rather than the character, but a couple of lines earlier 'John' has not been objected to (*UBF* 52) and after all even 'Horatio' has been introduced only indirectly, because Hamlet called him so (*UBF* 50). The French Ambassador seems to be represented – unlike his English colleague – as a habitual theatregoer, who is ready to infer the protagonists' names from the dialogue, but is perplexed by a speaking character who is killed without his role having been made clear. He appears to have accepted that Gertrude is interpreted by a man who literally crosses swords with the Danish prince while his friend Horatio is simultaneously attacked by the queen's anonymous allies, because Hamlet has addressed Kees as 'mother' (*UBF* 52), but no one has introduced the person hiding behind the arras. In his spotting an incongruous figure, the French diplomat may seem to be following the performance a little more than his colleague, but what both miss completely is the fact that the fight they are observing is not make-believe.

In the published version of the play, the English Ambassador goes even further in the unflinching assertion that what happens on stage must necessarily be part of the spectacle and therefore cannot be real: even when Isabelle states that Tom is actually dead, he replies with great composure 'no ma'am, 'tis but a play, never fear' (*UBF* 53). In the prompt book, this exchange is replaced with the Sultan's comment 'this is what happens when you disregard Aristotle',[45] which sparks a series of possibly funny connections. To begin with, it uses the slaves' revolt, apparently once more misunderstood as a dramatic incident, to support the classicist argument that Shakespeare's plots lack clarity because they do not abide by the Aristotelian unities of place, time and action, and perhaps it implies that when there is no respect for aesthetic rules, the infraction of all laws is soon to follow. Furthermore, the man who voices this opinion is an Arab, a representative of the people who preserved most of the ancient philosopher's works during the Middle Ages, but who did not have theatrical representations in their traditional culture; therefore it may be amusing that his judgement should express a scholarly knowledge of the *Poetics* while showing that the Sultan, just like the other spectators, cannot properly tell dramatic fiction from real-world action. Immediately after this remark, Hamlet takes hostage and threatens to kill the Sultan's daughter, in what may look like both a way to demonstrate once and for all that the fight is not part of the performance and a prompt retaliation against the classicist criticism of complex plots. The English diplomat epitomizes the Puritan condemnation of the theatre by concluding that 'this is what comes of watching plays' (*UBF* 53).

Most of *Under the Black Flag*'s spectators will probably miss some of these jokes, both because they are based on a knowledge, however basic, of Aristotle's *Poetics*, of *Hamlet* and of seventeenth-century debates on the theatre, and because these comments are easily upstaged by the simultaneous stage business. This is not really a problem, though, because the metatheatrical caricature of an uncomprehending audience does not bring any further meaning to the play. Its function is entertainment, and in placing it side by side with a sword fight Bent seems to be thinking of the Globe's various patrons: combining a typical piece of buccaneering action with a few gags based on notions that the more cognisant and classical-minded theatregoers are likely to share, the scene caters for different backgrounds and tastes at the same time.

Representations of the theatre seem to be intended merely as a source of amusement in Samuel Adamson's *Gabriel* too. Not by chance subtitled *An Entertainment with Trumpet*, it satirizes the ambitions of actors, the contentiousness of musicians, the stinginess of managers and the extravagance of directors not in order to convey a serious critique but essentially for fun (*G* 55–8, 84–94), and in the same spirit one of its playlets, 'The Rake' (*G* 52–4), is centred on spectators. In a two-page flowing monologue its protagonist pithily censors Purcell's 'English opera' *King Arthur* but mainly directs his trenchant judgements against his fellow spectators, ridiculous, incompetent and utterly uninterested in the performance they are witnessing; after refusing to buy an orange and concluding that the whole occasion is a 'spectacle of ignominy' (*G* 54), he suddenly stands, bows to the ladies beside him and leaves; one of his neighbours deplores the departure of what 'looked like a gentleman of the best quality' (*G* 54) before discovering that while venting all his disgust he has robbed the other woman of her purse. The sustained rhythm and lexical richness of the piece make it an excellent vehicle for an awesome performance on the part of the actor (James Garnon at Shakespeare's Globe), and some traits in the vitriolic description of the inattentive 'coffee-soaked gobblers' (*G* 53) in the audience are likely to remind spectators of themselves or the people around them, but without implying any further reflection.

Other plays, on the contrary, employ their metatheatrical aspects to provide some food for thought. Trevor Griffiths takes this path only briefly, and without directly representing the audience, when his Danton prepares for the Jacobin Club as if he were putting on costume and make-up for a dramatic performance and explains to Paine that in front of the public all personages are actors, who improvise their roles but must never forget to consider, along with their listeners' minds, their feelings and instincts (*TAT* 134–5). It is a short but effective reminder that spectators can be such outside the playhouse too.

The connection between theatre and politics appears much more constantly in Glyn Maxwell's *Liberty*, starting with the association of its title with its character list, which features among its six protagonists 'a comedienne', Rose, and 'a puppet-maker', Maurice (*L* 5). The former repeatedly discusses the subject of theatre with Evariste. An orthodox revolutionary, he despises all plays that feature aristocratic characters (*L* 18–21) and sees the performers that interpret them as dangerously near to the ruling classes and far from the people (*L* 21, 66, 81), while the young woman at first only defends her job (*L* 18–21), except for a hint at the fact that Evariste should read texts before condemning them (*L* 18), but later on she denounces censorship (*L* 66) and the imposition of educational plays selected by the politicians in power (*L* 67). The magistrate's view of the theatre is shared by other revolutionaries that consider Rose's profession suspect to say the least (*L* 73–80, 104–5, 112–14).

But the same people who despise the theatre as an institution and as an art form rely in various ways on the power of performance. Guards use it to humiliate Rose and Maurice by compelling them to enact specific scenarios: the old man is forced, in front of the woman he loves, to mime having sex with a puppet resembling her (L 78–9); the comedienne has to earn her bread by repeating some ambiguous lines concerning her job (L 113–14). Furthermore, revolutionary leaders act too: Evariste frequently rehearses speeches (L 7–8, 94,[46] 98, 107, 115) and when he delivers them, they can be cheered and praised as performances (L 37–9); he is so accustomed to this sort of staged rhetoric that he adopts it even when there is no public occasion (L 81), triggering Rose's protest, 'is that it? That your speech? Do we applaud? Do we weep?' (L 82).

This sort of revolutionary theatre is so strong that also those who belong neither to its world nor to the professional field of the performing arts must nevertheless adopt its methods and forms. Philippe has to rehearse his defence in order to be released when interrogated (L 95–7). Elodie is 'being trained', 'like a monkey in a costume' (L 57): at first it is only the protocol she needs to make hers, 'learning lines like you do' (L 65), as she announces with pride and enthusiasm to Rose, but as her relationship with Evariste evolves, it takes more and more the shape of revolutionary-themed role-play (L 68–9, 91–92), until she starts to interpret Marianne, the personification of France, speaking nothing but the allegorical statements her husband teaches her (L 107–8), and when Philippe finds her after the Thermidor, lost and confused, she seems to have been brainwashed into her part, so that she keeps repeating those words (L 121–2).

*Liberty* is thus imbued with a metatheatrical theme, but audiences are strangely absent from almost all of the scenes mentioned. With the only exception of Elodie eavesdropping on the initial rehearsal (L 7–8), the five friends listening to Evariste's maiden speech (L 37–9) and Rose being compelled to witness Maurice's humiliation (L 78–9), the only spectators of these performances are their producers themselves (the Guards, Evariste). In fact, the question of the audience is addressed at the beginning of the play, when Elodie tells Evariste that he is an orator 'when no one is looking' (L 8), but more importantly underlines that he has 'found a natural audience in the meadows' (L 8); the young man has been speaking to the auditorium, so the 'trees' (L 39) that have been hearing him since the beginning are the Globe patrons. It seems legitimate to suppose that Maxwell thus indicates in the play's first scene that they must observe themselves as the missing spectators and question their own response to *Liberty*'s many metatheatrical representations.

Other scripts take the audience's attitude as a theme and even express some specific criticisms. In *Holding Fire*, the morbid curiosity of the public towards Lizzie and Will's story is only hinted at, by means of the street ballad, which shows how their experiences are perceived by strangers, representing the sensationalism of its treatment in a form that twenty-first-century spectators can consider with a certain detachment because of its old-fashioned features. Listening to the popular song together with characters, in a tavern (*HF* 69–70) and in a prison yard (*HF* 106–7), theatregoers are encouraged to share Beth's refusal rather than her father's drunken indifference (*HF* 70) and they may be led to think about their own reaction to the play's gruesome spectacle of the two lovers quarrelling over Eli's corpse (*HF* 66–8). Nevertheless, the audience's taste for scandal is far from being one of the main themes of the play; on the contrary, the most distinctly metatheatrical scene in Shepherd's drama is centred on a coup de théâtre with a light tone and a very practical function: the second act opens with a dialogue between Princess Victoria and Prince Albert of Saxe Coburg Gotha (*HF* 54–7);[47] then the royal couple bursts into a rather unexpected song, almost childish in its naivety, full of funny rhymes (*HF* 57–8); 'the song ends on a high note, just a little too high perhaps for both singers, who are revealed as Molly and Jenkins, rehearsing for the Christmas concert' (*HF* 58). The Globe's almost unavoidably fixed scenery and the habit to have actors play several roles make the audience initially accept at face value the radical change in setting and characters, which is made even more believable by its position, right after the interval. So the spectators can be at first unsettled by the apparent new surreal tone in a script that was hitherto realistic, and then startled when the play-within-the-play is interrupted and exposed. Their attention is thus efficiently re-captured after the act break with a double surprise that quickly brings them to a humorously depicted Windsor Palace and then back to the servants' quarters of Harrington Hall. The scene thus constitutes a striking example of how the peculiarities of the reconstructed theatre are put to good use against its possible weaknesses, but it does not advance any specific reflection on the spectators' attitude.

Morbid curiosity occupies a more prominent position in *The Golden Ass*. As the subtitle *The Curious Man* suggests, it is, after all, what brings Lucius to be turned into a donkey, but it is by no means limited to the text's protagonist. To begin with, Oswald expands the roles of two travellers the young man meets at the beginning of his adventures, Aristomenus and Clytus in the play. As in Apuleius's novel, the former tells the first of the many stories that cross Lucius's, a tale full of magic and horrors, which the latter refuses to believe (*GA* 11–17; Apuleius, *The Golden Ass*, book I, § 2–20). While these companions never reappear in the Latin text after they reach Hypata with the protagonist, the playwright has them come back on stage three times (*GA* 45–6, 74–5, 93–4), twice to introduce the intervals and the last time without any such practical reason. Because of these reiterations, Clytus's attitude does not appear as clear-cut as that of his anonymous model: he keeps saying he cannot stand to hear such rubbish, but he never really stops listening to it. He thus embodies a sort of hypocritical audience that condemns the 'pornographic imagination' (*GA* 12) spinning unbelievable yarns full of prurient details but never fails to keep up with them.

His ambiguous interest reaches an apex the last time this double act comes on stage, when Clytus interrupts the action in a burst of indignation because the donkey Lucius is becoming a woman's lover. His protest is soon diverted, though, because after exclaiming that 'this is going too far' (*GA* 93), he adds that 'this filth' cannot be 'in the original book' (*GA* 93), and Aristomenus hands him a copy of the Latin text, from which Clytus reads and translates part of the disputed passage (*GA* 93–4),[48] concluding 'so that was alright then!' (*GA* 94). What begins as an attempt to prevent a morbid spectacle actually ends up making it more explicit, because Massima and Lucius have disappeared 'behind a veil' (*GA* 93) after she has declared her love and desire for him, whereas the would-be censor's words supply an account of what they do. By moving the question of the representation's legitimacy from the plane of ethics or propriety to that of authorship, Clytus obtains, first of all for himself and indirectly for the audience, the occasion to dwell on Massima and Lucius's love-making and his moral qualms are visibly replaced by a prurient curiosity.

This passage also makes clear that Clytus is a spectator of *The Golden Ass* and not just Aristomenus's listener. The fact that his friend's initial narrative is acted out in front of the audience (*GA* 14–17) can be interpreted as conventionally showing what is only being said, just like Tim Carroll's staging did for Bellepheron's adventure too (*GA* 32–3), but the moment Clytus calls Apuleius's text 'the original book' (*GA* 93), the object of his comments must necessarily be its adaptation, i.e. Peter Oswald's *The Golden Ass*. Apart from the paradox of a character being a spectator of the play to which he belongs, the main consequence of this observation is that this ambiguously curious censor turns out to be presented as a member of the Globe's audience watching the performance, so that theatregoers are encouraged to compare their own attitude with his and ask themselves if his mixture of outrage and interest is not theirs too.

This effect is immediately reinforced by the following scene. The Ringmaster callously presents a far worse spectacle, because the donkey Lucius is supposed to publicly rape a condemned woman, and the man's patently hypocritical 'horror! But I put the blame on Fortune!' (*GA* 95), immediately followed by attempts to egg on the recalcitrant ass, is contrasted with the animal's staunch refusal to perform such a deed. The donkey tries to harangue the audience, warning them that they are 'sailing into devastation' (*GA* 95) and urging them to repent. 'She who cursed me will not spare you' (*GA* 95), he explains: the people he wants to convert are those who display the same morbid curiosity that was his, i.e. the spectators. When the Ringmaster's cruelty is suddenly put an end to by the very lions he was keen to show devouring people, the audience is likely to feel not only relieved for Lucius's escape but also satisfied for the sadistic entertainer's appropriately gruesome punishment. But then the protagonist's words remind them that 'this is not justice' (*GA* 95) either and that after all they are once again rejoicing for the unpredictable bloody demise of a human being. Since it is after the circus ambience has disappeared that the ass, alone on stage, facing the auditorium, prays the ocean to hide him 'from these human lions' (*GA* 95) of which he was one (*GA* 96),[49] it is definitely the spectators' thirst for blood that he is denouncing.

So in spite of its light-hearted tones *The Golden Ass* may well be said to question rather seriously its audience's attitude, even though this theme probably runs the danger of being drowned by the play's more ostensible madcap comedy aspects.[50] Other scripts written for Shakespeare's Globe have given this self-reflexivity a more prominent position. Howard Brenton's *In Extremis* and *Anne Boleyn* will be analysed from this point of view in Chapter 5, but the text that more explicitly focuses on the action of spectating is Chris Hannan's portrayal of celebrity culture, *The God of Soho*.

When the playwright first presented this work to the press, he declared its main characters were inspired by reality-show stars and more generally by those people whose fame does not rest on any exceptional quality or feat (Sharp 2011), comparing them to the sovereigns and nobles of Shakespeare's plays (Brooks 2011; Jury 2011); 'we call them our gods and goddesses' (ibid.), he added. These statements made it clear that the script would be centred on the way its protagonists are perceived, on the public gaze constantly following them with no apparent reason, as well as on their personal story.

Hannan represents the audience's role and their relationship with the celebrities not by including any fans among the dramatis personae but by involving the performance's spectators themselves in two ways: by means of figures that mirror their position on stage and directly, because it is before their eyes that Natty and Baz live their 'private' life, 'tearing each other up in the tabloids slash home' (GS 17).

In what may look like a peculiar reversal of the writer's theoretical statements, it is essentially the deities that act as deputy audience members, in various scenes, by witnessing the main action and occasionally commenting on it while the other characters ignore their presence. In these conditions New God observes Clem sleeping and then waking up with the mysterious Kelly bag beside her (GS 31–3). Even more significantly, Big God and Mrs God watch several scenes (GS 45–54, 63–5) without being able to intervene; when they find someone who can hear them, it is a person afflicted by mental illness, who refuses to consider them anything more than a delusion (GS 63–5). If these supernatural beings cannot actually be seen by anybody, the former Goddess of Love, Clem, occupies a similar position throughout several scenes even though she has become a mortal and quite perceptible: when after silently witnessing several moments of Natty's life (GS 38–43, 49–54) she tries to communicate with her indirectly, the publicist's answer is tellingly, 'she don't know you, babes' (GS 43). Finally, the only person accused of eavesdropping (GS 48) is the former New God, Tony Goldilocks, who has actually been watching Clem's dialogue with Baz (GS 46–8), although Hannan does not give him any line manifestly responding to what he has seen and heard.

The paradoxical identification of the audience with divinities, apart from the possible pun on the phrase 'gallery gods', has two significant motivations. From the point of view of the play's contents, it supports the idea, expressed by Baz, that spectators ultimately look down on celebrities (GS 59). What is more, because of these scenes' structure, the utterly disempowered deities mirror very precisely the spectators' condition of omnipresent witnesses who have no possibility to intervene because even their voice cannot be heard. The traditional eavesdropping setting, 'by emphasizing discrepant levels of awareness and control, ... creates a situation that confirms the audience's superior perspective vis-à-vis the stage characters, while at the same time calling into question the ultimate extent of that audience's autonomy and omniscience' (Howard 1984: 59). These supernatural observers also highlight another contradiction in the theatregoers' relation to the action, because they seem to confirm their omniscience but also to embody their inability to influence the events on stage.

An especially complex mise en abyme of the spectators' role concludes the first act of *The God of Soho*, in which the patrons of Shakespeare's Globe could see three different levels of onlookers beside the central confrontation between Natty and Baz: Clem observes the couple without ever speaking,[51] while her parents, Big God and Mrs God, watch both the scene and their daughter's reactions, and the spectators spy on them all. Big God's consideration that the former goddess is 'double lost. it's like she's on a trip inside a trip' (*GS* 54) seems to point out, besides the young woman's confusion, this Chinese-box structure. The artifice is not only interesting in itself, though, or as a general reminder of the audience's position; more substantially, it provides the occasion for a key moment because it allows some characters to comment on another's gaze. Clem moves towards the traces of the violence she has just witnessed and her parents remark that 'she likes the blood', 'she likes ... the violence' (*GS* 54).

The object of these multiple looks is not indifferent either, since the spectacle of violence and its fascination are a recurring theme in the play. Several characters assert the tabloids (and indirectly their readers) are mainly interested in the couple's 'beating the shit out of each other' (*GS* 17–19, 36, 50, 53–4; the quotation is from p. 18), while Teresa and Edwardo separately show that the best way to get everybody's attention is to attempt suicide in public (*GS* 78–9).

At the same time, spectators are drawn to consider their own attitude towards the voyeurism mass media often display because they are clearly identified as representatives of the audience society that makes celebrities what they are. They are constantly reminded of their role by the sight of fellow theatregoers watching the couple live their private life on a stage, but not only. Their presence is also highlighted by lines such as Baz's answer to Clem's question if he minds talking to Natty in public: 'no man, it'll be more private in public. In the bedroom she acts like she has to project herself or the public won't know what she's feeling' (GS 58). This specific speech is particularly interesting because it focuses on the necessity in performance to project, an idea that can be applied to other contexts but is especially linked to the theatre, and even more to acting in the open air, where special attention must be paid for the voice to carry. Baz's image thus reflects the world of Shakespeare's Globe and of the theatregoers in front of him rather than the environment of tabloids or television, to which celebrities usually belong.

In this perspective, the moments when the audience witnesses acts of violence or intimacy, such as Natty and Baz making love (GS 67–9), can be especially meaningful, because spectators have a chance to interrogate their own and their neighbours' reaction. Yet these scenes can also backfire on the critique of the public's voyeurism, because they offer the kind of spectacle the play denounces. These actions are not sensationalised, they are on the contrary played down with humour, but this careful choice does not quite solve the problem: it prevents the characters from being objectified in an erotic or sentimental way, but it may lead the audience to look down on these figures that are not sensual even when they make love, nor moving when they are beaten, nor frightening when they are violent, nor heartbreaking when they are on the verge of suicide. The God of Soho seems to support the view that celebrities without any quality are put on a pedestal so that people who loathe themselves can despise them instead of changing their own lives (GS 58–9), and it is precisely this attitude that the understated presentation of very delicate scenes runs the danger of fostering. Nevertheless, it may be a risk worth taking, maybe relying on the much warmer presentation of Natty and Baz in the final scene (GS 83, 84–5) to establish incontrovertibly their human dignity.

What emerges beyond doubt, from the case of The God of Soho as well as from those in which this theme occupies a less prominent position, is that the visibility of the audience in the reconstructed Globe makes it an ideal venue for reflections on the role of spectators in relation both to the performing arts and to our heavily mediatized society at large.

# PART TWO

# Brenton's Globe

# 4

# The Weight of the Past

With three plays being performed across six seasons in the last decade (*In Extremis* in 2006 and 2007; *Anne Boleyn* in 2010, 2011 and 2012; *Doctor Scroggy's War* in 2014), Howard Brenton is certainly one of the most successful new playwrights at Shakespeare's Globe. When at his debut in the reconstructed Elizabethan playhouse reviewer Tim Walker commented 'it will … be a while yet before anyone talks about Brenton's Globe' (Walker 2006), the paradox, which was meant to check a widespread enthusiasm, actually confirmed that the text related to the theatre in an effective way. The fruitfulness of the Globe-Brenton combination soon gained further evidence in the case of *Anne Boleyn* and, recently, in his review of *Doctor Scroggy's War*, Andrzej Lukowski has suggested, although in a very cautious form, that Brenton's plays are attuned to the venue just like Shakespeare's: 'would it be controversial to say that the only two playwrights who've really cracked writing for the Globe are William Shakespeare and Howard Brenton?' (Lukowski 2014).

It stands to reason that the bases of these achievements should reside in the two components' natural compatibility as well as in the artist's ability to harmonize his work with the peculiarities of its destination. Looking at the dramatist's overall output, it is possible to point out some essential traits that chime with the theatre's uniqueness, while a detailed analysis of his scripts produced by the Globe shows how they have been tailored to fit this context's needs and to capitalize on its assets. Both continuity and specificity characterize the three plays examined here in relation to the rest of Brenton's works, because several recurring themes and stylistic traits of his appear to be enhanced and fine-tuned for the occasion rather than forcibly imposed on an incongruous context or removed from his habitual sensibility and technique.

The same two strands of thought applied in the first part of this book to the peculiarities of Shakespeare's Globe and of its new plays in general can actually be highly conducive to a deeper understanding of its three Brenton productions too. The present chapter will therefore focus on the playwright's unwavering attention for the past and its bearing on the present, which is probably the main aspect of the affinity between his poetics and the ethos of the reconstructed theatre. The next one will complementarily examine his determined pursuit of increasingly wide and difficult audiences and the insightful characteristic modes of address he has chosen for the Globe's spectators.

# Virtuoso meets Steinway

Brenton's collaboration with Shakespeare's Globe is an interesting example of how theatre and playwright can build a fruitful connection that fosters the production of plays conceived for a specific architectural and spectatorial environment. The plays issuing from this partnership derive from different creative processes that match successive phases in the relationship.

*In Extremis*, based on the well-known story of Abelard and Heloise, was first written in 1997 at University of California, Davis, where Brenton was Visiting Granada Artist, for a traditionally structured theatre (Reinelt 2007: 172).[1] Dominic Dromgoole, who had already described the playwright as 'one of our most consistent, surprising and rich dramatists' (Dromgoole 2002: 38), chose the play for his first season as artistic director of Shakespeare's Globe, entitled 'The Edges of Rome'. In that context, the famous lovers, a couple of twelfth-century scholars that upheld the value of ancient philosophy against the prevailing idea that pagan authors could never be trusted, represented the permanence of classical culture in the Middle Ages and perhaps its rediscovery in a perspective that anticipates the Renaissance. Brenton was ready to rewrite his text for the reconstructed Elizabethan playhouse, he talked about it with director John Dove before rehearsals began and then reworked it on the basis of the company's observations, but he realized that there was less to do than he thought: 'there was a little stitching needed, but we found that the stage was very friendly to the play' (Brenton 2007). Actually, statements he successively made[2] as well as interventions that can be evinced from the prompt book suggest that the changes responded to new possibilities the theatre offered rather than to problems it posed. In this situation, Howard Brenton verified that 'the Globe is proving to be a Steinway grand of a theatre, not a joanna in a pub to bash out songs, which is what people once thought Shakespeare's theatre was' (Neill 2006: 9), and at the same time he proved to be the kind of 'composer' that could display the richness of its sound in full. These were the best possible conditions not only for the successful revival of *In Extremis* in the 2007 'Renaissance and Revolution' season (a title that seems to be modelled on Brenton's radical proto-humanist protagonists), but also, more suggestively, for further collaboration between the writer and the theatre.

Unsurprisingly, then, a couple of years later Dromgoole commissioned Brenton a new play for the Globe. The request seemed to depend on the playwright's ability to present complex questions in a thought-provoking yet attractive and entertaining way, just as he had done with *In Extremis*, combining 'weighty intellectual discourse, ribald humour and passionate romance' (Marlowe 2007), since the artistic director asked him to write a play on the King James Bible for the season that would celebrate its fourth centenary, 'The Word is God'. Brenton, who had been researching the Tudor dynasty for a different project,[3] chose to dramatize the link between the Authorized Version and William Tyndale's banned translations of the Scriptures, by having the recently crowned James I find Anne Boleyn's copies of the 'heretic' New Testament and *The Obedience of a Christian Man*. As a result, the play focused on the religious policy of two reigns, and the main characters of its Tudor part were mostly the same as those of *Henry VIII*, with which it was paired to be introduced, as soon as it was ready, in the 'Kings and Rogues' 2010 season. The following year, for the programme of which *Anne Boleyn* had originally been planned, saw its acclaimed comeback, and in 2012 Howard Brenton's play was the first non-Shakespearean production the Globe toured autonomously.[4]

In a further example of ongoing creative collaboration among the reconstructed theatre's artists, it was John Dove, the director of both *In Extremis* and *Anne Boleyn* (and several other Globe productions, among which Jessica Swale's *Blue Stockings* in 2013), who suggested Harold Gillies as the possible subject of Brenton's third commission. The result, *Doctor Scroggy's War*, occupied a particularly relevant position in the 2014 'Arms and the Man' season, prompted by the centenary of the Great War, because it was the only play representing that conflict directly.

Introducing her review of *Anne Boleyn*'s 2011 revival, Caroline McGinn stated that 'Howard Brenton has been a living hit for Shakespeare's Globe, writing history plays with a verve and revisionist wit surely inspired by the big man himself' (McGinn 2011); after the play's première, Paul Taylor had already remarked that 'Brenton understands how to work the audience at the Globe, which is a brilliant forum for intellectual debate provided it is leavened with irreverent humour' (Taylor 2010). These two acknowledgements of the results achieved by the playwright's collaboration with the reconstructed playhouse highlight two essential aspects of its fruits, a specific approach to the historical genre and the relationship the texts build with the audience. The former will be the object of the present chapter, while the latter will be at the core of the next one.

# History plays for now

Since his beginnings, Brenton has been labelled a 'political' writer and, though obviously rejecting the drabby connotations the term usually entails and stressing that all plays are actually political (Hay and Roberts 1979: 135), he has never denied or concealed his engagement and his leftist ideas.[5] It may therefore surprise some that he should repeatedly choose to write for a commercial (at least in the sense that it is neither fringe nor publicly subsidised) theatre;[6] even more so, if the reconstructed Globe's manifest connection with the past is contrasted with the playwright's forward-looking concern for the present. The socio-economical aspect of the question, that is part of Brenton's relationship with his audience, will be addressed in the next chapter, while the role of history in his oeuvre will be the main subject of the present one.

Several of Howard Brenton's plays can be regarded as instances of the historical genre, but of a kind that is actually quite consistent with orthodox historical materialism: they scrutinize recent or remote events as the source of the present and tend to draw a parallel between then and now that evokes suggestions and warnings, rather than celebrate the past or use distant ages as a temporally exotic background and a pretext for lavish productions. *Never So Good* (2008), for example, sheds some light on contemporary British politics by outlining the way it has evolved in the twentieth century through the depiction of some key moments in Harold Macmillan's career, while *The Romans in Britain* (1980) connects ancient and contemporary scenes in a way that suggests both causality and similarity.

Brenton's works for the Globe fit this description too, and in articles and interviews the playwright explicitly links their characters and plots to twenty-first-century themes both by highlighting the historical turning points they dramatize, and so their bearing on present-day reality, and by drawing comparisons between the time in which they are set and ours. When commenting on the philosophical conflict at the core of *In Extremis*, for instance, he underlines its relevance for contemporary issues:

> It is the struggle at the heart of the Enlightenment, which took off hundreds of years later. It goes on now, with Christian and Islamic fanatics on the one hand and the rest of us on the other, with our Western values of scientific progress, personal struggle and liberty (and the right to shop in a Godless world! For Bernard[7] sensed Abelard's thought would end in an atheistic hedonism and, in a way, he was right.) (Neill 2006: 7)[8]

Similarly, introducing *Anne Boleyn*, both in the theatre programme and in the preface to the printed text, Brenton declares that he wrote the play 'to celebrate her life and her legacy as a great English woman who helped change the course of our history' (Brenton 2010). Once again, he portrays his historical subject, here the Tudors and specifically Henry VIII's reign, as both the origin of modern-day realities ('power struggle. The establishment of a regime who founded us really. We're their heirs', Woddis 2010) and a time characterized by correspondences with the present ('you find the resonances in it are of our time; religion is killing people at the moment', ibid.).

Addressing contemporary problems by means of past events is a technique Howard Brenton has not only constantly practised but also reflected on throughout his career. Recently, mainly referring to *Anne Boleyn*, he has stressed that distant subject matter offers the writer a greater freedom to tackle existential themes and political mechanisms directly:

> History plays are not exactly parables but you can show the workings of society more clearly in some way, and hope that there's a resonance ... It's a way of addressing first and last things in a way that you can't in a satire or modern play, like death and the great clashes in society between poverty and the rich. (Woddis 2010)

So histories share with parables the possibility to unveil the ultimate facts and processes of life and society in a depiction that is rendered more distinct by abstraction in the latter and by distance in the former. But representing past events has the undisputed strength of actuality, which carries with it credibility[9] as well as causal connections with the present, while stylization may easily lapse into schematism, and thus engender a lack of liveliness in characters and scenes. Although on this occasion Brenton did not explain his preference for the historical genre, this is very likely to be one of its main reasons, since he analysed this pitfall of parables in his criticism of Brecht's oeuvre (Brenton 1986a: 5–7).

As for the historical perspective that seeks to outline past events as the source of the present, the playwright set it forth rather early in his career: when asked why writers of his generation often focused on the previous thirty or forty years, he stated it was 'because of the old truth – that if you don't understand the past, you'll never understand the present, let alone the future' (Hay and Roberts 1979: 136). He went on to explain the importance of the theatre in developing this perception and knowledge, advocating the representation of history, even recent history, as a necessary antidote to the contemporary drift towards instantaneous oblivion (ibid.), a risk that appears much greater in the fast-paced twenty-first century, making Brenton's argument even more persuasive.

In line with these ideas, Shakespeare's Globe is an especially appropriate setting for 'history plays for now' (Hay and Roberts 1979: 138), as he defined this kind of drama set in the past but directed towards the future, because it evokes both consequentiality and similarity. A reconstructed Elizabethan playhouse obviously symbolizes a seminal moment for English theatre, and thus exemplifies the past's influence on the present, while the fact that it makes spectators and performers visible as parts of the same picture effectively suggests that characters and audience share the same predicaments.

# A British epic theatre

Howard Brenton's criticism of Bertolt Brecht's parable dramas is only one episode in what looks almost like a haunting: in the second half of the twentieth century, a committed left-wing playwright could not avoid confronting the author whose engaged theatre revolutionized Western drama and stage practice, but Brenton seems to have gone far beyond the due homage or revolt. More than once Janelle Reinelt has described him as 'what a successor to Brecht might be like' (Reinelt 1994: 17),[10] and he has behaved like a proper 'son', rebelling against this perspicuous 'father' as well as acknowledging the parentage.

Perhaps because of the critics' and interviewers' insistence on this point, Brenton has been facing Brecht's model throughout his whole career. His ideas on this subject have been evolving in relation to his artistic experiences as well as to the changing political and cultural context. Back in 1974, he explicitly declared, 'I'm an anti-Brechtian, a Left anti-Brechtian. I think his plays are museum pieces now and are messing up a lot of young theatre workers. Brecht's plays don't work' (Itzin and Trussler 1975: 14).[11] Nevertheless, a more ambivalent relationship with the deviser of the Verfremdungseffekt was implicitly expressed in passing, when he explained a stylistic choice in *Christie in Love* (1969) as a sort of alienation device and commented that 'the search for something other than what Brecht was doing goes on endlessly amongst the writers of my generation' (Itzin and Trussler 1981: 90). The German playwright was an obvious example, though one the young Brenton meant to transcend by developing 'an epic style that has nothing to do with Brecht' (ibid.: 94).

A radical change in Brenton's reading of Brecht came about when he wrote the English translation of *Leben des Galilei* (*The Life of Galileo*, 1980).[12] A few years later, he stated he did it 'to find out what made that playwright tick' (Mitchell 1987: 199); on that occasion, after declaring once again that he had 'always disliked him', he avowed 'to be frank, he frightened me' (ibid.). In a later interview, he explained the reasons of fear and dislike, recalling that when he began writing Brecht was 'a deadening influence' (Reinelt 1992: 39) because, from a political point of view, 'a lot of scholars would hit you over the head with Brecht, demanding some sort of ideological purity that actually Brecht's work doesn't have, because it is very dialectical writing' (ibid.); at the same time, on an aesthetic plane, a widespread incorrect reading of his theories led to the conviction that in epic theatre 'it's not necessary to act' (ibid.).

After confronting the 'bogeyman', Brenton took an articulated stance. On the one hand, he highlighted the consequences of erroneous interpretations and faulty translations in the British reception of Brecht's works and ideas (Reinelt 1992: 39–40) and he expressed admiration for him, as the creator of complex, meaningful characters and scenes, as the author of some masterpieces (notably *Die Mutter* and *Leben des Galilei*), and as a truly committed artist (Brenton 1986a: 5–6; Mitchell 1987: 200; Reinelt 1992: 43–4). On the other hand, he did not refrain from defining much of his dramatic writing 'thin' (Brenton 1986a: 6), expressing the dialectic in 'banal and obvious parables' (ibid.). Nevertheless, he also acknowledged Brecht's direct influence on his own writing (ibid.; Reinelt 1992: 44–5, 47). This thoughtful and somewhat conflicted attitude can be seen as the elucidation of his desire to develop 'a British epic theatre' (Brenton 1986b: xii), a dramatic form that would secure the best of the German writer and theorist's concepts and practices while avoiding his mistakes and adjusting his solutions to the very different artistic and political context of the United Kingdom in the 1980s.

Throughout these evolutions, however, the most interesting thing is how Brenton's own output can be compared to Brecht's, and especially to the way the British playwright read him. Rather early in his career, Brenton already defined his own plays 'epic', although he added that 'measured against the Brechtian, received idea of an epic they are far from being "pure epics"' (Hay and Roberts 1979: 139).[13] His explanation of the term was specific and multifaceted, and listed characteristics that apply to most of Brecht's works too: 'they are epic in that they are many scened, full of stories, ironic and argumentative, and deliberately written as "history plays for now"' (ibid.: 138). After his close scrutiny of *Leben des Galilei*, Brenton changed his view on the first point he had emphasized. Although he still thought each scene must consist of a 'window' on an episode that is true in itself and at the same time constitutes a step in the overall argument of the plot, he realized Brecht usually wrote scenes that are not fragments but complete structures, almost whole short plays; believing that this configuration enabled the playwright to combine complex political reasoning with a simple storytelling set-up, Brenton openly adopted it in his own subsequent works.[14]

When asserting Brecht's positive influence, Brenton credited him with inventing 'a way of busting the decayed Ibsenite drama of closed rooms and closed minds wide open' (Brenton 1986a: 6). With this statement, he recognized Brecht's fundamental role in an artistic battle he had been fighting (and was going to continue) throughout his career (see Hay and Roberts 1979: 135–6; Reinelt 1992: 4; Wu 2000: 29–31; Wilkinson 2006), against the psychological 'revelatory' conception of human nature, according to which characters are represented as having a core truth the play guides its audience to discover. Brenton has always maintained that consciousness is chaotic, contradictory, to the point that people's identity can ultimately be recognized only in their actions. While the philosophical foundations of this idea are basically existentialist,[15] their dramatic expression can certainly be found in the 'distanced' portrayals created by Brechtian writing and acting, or by other techniques aiming at an alienation effect, as Brenton's plays showed even before he acknowledged this connection.

This way of presenting human beings is clearly linked to another trait shared by Brecht's and Brenton's characters: they can never be classified as 'good' or 'bad', not even with an attenuating adjective.

[Brecht's] heroes and heroines are a mixed bag of what many would call 'morally ambiguous' figures. Azdak, Galileo, Courage, even Mother are, in themselves, remarkable. They are not 'great persons'. They do not embody great virtues, or even flawed virtues. (Brenton 1986a: 5)

This description might as well be applied to the British playwright's creations, a gallery of 'perverse saints' (Itzin and Trussler 1981: 93), 'over-reachers' (Neill 2006: 9) and the 'millions [who] do not have that vision, confidence and heroism, and some [of which] are traumatised by defeat' (Brenton 1986b: xv). Their recurring traits will be discussed in the next paragraph, but their moral ambiguity is already apparent in the way Brenton defines them.

Moreover, as remarked by Janelle Reinelt (1985: 30–1), Brenton's use of the historical genre as a means for addressing contemporary issues is quite in line with Brecht's concept of historicization. It only differs in that it shifts the responsibility for the alienation effect from the performer to the playwright: while one of the main texts concerning the Verfremdungseffekt explains that 'it is up to the actor to treat present-day events and modes of behaviour with the same detachment as the historian adopts with regard to those of the past' (Brecht 1964 [1940]: 140), historical drama may anticipate this need by setting the action in a different time-frame, even though it refers to contemporary reality. This sort of displacement was employed by Brecht himself, after all, in such plays as *Leben des Galilei* and *Mutter Courage und ihre Kinder*.[16] It may at first sight contrast with his specification that 'historical incidents are unique, transitory incidents associated with particular periods' (Brecht 1964 [1940]: 140) and that 'the conduct of the persons involved in them is not fixed and "universally human"' (ibid.). Yet a closer examination shows that this is not the case, as similarities between an epoch or situation in the past and the present can be recognized and foregrounded, without implying that they are determined by some overwhelming constant in human nature. On the contrary, such analogies may encourage a reflection on what financial, social or political factors and mechanisms can explain the differences and the points in common between the two contexts, and consequently offer the possibility to direct future action according to the analysis of previous events, the issue of which is already known.

Of course, this is not to say that such a play must be heavy with theory and speculation. In *Anne Boleyn*, for instance, a crucial question is expressed with a comic mixture of provoking wit and palpable difficulties by the evidently intoxicated King James:

God's Word my Word, God's Word my Word. My my my Word. I ... Tell me this, Queen Anne, great Queen. *(Takes a great breath.)* Why ... *(Takes another great breath.)* Why is it that all we do in the name of God is always exactly the same as what we need to do in our own self-interest? *(AB 115)*

The distance between the fictional reality's times and ours is also emphasized in the same play by an ostensibly funny dialogue on birth control methods (*AB* 30–1).

This process of historicization has already been shown to operate in the plays Brenton wrote for Shakespeare's Globe, while the complexity and ambiguity of their protagonists are analysed in the next paragraph; here, it may be interesting to exemplify the 'Brechtian' structure of their scenes. A typical instance is Scene 1.11 of *In Extremis* (*IE* 45–8), which represents Abelard and Heloise's reunion at the end of the time during which she had to take shelter in his family's farm, in Brittany, after discovering she was pregnant. The 'window' it opens is detached from the previous scene, set two years before in Paris, and from the following one, which takes place some days after they have returned to the capital. In spite of being rather short, it has the structure of a complete piece, with a beginning that outlines the situation (Heloise and Abelard's sister, Denise, looking down from a cliff-top, watch the latter's father and comment on the former's refusal to become part of the family), a development in which a conflict is exposed (the two women disagree about the lovers' duties towards their child, Astrolabe), a main event (the man's arrival) and a consequent conclusion (Abelard and Heloise are reunited and can plan to go back to Paris together). The episode constitutes a relevant passage in the play's overall argument because it displays the protagonists' recklessness by contrasting their eagerness to return to the situation they had to flee with Denise's foreseeing worries (*IE* 47–8) and by throwing light on Astrolabe's condition as a 'war orphan' in the 'war of ideas' (*IE* 47) they are fighting.

Similar features can be recognized, for instance, in *Anne Boleyn* 2.7 (*AB* 33–9), which focuses on the long wait before Anne and Henry can marry. The scene starts with a 'spoken stage direction'[17] informing the audience it takes place five years after the previous one, and the first lines of the following one manifest a time gap quite as effectively, although implicitly (Anne, who has just exited hand-in-hand with the king, is said to be missing from the hunt he is attending). From the point of view of place, too, the distinctions are clear, though not explicit, a public situation (the royal divorce being discussed as a matter of state) coming after a private one (the protagonist chatting with her friends) and before a secret one (Cromwell's intelligence work). The scene begins in medias res (with Henry's request of explanations enabling the audience to understand what is happening), develops through various small incidents (Anne repeatedly interrupts Wolsey's exposition of how the Legatine Court will proceed, until the king dismisses everyone but her) that reveal conflicts (between Anne and Wolsey) and troubles (in the way of the royal divorce and second marriage) and ends with a reassertion of the lovers' mix of patience and desire. In the overall design of the play, this scene displays the protagonist's powers (since by means of her strong will, her intelligence and her quick temper she temporarily manages to rule the court and the king himself), but also the dangerous intermingling of the public and private spheres that will eventually bring about her downfall.

In *Doctor Scroggy's War* 2.4 (*DSW* 83–7), framed between two scenes set at Sidcup hospital, Penelope and Ralph meet during a sort of army celebration at the Ritz. Both have last been seen by the audience on the front. Their dialogue begins with their encounter and as they catch up on each other's situation spectators learn that the man is a war hero, while the woman has quit working as a Voluntary Aid Detachment (VAD) nurse. As the conversation progresses, they do not articulate their opinions, but the contrast between Penelope's hysterical laughter and disillusioned irony on one side and Ralph's composed and resolute avowal that battles can be fun on the other represents antithetical views of war no less clearly than the more explicit confrontation between the young woman and Jack which will mark their separation (*DSW* 99–101). The conflict between all sorts of oppositions to war and its mysterious fascination is probably the core theme of the play, but this scene closes on a more positive note, with Penelope and Ralph agreeing to go visit Jack at the hospital where Gillies treats facial injuries (*DSW* 87). This arrangement paves the way for the following development of the plot, but it also provides an appropriate conclusion for the narrative arc of the episode, which depicts the two friends' difficult reunion after their similar and yet contrasting experiences on the front.

The scenes taken as examples here feature also other notable Brechtian devices, such as irony (e.g. when Heloise cannot recognize her lover just because he limps and he has no horse, *IE* 47, or when Anne states, 'I'll never say anything against Catherine. Ever. I just wish the bitch would piss off to a convent', *AB* 34), the dialectical confrontation of opposite theses (e.g. Denise's and

Heloise's concerning what is 'real life', *IE* 46) and other techniques of alienation (such as the spoken stage direction mentioned above, *AB* 33, or the ostensibly absurd presence of a football at a military celebration in a stylish hotel, *DSW* 83–4).

In *Extremis*, *Anne Boleyn* and *Doctor Scroggy's War* also exemplify two more traits shared by most of Brecht's and Brenton's plays, though the British playwright did not highlight their presence in the works of his German predecessor: variety and amplitude. Brenton has always pointed out the abrupt changes in style and content as characteristic of his own writing (see e.g. Ansorge 1973: 23; Mitchell 1987: 198; Wu 2000: 40; Brenton 2007). Remarking the lack of critical criteria to judge an epic production, he stressed that 'experts' tend to pick out single scenes, bewildered by the absence of a constant tone, while 'audiences can sit quite happily through shows which have serious, terrible speeches about torture, and silly songs' (Reinelt 1992: 56), thus linking a feature of his own output with the definition of epic drama and with a description that evokes Brecht's works too. Also, the wide range of moods in both authors' plays can be linked to their ample scope, often encompassing rather distant times and places, in which a remarkable array of characters interact, so as to challenge the three Aristotelian unities of place, time and action.

The vicissitudes of Abelard and Heloise, themselves a potentially odd mixture of theology and sex, are thus intertwined with scenes centred on what Brenton defines 'a kind of Rosencrantz and Guildenstern double act' (Neill 2006: 9), Alberic and Lotholf, in the first act two disciples of philosopher William of Champeaux, then a powerful bishop and a wealthy entrepreneur. As for width, the plot of *In Extremis* spans throughout most of the lovers' lives and brings on stage such different characters as king Louis VI and Bernard of Clairvaux, countrywomen and courtiers, prostitutes and nuns, in environments that range from Notre Dame in Paris to the coast of Brittany, from open fields to cloisters.

*Anne Boleyn* is less varied with respect to settings, only two of its scenes taking place out of the royal palace, in a wood; from the chronological point of view, on the contrary, it goes beyond a human life-span, because it features episodes from the reigns of Henry VIII and James I. Most characters in the play are somehow part of the court, but notable exceptions are constituted by William Tyndale and his supporters with whom Anne meets, and by the diverse crowd of religious representatives summoned by James. An interesting example of multiple changes in tone can be found in 1.5 and 1.6, in which the same subject, love, is treated in several different ways: it is first debated by Anne and Henry in the terms of witty court poetry (*AB* 26–8), then the king addresses the point directly in a 'ripe' monologue (*AB* 29) followed by a less explicit but very matter-of-fact letter (*AB* 29–30), a group of ladies reduce it to the material (and for the audience comic) details of sixteenth-century birth-control techniques (*AB* 30–1), and finally the protagonist incorporates it with cool determination into her plans for the future (*AB* 31–2).

Usually distant situations and people are brought together by the centripetal force of the conflict in *Doctor Scroggy's War*. In a couple of momentous years its protagonists' lives are transformed by war and its consequences. The parable of 'temporary gentleman' Jack Twigg and more succinctly the case of VAD nurse Tilly, who turns out to be a personal acquaintance of the Queen's (*DSW* 90–1), epitomize the way war temporarily upsets social distinctions. The characters' constant awareness of this anomaly (see e.g. *DSW* 22, 24 or 57–8) suggests rather forcefully that this apparently egalitarian reshuffling will not outlast the emergencies that have caused it, but this peculiar context makes it possible for the play to connect such disparate settings as a working-class London house, the battlefields of France, a hospital and the Ritz, and to unite characters that range from a ship-chandler to the Queen. The play's stylistic mixture also finds an almost realistic explanation in the absurdity of mass suffering observed by Doctor Gillies (*DSW* 81–3) and in the medical genius's decision to fight it with the weapons of fun, embodied by his *alter ego* Doctor Scroggy.

Finally, *In Extremis*, *Anne Boleyn* and *Doctor Scroggy's War* have been produced in a particular 'epic' context, because the reconstructed Globe itself, with its multiple time layers and its eye-catching audience, is a historicizing location and a very conspicuous distancing device.

# Perverse saints

Four of Howard Brenton's most recent plays – *Paul* (2005), *In Extremis* (2006), *Anne Boleyn* (2010) and *55 Days* (2012) – have been more or less explicitly grouped, by several critics as well as by the author himself,[18] because of their religious theme. Their specificity is all the more remarkable because a professed Marxist is not expected to be interested in the nuances of faith, but a closer look at this surprising output makes it far more comprehensible and two main explanations of the playwright's take on Christian beliefs have already been expressed. In line with Brenton's statements, Janelle Reinelt has pointed out that he is once again addressing 'contemporary sociopolitical concerns' (2007: 167): 'we live in a moment when understanding how and why people believe in various spiritual realities is critical if we are to combat the intolerance, violence, and wars of religion that threaten our fledgling century' (ibid.).

At least one influential reviewer, Ian Shuttleworth, has suggested that the plays' perspective is actually a historical one that has very little to do with faith: 'Brenton is concerned not with theology, but with churches as a kind of political body against which more and less powerful individuals strove' (Shuttleworth 2010). This materialist view may be supported by the fact that all four texts deal with the relationship between church and state. *55 Days* represents the trial of Charles I, a political crisis regarding which all conflicting parties believed to be doing God's will (see Hemming 2012). *Anne Boleyn* focuses on two events that are founding and at the same time exemplary of the crown's religious power, the establishment of the Church of England and the commissioning of the King James Bible. Although Brenton has remarked that *In Extremis* is set in a time when the church was still defining its own tenets (Brenton 2006: 4; Neill 2006: 7), the play portrays its influence on secular life by tracing Lotholf's entrepreneurial success to Bernard of Clairvaux's protection (*IE* 69) and by presenting Louis VI's failed attempts to break free of the church's impositions (*IE* 31–2, 81–2). *Paul* represents a very early stage in the history of Christianity, when it was not institutionalized yet, but in a crucial scene Emperor Nero foresees a future in which the successors of Peter and Paul will 'have priests, … a good hierarchy of bribable gentlemen in fine robes, like any other religion', and 'will do business with the state', so that 'a hundred, two hundred years from now, Christianity could be the Empire's official religion' (Brenton 2006: 80).

There may be yet another reading of what religious belief stands for in these plays, a metaphorical one. Early in his career, Brenton used the word 'saint' to describe several of his main characters:

I'm very interested in people who could be called saints, perverse saints, who try to drive a straight line through very complex situations, and usually become honed down to the point of death. (Itzin and Trussler 1981: 93)

He made this remark in answer to a question concerning Wesley, the founder of Methodism, but he immediately went on to specify that 'Scott was one of those' (ibid.),[19] thus suggesting that religious fanaticism could be a metaphor for any kind of blind, absolute belief. As Duncan Wu observed, Brenton has always been 'concerned with whether moral inconsistency, even failure, invalidates the larger political project' (Wu 2000: 14). A combination of these two core traits – a 'saintly' conviction and a fatal fault – characterizes most of the playwright's revolutionary figures, from the 'Stalinist Macbeth' of *Thirteenth Night* (1987 [1981]), who sets out to establish freedom and peace and ends up at the head of a terror state, to the Romantics of *Bloody Poetry* (1987 [1984]), whose free-love utopia is tainted by a selfish insensibility that causes suffering and death; an especially interesting case is Paul, who lives and dies for a great ideal that may be (consciously or not) based on erroneous premises, thus putting into question the validity of all his teachings.[20]

The three protagonists of *In Extremis* – Abelard, Heloise and Bernard – all fit this model. The two lovers see themselves as 'philosophical warriors ... fighting in a war of ideas' (*IE* 67), 'running, full tilt, towards a wonderful future' (*IE* 18) in which mystery and confusion 'will flee before the light of philosophy' (*IE* 14), but they cannot see the dangers Denise warns them of (*IE* 17–18, 47–8, 78) and they overlook the suffering they cause to those who love them or depend on them (*IE* 47–8, 76–7). Abelard expounds beautiful ideas regarding the power and the elevated nature of human reason (*IE* 13–14, 26–9), but he is patronizing towards the woman he loves (*IE* 43–4) and generally self-important (e.g. *IE* 75–6). Heloise asserts the value of 'man and woman, equal in love' (*IE* 43), but her rejection of marriage borders on a refusal to grow old (*IE* 44–5) or to accept responsibilities (*IE* 47), and her little understanding of the life of other women can drive her to believe that her experiences should be easily accepted by other people (*IE* 58), or that no one ever did the same (*IE* 67). On the other hand, Bernard is guided by sincere faith (*IE* 34–5, 79), free of material interests and willing to spread salvation (*IE* 24–5, 33–6) but he lacks humanity (*IE* 83–6, 89) and in order to uphold his ideals and make Clairvaux 'an instrument for the purpose of God' (*IE* 25) he is ready to mythologize his own life (*IE* 70–1, 83–5, 89–90), to politick (*IE* 71–2, 90), even to cheat (*IE* 72–3, 80–1, 83).

Abelard's exemplification of the 'ethics of intention' he propounds may be very telling: 'even if religion were found to be false, the harm we did preaching it would have to be forgiven. For, with all our hearts, you and I always intended only to do good' (*IE* 85). Both he and Bernard have tried to defend truth and make it known, and in doing so they have damaged other people (*IE* 86); according to Abelard's doctrine, they should not be condemned because they erred in good faith, but their faults inevitably throw a shadow on the validity of their ideas. That the contrast between their views remains unresolved is attested by the play's ambiguous representation of divine manifestations. Bernard behaves as a man to whom God speaks and appears (*IE* 33–6, 79) and considers events as caused by His direct intervention (*IE* 33–6, 79, 83–4), while Abelard challenges both these visions and these readings (*IE* 33–6, 83–4). The spectators do not see nor hear as Bernard seems to, but they are not given a clear, definitive explanation of such events as Abelard's unexpected silence at the Council of Sens (*IE* 81–3), so they are drawn to weigh the different ideas on stage carefully, apprehend each position's merits and contradictions and possibly search for their own truth.

*Anne Boleyn*, as the title suggests, is rather centred on its heroine: although there are many other carefully drawn characters, the text appears to be focalised on her, since she opens and closes the play with monologues that address the audience directly (1.1, *AB* 11–12, and 2.12, *AB* 115) and she repeatedly speaks her mind, in soliloquies (*AB* 41, 50, 59, 60, 97) in confidences she makes to her friends (*AB* 23, 30–2) and in a feverish outburst (*AB* 83–4). Another instance of a person who pursues a high ideal but is somehow impaired by her own moral shortcomings, Anne expresses the ambiguity of her goal when she words it: 'I will be a new queen. For a new England ... A Protestant Queen for England' (*AB* 32). Throughout the first act of the play, her personal and disinterested ends coincide, and thus give her will an exceptional strength, but her second meeting with Tyndale and his followers, who insist that her marriage with Henry is not part of God's plans, marks the beginning of her decline (*AB* 92–7).

Anne protests that she does look into her heart, as Tyndale advises her to do (*AB* 97), but she does not seem to see the ambivalence which is, on the contrary, clear to other people's eyes. Right from the beginning, when she asserts that her ambition 'could be God's Will', her friend, Lady Rocheford, immediately replies, 'your will!', but Anne confidently repeats, 'God's Will. This may be his purpose for me on earth' (*AB* 32). On first encountering Tyndale, the young woman asks, 'how can any of us know that we are God's instrument?'; the 'wise man' (*AB* 83) cannot answer, but he offers a rule of thumb: 'they who claim to be God's instruments, never are' (*AB* 48). The queen-to-be does not realize this definition applies to herself, and as soon as she is alone, she asks for God's help in her mission (*AB* 50). Even after her death, when James asks, 'why is it that all we do in the name of God is always exactly the same as what we need to do in our own self-interest?', she dismisses the problem as 'a demon thought' (*AB* 115). The fact that Anne is now a spirit (while James's question is the last sentence he manages to articulate before passing out, helplessly drunk), may give her words greater reliability, and suggest that the argument is closed and she was right to trust herself. But 'demons' is the word Anne has used, and will use again, to define all people of the future, James as well as the spectators (*AB* 114, 115), so her statement may come to mean that the doubt concerning God's will is actually a 'modern' thought.

After all, James's perspective is at the heart of the whole play, of which Anne is the eponymous heroine but not quite the only protagonist. If the first act is decidedly hers (15 scenes out of 16 and 50 pages out of 59), the second is almost equally divided between the two sovereigns: 5 scenes out of 12, amounting to approximately 21 pages out of 46, are set in the Stuart king's times. The queen opens and closes the play with monologues resembling a prologue and an epilogue because, alone on stage, she talks directly to the spectators, almost ushering them in and out of the performance (*AB* 11–12, 115), but James begins and ends the action proper, that starts with his curiosity on arriving in London (*AB* 12) and reaches completion when he achieves a possible understanding of her fall (*AB* 114) and manages to talk to her (*AB* 113–15). As a matter of fact, the Tudor strand of the plot appears to be evoked by James's summons, that always anticipate its sequences ('Anne, you hussy! Where are you? Anne!', *AB* 21; 'Anne. Anne. Tell me what you began and I will end it', *AB* 82; 'Anne. Anne, who pulled you down?', *AB* 102).

James asks the questions that are on the spectators' minds: what was the young woman doing with Tyndale's forbidden books (*AB* 16) and who caused her ruin (*AB* 102). Moreover, Anne herself seems to consider him an exponent of the 'demons of the future' (*AB* 114) in the auditorium, and in this perspective the phrase with which she introduces him, 'come to rule you all' (*AB* 12), may refer not only to the English people he was going to reign over but also to the spectators he is going to lead from the traditional image of 'the harlot Queen' (*AB* 14) to a deeper reflection on the power struggle in which she took part and on her role in the birth of the Church of England. Yet, from an essential point of view, King James is far from being an audience member: his investigation of Anne's life is aimed at completing her work ('tell me what you began and I will end it', *AB* 82), and Howard Brenton dramatizes the Stuart king's part in the history of Anglicanism too. The play was commissioned to celebrate the 400th anniversary of the Authorised Version of the Bible, after all, and the 'Protestant Queen of England' (*AB* 32) is essentially presented as a precursor who contributed to King James's achievement.

The combination of the two time planes in *Anne Boleyn*, cross-cut and framed by the present of Anne's speeches directly addressed to the audience, actually constitutes a new take on a theme that has characterised most of Brenton's work, i.e. the power of history. Most of his plays deal with ways in which the past and its perception can shape what follows (even when, as in *Greenland* [1988], both the fictional present and its past are presented as the audience's future); furthermore, the relationship between James and Anne can be usefully compared to a recurring pattern highlighted by Richard Boon, that of the 'dirty old man' and the resurrection of his ghost (Boon 1991: 23–4, 138–9). In what amounts almost to a trope of Brenton's playwriting, a man from a previous generation exerts a usually malign influence on younger characters, his being a representative of an era that has a hold on the present sometimes emphasized by the fact that he is 'a long-dead figure from history' (ibid.: 139), 'resurrected from the past to lay a hand on the present' (ibid.: 138). The most obvious examples are the Nazi soldier Hans in *Hitler Dances* (1982) and Winston Churchill in the play within *The Churchill Play* (1974 and 1978).

Anne could be defined the 'pretty young woman', an opposite and yet parallel embodiment of that figure. Sixty-seven years after her death, she is conjured up by a man whom she evidently fascinates (to the point that he enjoys dancing in her coronation dress, *AB* 70) and whose actions she influences, indirectly guiding his thoughts towards the question of the relationship between religion and state (*AB* 16). She does not have the menacing traits of the dirty old man, because she is young, attractive and in Brenton's portrayal even considerably pure (*AB* 32). Yet these features are precisely those that make her dangerous. Her beauty is seductive and evokes 'the stink of witchcraft' (*AB* 15); her being an 'insufferably holy cow' (*AB* 115) suggests the ambiguous overlapping of 'God's will' (*AB* 114) with 'our own self-interest' (*AB* 115). She has the appearance of a victim, but she is also a 'perverse saint'. What appears to be the main difference between Anne and the typical 'dirty old man' is that she does not 'exert a malign and violent influence on the present' (Boon 1991: 37). On the contrary, following her trail makes James reconsider some historiographical received ideas and work on a fundamental problem of his own time. The result is not unquestionably good, though. On the one hand he establishes 'a new way in [his] Kingdom, in which all are included' (*AB* 75), but on the other he enforces it by threatening violence (*AB* 71, 75, 79) and by consolidating first of all his own power and control (*AB* 78–9, 100–1), so his action resembles the 'stony path' (*AB* 91) of impositions Anne and Cromwell follow to foster the Reformation more than the heroine's utopian image of 'a woman standing naked before her God' (*AB* 59). Moreover, his reflection that 'all we do in the name of God is always exactly what we need to do in our own self-interest' (*AB* 115) applies to him as well as to her. All in all, Anne is not for James an indisputably good model; the best fruit of their peculiar relationship is probably the consciousness that allows the king to question his own motives as well as other people's.

In fact, while one of the main subjects of both *Anne Boleyn* and *In Extremis* is 'belief', their core message seems to be 'doubt', and this effect is achieved by means of the protagonists' ambiguity. Unfortunately, this choice has led to some misunderstandings, especially in the case of the earlier play, because a central character that is morally questionable seems to be easier to accept (or to ignore, as the critics' silence on this aspect of Brenton's Anne may suggest) than a clear-cut division that does not boil down to the opposition of 'good' and 'bad'. As a result, some reviewers have remarked the lovers' shortcomings or their nemesis' fascination as odd or even wrong.[21] These observations are rather obviously accompanied by the conviction that 'Bernard is nasty and deluded' (Hart 2006b), 'no longer a mystic but a devious politician who is not at all beneath using spiritualist-style trickery to advance … mindless fundamentalism' (Nightingale 2006), and that his 'sanctity is barely more than a ruse to obtain power' (Shore 2006b), because ultimately 'Brenton obviously has little feeling for religious mysticism' (ibid.).

A rough interpretation of the playwright's assertions concerning the play's topicality may have supported these readings, but most of the critics have rather credited Brenton with creating a balanced ensemble of complex figures (e.g. Cavendish 2006; Taylor 2006b; Gardner 2007; Marlowe 2007). An interesting, more nuanced view, has been expressed by Michael Billington, whose review states that *In Extremis* 'reveals the intellectual contradictions that make Brenton such a fascinating dramatist' (Billington 2006b), essentially recognizing the play's design, but attributing it to the artist's unconscious sensibility instead of considering it the product of deliberate choices:

> It is the rabid, flesh-loathing fundamentalist Bernard, supposedly representing everything Brenton deplores, who emerges not only as the most gripping figure but also the real revolutionary.
>     This strikes me as being Brenton's dramatic strength.… It isn't simply a case of giving the devil the best tunes. Brenton lends the Cistercian a missionary zeal that carries echoes of early political militants. Brenton's head may be with Abelard but his heart is secretly with Bernard. (Billington 2006b)

Howard Brenton's plays have already suffered from this kind of interpretive problems in the past and his characters have been misunderstood by some performers too. Since the most conspicuous episodes concerned the Los Angeles production of *The Genius* (1984) and the 1987 New York staging of *Bloody Poetry* (Reinelt 1992: 51–2), he attributed the difficulties to a cultural difference. He stressed that 'in America, there is no notion of what opposition is' (ibid.: 52), adding that, what is more, 'the Christian moralism which is at the root of American sensibility' (Brenton 1986a: 5) prevents spectators and professionals alike from accepting such ambiguous heroes as Brecht's and to comprehend that, in the case of *The Genius* (1983), for instance, the protagonist 'may well be a brilliant man, but whether he's fine or not, as in *Galileo*, is really up to question' (Reinelt 1992: 51). He also remarked that method acting, which requires the performer to identify with the character, is not appropriate to this kind of figure, while better results may be achieved by means of the 'sardonic attitude toward the role' (ibid.: 49–50) that is characteristic of English players.[22]

The playwright's considerations on these two episodes and his reflections on Brecht's main characters contradict the interpretations according to which his Bernard is too appealing and his Abelard and Heloise too self-conceited by mistake, and weakens Billington's 'split' theory: whatever his thoughts or feelings may be, Brenton deliberately avoids creating figures that embody 'right' or 'wrong'. He guards himself from the danger of representing one of the possibilities as '"the" option within the world of the play' (Reinelt 1992: 48) and thus using the great power of drama to convince the spectators and make them think they have been given the solution to a problem.

The same attitude has not been misunderstood or criticized in the case of *Doctor Scroggy's War*. This different reception may in part be due to the fact that in the meantime Brenton has come to be recognized as one of the best twenty-first-century Globe authors, but that is certainly not all. Although the most hostile review formulates the opposite accusation of portraying his characters according to socially Manichaean stereotypes (Evans 2014), a change in the playwright's approach does not seem to have actually occurred. His willingness to portray both sides of the argument with equal doubtfulness rather seems to have been accepted. Several critics approve, for instance, his relatively sympathetic portrayal of Field Marshal French, even though it contrasts with the undeniably atrocious responsibilities he is attributed (e.g. Billington 2014; Curtis 2014). The reason for this generally more favourable response to Brenton's ostensibly contradictory depictions may rest in the widespread conflicted feelings aroused nowadays by the First World War. The need to honour the sacrifices of a still recent generation clashes with the impossibility of celebrating a largely senseless massacre, and *Doctor Scroggy's War* is seen to avoid 'the centennial pitfalls – prurient wallowing in misery or simplistic hostility towards the officer class' (Purves 2014).

All these readings tend to focus on commanders and soldiers who are secondary characters in the play, though, rather than on its protagonists, those that are more likely to represent a new embodiment of the 'perverse saint'. And there a more controversial image can be found, that of a whole generation of 'perverse martyrs', represented by Jack and Ralph (and Fergal), who acknowledge the mysterious fascination of the front line (*DSW* 59, 73–4, 84, 100–1). An abstract sense of duty (*DSW* 101) and the paradoxically powerful feeling of being alive while facing probable death, at least in Gillies's interpretation (*DSW* 106), make these young men ready for a self-sacrifice that is perverse because it survives not only the first-hand knowledge of the military high ranks' shortcomings (*DSW* 45–8, 56, 93) and the personal experience of horror (*DSW* 48–50, 67–9, 85) but even the thorough demolition of all declared reasons for fighting (*DSW* 103–5). Actually, what prompted Brenton to dramatize this story is precisely the surprising fact that most of the real Doctor Gillies's patients wished to go back to active service on the front as soon as their terrible wounds started to heal (Curtis 2014).

The 'perverse martyrs' of war are criticized by civilians who cannot understand them, even though they have experienced the battles first-hand, like Penelope (*DSW* 86, 100–1), as well as by Gillies, whose 'diagnosis' of their problem is warranted by his professional position. The young men reject these objections, but they cannot really argue their case (*DSW* 86, 100–1, 106–7). Nevertheless, their attitude is not condemned by the play. On the contrary, their unquestionable bravery (*DSW* 85, 106) and remarkable composure throughout the script are favourably contrasted with the weaknesses of their opponents: fear and horror repeatedly overwhelm Jack's father (*DSW* 20, 67–8) and Penelope, before engaging in the pacifist movement, appears slightly drunk and prone to hysterical laughter after she has returned from the front because she has lost her nerve (*DSW* 60, 83–6).

Gillies himself combines medical genius and absolute commitment to his patients' well-being with an impressive array of oddities, such as smashing beer bottles for a golf swing experiment (*DSW* 9–10) or carrying around a rowing boat oar because it helps him think (*DSW* 65, 70), so that Jack's reiterated suggestion that the doctor may not be entirely in his right mind (*DSW* 70, 106) does not appear to be completely groundless. His comic alter ego Doctor

Scroggy may be not only the pivot of a 'fun therapy' designed to heal his traumatised patients' spirits but also an expression of the toll the conflict's 'conga of suffering' (see *DSW* 82) takes on him too. Because of his ostensibly light-hearted attitude, Gillies does not seem to be as driven as Brenton's perverse saints usually are, but he too is fighting a personal war, as the play's title makes clear. What is more, he is losing his battle, it seems, since the young men to whom he has given a new face (and thus symbolically a renewed humanity, *DSW* 95) overcome horror and despair (*DSW* 69–70, 77–80) only to go back to the front, making him 'feel that all [his] work is for nothing' (*DSW* 107).

In conclusion, *Doctor Scroggy's War* is once again centred on a set of complex, sometimes contradictory, characters who carry opposite views on fundamental issues and Brenton carefully avoids espousing any of their positions but calls them all to question. After all, he believes that 'the democratic way is almost certainly to stir it up' (Reinelt 1992: 49), the dialectical way, the path also Brecht pursued (ibid.), because 'there's a great thirst for wisdom in an audience' (ibid.), but the playwright must 'be both arrogant enough to say I understand what's going on and dramatize it and also humble enough to say, well, actually I'm in no higher position of wisdom than the audience' (ibid.).[23] Morally ambiguous characters are certainly a useful instrument to raise questions rather than answer them.[24]

# Historiographic metatheatre

Plays concerning historical events have a contradictory nature: their narratives are based on facts, but they are meant to engender a patently fictional construct, viz. a performance. As Freddie Rokem has remarked, 'in order to cope with this kind of hybridity, performances about history frequently also draw attention to different metatheatrical dimensions of the performance, frequently showing directly on the stage how performances about history are constructed' (Rokem 2000: 7). In line with this observation, Alexander Feldman has even coined a term, 'historiographic metatheatre',[25] for 'all of those works, and parts of works, in which self-reflexive engagements with the traditions and forms of dramatic art illuminate historical themes and aid in the representation of historical events' (Feldman 2013: 2–3). For Rokem, such an awareness fosters the audience's perception 'that, even if what is presented on the stage is a theatrical performance, it actually presents or refers to events that have really taken place' (Rokem 2000: 7), while Feldman chooses the word 'historiographic', rather than 'historical', in order to stress that the playwrights' interest is directed to 'not only the events of the past but also the way in which they are constituted in the discourse of history' (Feldman 2013: 3). Thus, they highlight the two sides of a genre that acknowledges its contradictions in order to harness their revelatory potential. 'The theatre is the ideal medium in which to consider the versions of history, in all their instability, because the provisionality of the stage and the ephemeral nature of its representations complement postmodernism's sense of the plurality of historical truths' (ibid.: 25).

The historical plays Howard Brenton has written for Shakespeare's Globe do not seem to adopt this model, because they neither contain a play-within-the-play nor explicitly focus on the production of chronicles. This impression may be supported by the comparison with other works of his: *The Churchill Play* (1974 and 1978), for instance, embodies historiographic metatheatre so precisely that Feldman chooses it as an example (Feldman 2013: 109–51), and *H.I.D.* (1989) employs a variety of techniques to foreground its theatricality and to show the way a historical narrative can be forged. Nevertheless, while *Doctor Scroggy's War* touches this theme only in passing,[26] both *In Extremis* and *Anne Boleyn* deal with how history is handed down to (or withheld from, or fabricated for) future generations and display some notable metatheatrical features; what is more, these aspects of the texts are thrown into relief by the playhouse itself, with its Elizabethan architecture and its ever-so-visible audience; so it may be interesting to see them in this light and consider them two instances of 'implicit' historiographic metatheatre.[27]

The mythologization of Bernard's life is explicitly discussed in more than one scene of *In Extremis*. The subject is first addressed by what is usually considered a comic duo, Alberic and Lotholf, at the beginning of Act 3 (*IE* 70–1), just before Bernard renews the gesture of licking one of the pilgrim's feet (*IE* 71) and shortly after the bizarre apparitions of some mad monks (*IE* 69–70), that is between two oddly funny sketches. This placement is meaningful:

the opening of the play's last section announces one of its main themes and its philosophical weight is lightened by the association with two humorous moments. 'You have no idea that you live in a mythic time, do you?' (*IE* 71) is Alberic's conclusion, after explaining to his friend that Bernard cannot cure his aching back instead of performing the foot-licking action once again, because the latter is part of the abbot's 'official life story' (*IE* 70). This unnaturally self-conscious reflection, comically set forth by an apparently minor character as if it were obvious, is possibly one of the reasons why Brenton compared Alberic and Lotholf to Rosencrantz and Guildenstern (Neill 2006: 9). The dialogue reveals that Bernard's biography is partly a forged one, but without any explicit condemnation of such practices: 'the curing of [Lotholf's] feet could be one of the miracles that confirms Bernard in his sainthood' even though actually 'he didn't cure them', 'he just licked them' (*IE* 70–1), but after all the abbot 'has been [Alberic's] saviour', 'the mother of [his] soul' (*IE* 72), so there is nothing wrong with substituting a material, 'verifiable' miracle, for a less tangible proof of his saintliness.

A much harsher criticism of Bernard's fabricating his own biography is in Heloise's reply to his repeated assertion that he was reconciled with Abelard before the latter died (which the audience knows to be a lie, because their meeting in 3.4 ended up in reciprocal accusations):

> You were not. But you will make it part of your life story. As you hope coming to console me, will be part of your life story. You are all story, Abbot. You are not really living at all. (*IE* 89)[28]

This conclusion bears an interesting echo of what Helene, the mother superior of the convent, had told Heloise about her love affair with Abelard:

> Do you think that was *in* life? ... You and Peter weren't in real life, or real time at all. Even as your affair happened, it was a memory. Think.... Even the memory of love isn't real. It becomes just a beautiful story. Not life. (*IE* 67)

All ideals, whether religious or secular, are questioned and revealed as somehow fictional, regardless of their having been confirmed or denied on stage, and 'perfect' moments are just wonderful narratives, even for the people who have lived them.

Therefore, Heloise's well-supported assertion, in the last scene, that Bernard has lost, does not mean that truth has triumphed. In the future, Abelard's autobiography and the two lovers' letters will circulate far more widely than Bernard's writings, as the woman proves by holding out a twenty-first-century paperback (*IE* 90), and so their story will prevail over his, but this popularity does not necessarily imply veracity. On the contrary, Heloise herself, commenting on the title *History of My Sorrows*, remarks that 'Peter was always a little self-dramatising' (*IE* 90).

John Bull has foregrounded this final ostension of the book and thus linked *In Extremis* with *Anne Boleyn* and with Howard Brenton's version of *The Life of Galileo* to stress a common emphasis on the importance of the written word and more specifically of the printed word (Bull 2013).[29] The contrast between hand-written and printed volumes may be not quite so relevant in Brenton's plays, in which the transition from the one to the other only seems to constitute a technical improvement,[30] but the importance they attach to books is unquestionable. As Bull points out (Bull 2013: 179), the last scene of *Leben des Galilei*, which the British playwright passionately defended from the threat of being cut (see e.g. Reinelt 1992: 42),[31] is centred on a smuggled book, which becomes the symbol of culture being spread in spite of any hindrance, and thus embodies a hopeful message that underlies all three plays.

The same irresistibility characterizes Tyndale's works in *Anne Boleyn*, a text that was certainly intended to celebrate books, since it was commissioned in view of the fourth centenary of the King James Bible and as part of a season entitled 'The Word is God'. In the opening scene, the unauthorized translation of the Scriptures is, together with her severed head, in the bag Anne carries after her death,[32] and it is actually the object of the play's first line, 'do you want to see it?' (*AB* 11), even though its listeners are very likely to misinterpret the reference and think she is talking about her head. By showing this little volume to the audience, the protagonist herself presents it, with hindsight, as the most important thing in her life, and consequently in the dramatization they are going to see. In the following scene, which introduces the second strand of the plot, the two books trigger both James's interest for Anne and his need to 'settle religion in England' (*AB* 16), thus establishing the connection between the two storylines of the play and setting the later one in motion.

Besides, this crucial moment foregrounds the possibility to bootleg books, by showing it on stage as well as by having a character reflect on it: James finds the volumes, carefully hidden, under the lining of a chest that had been previously searched (*AB* 15–17), and comments that they are printed so small 'to be smuggled into the country' (*AB* 16). Hidden books are also discussed by Anne and Tyndale during their first meeting, the object of which is precisely the woman's request to read *The Obedience of a Christian Man* (*AB* 48–9). The scholar's comment that 'a book won't break the Pope's power in England. That will take a King' (*AB* 50) proves to be only partly right when his work, by means of Anne, reaches the king and prompts his action in that sense (*AB* 63–5), but before this happens that same forbidden book causes a lot of curiosity, scandal, conflict and danger in the court (*AB* 51–9, 63–4). It is interesting to note that in the second act, dramatizing Anne's decline and downfall, the two volumes are no longer seen on stage, and Tyndale's works are only referred to by James, who orders the new translation of the Bible to be based on his (*AB* 100).

*In Extremis* also features some prohibited books, Abelard's, and in that case too bans and threats cannot destroy them: Bernard does all he can to fight their circulation, but to no avail (*IE* 71–2); at the Council of Sens he demands 'that [Abelard's] books be burnt, and that [he] be shut up in a monastery for the rest of [his] life, condemned to silence' (*IE* 81), meaning by 'silence' the impossibility to write or teach, and his request is sanctioned (*IE* 79–82), but in the end Abelard's works will be read throughout the world (*IE* 89–90).

The resilience of culture is central to *In Extremis*, after all. One of the main theories Abelard and Heloise uphold is the validity of ancient philosophy in a world that has been transformed by the Revelation and by the spread of Christianity (*IE* 12–15, 28–9). The books that individually[33] appear on stage are not copies of classical tracts, though: in 3.2, Heloise and Helene are reading Thomas of Britain's *Tristan*, a contemporary poem, which Abelard calls 'a trashy love story' (*IE* 74, 76), while at the beginning of 3.6 Heloise is studying an Arabic grammar (*IE* 88–9). Brenton's irony has both volumes called 'devotions' (the first one, humorously, by Abelard; the second, mistakenly, by Bernard), thus highlighting the contrast between what is expected to be the only kind of book a nun should peruse and the variety of readings that are worthy of consideration, from the products of distant cultures to what may be scoffed as lowbrow (but could become a classic in the future).

Two more books frame the love story of Abelard and Heloise. One consists of their letters, which will eternalize their passion, as the play's ending shows; the other is St Jerome's *Against Jovinian*, which on their first meeting the lovers literally devour (*IE* 11), prompted by Fulbert's assertion that his niece can 'eat a book by St Jerome for breakfast' (*IE* 9). This gesture may look like a rejection of the text, since it results in the destruction of the manuscript and in the couple's intentional abandonment to the sensual pleasures St Jerome denounces. It also marks a transition from the realm of words to the sphere of action, not only because it is the literal realization of a figure of speech, but also because by means of the book Abelard and Heloise gradually slip from the description of a passion to its embodiment, and from this point of view, reading the treatise and making love are not opposed but almost consequential acts. Even more so, if eating the manuscript is also interpreted as the visual rendering of another metaphor: their love being nourished by their shared intellectual passion.

The iconic image of Abelard and Heloise biting the book has the effect of foregrounding the volume's materiality, an aspect that should be kept in mind also with reference to *Anne Boleyn*, since in the case of Brenton's second Globe play, the historiographical relevance of books does not lie, as in the final scene of *In Extremis*, in their content, but in their existence as objects. In fact, it is not by reading Tyndale's works that James discovers a hitherto unknown facet of Anne's life, but by finding out the queen owned them (*AB* 15–16); the hidden volumes signify her Protestant piety just like rosary beads might have manifested Catherine of Aragon's Catholic devotion. This scene exposes official and popular history as biased, censored and undependable by contrasting Anne's religious zeal, which the whole play will confirm, with the received opinion that she was a sensual witch (or, in a rationalist reading, a scheming seductress), colourfully expressed by James's morbid interest (*AB* 14–15), but what reveals the hidden truth is an archaeological find, not a reliable narrative.

*In Extremis* represents an unwritten aspect of historiography too: the oral tradition, depicted in its earliest stage as information spread by word of mouth, i.e. basically gossip. This kind of communication is portrayed directly in the young nuns' chatter regarding the lovers' encounter in the chapel (*IE* 61–2) and Abelard's castration (*IE* 64–5) and its effectiveness repeatedly witnessed: Denise has heard the details of her brother's love affair in a convent out of town (*IE* 17–18); Mother Helene already knows of their secret marriage two days after it took place (*IE* 58); their passion is so renowned that 'Heloise' is a favourite among prostitutes' pseudonyms (*IE* 70). The prurience that animates these discourses and the correctness of the news they carry (with only one exception, Heloise's age being minimized in the early accounts of the love affair, *IE* 18) raise opposite questions concerning the reliability of oral tradition.

Just as the meta-historiographical elements of Brenton's Globe plays are of the implicit kind, so their metatheatrical dimension is based on self-conscious alienating techniques rather than on the representation of performances, but there are some exceptions. A minor one is Cromwell's feigned hunger (*AB* 87–8), while more relevant is the use of costumes. In *Anne Boleyn*, the heroine's coronation dress is used to emblematize the role she fears to lose after the birth of Elizabeth (*AB* 83–84) and, even more significantly, to mark James's identification with her (*AB* 70–1, immediately before he begins to 'settle religion in England', as he said after finding her books, *AB* 16). As for *In Extremis*, Heloise is disguised as a nun twice before she actually 'takes the habit' (*IE* 46, 58–9). The second time, Mother Helene remarks her inappropriate dress and makes a comment that seems to anticipate the heroine's well-known destiny: 'many kinds of women have worn a habit, for many reasons. But perhaps you assume the clothes of what you are not, *too readily*' (*IE* 59, my emphasis). So in both plays clothes become costumes, although in different ways, and thus acquire a specific meaning, but in neither this metatheatrical device seems to be directly connected with the historiographical theme.

Artistic and historiographical self-consciousness merge in another element of these plays, the importance of which requires a separate treatment, and will therefore be the object of the next chapter: the role Howard Brenton assigns to the audience.

# 5

# Playing to the Crowd

## Aiming at an audience

Looking back on Brenton's long and productive career, the different venues where his works have been performed suggest a rather distinct periodization: up to 1969, they were rather constantly non-conventional and small;[1] between 1969 and 1972 non-theatrical environments still predominated, but usually larger ones;[2] by way of a two-year residency at the Royal Court Theatre (1972–73), well-known for its daring new-writing policy, Brenton increasingly collaborated with institutional, publicly funded theatres, where approximately three quarters of his plays between 1980 and 1992 premièred,[3] in spite of the *Romans in Britain* scandal;[4] his three works presented at Shakespeare's Globe in the last decade and possibly his recent frequentation of Hampstead Theatre (*55 Days*, 2012; *The Arrest of Ai Weiwei*, 2013; *Drawing the Line*, 2013; *Lawrence after Arabia*, 2016) manifest still another change in the kind of situation and audience he chooses. All of these distinctions have exceptions and grey areas, of course, especially because the playwright does not abandon his previous connections when he begins writing for new ones, but they seem to trace an overall course, constantly aimed at unfamiliar environments.

The coherence of these incessant movements is only apparently paradoxical. Brenton actually explained its rationale since the very first steps in this ongoing journey: 'I don't like knowing the score ... when you get to know the audience almost by name in the theatre, it's very bad. So I feel very restless' (Hammond 1973: 32). Although expressed in personal terms, this view is part of a wider reflection on the risks of establishing a 'tradition': 'a theatre becomes successful, with new work and a new artistic policy; but a few years on what made the success becomes a routine, then a habit, then rank decadence' (Brenton 1986b: xiii). In his own case, writing for companies that toured in non-conventional spaces gradually became less fruitful because, on the one hand, 'the fringe circuit audiences became spuriously sophisticated' (Itzin and Trussler 1981: 92), and on the other 'we began to know the circuit too well. Those two things made it not dangerous any more. And somehow it had to be risky, it had to be dangerous, it had to be a gut operation or else it was no good' (Hammond 1973: 27). As a matter of fact, what had driven him towards places where people were not used to attending performances was the thought that

> if you could take what was meant to be good from straight good writing and then put it into a context of an audience that ... hadn't heard of any of this, hadn't even seen plays quite a lot of the time, then you get a new kind of relationship, which in a way is straight to the content of the piece. (ibid.: 25–6)

So the playwright's 'restlessness' guided him towards institutions, like the National Theatre and the Royal Shakespeare Company, that usually catered for spectators acquainted with the classics of drama, but not with the kind of fringe theatre Brenton was coming from. Commenting on this change, he declared that he wished 'to get into bigger theatres, because they are, in a sense, more public' (Itzin and Trussler 1981: 91), where 'public' is 'a better word for political' (ibid.), as he had just explained with reference to how his plays should be defined. He thus left the 'intimate' atmosphere of a touring circuit that had grown accustomed to fringe productions and confronted the 'bourgeois institution' (ibid.) of purpose-built performing spaces to address new spectators, unknown and unknowing.

Approaching progressively wider and more heterogeneous audiences enabled him to maintain the dialectic quality of his plays, as he explained:

> the conflict isn't played out on the stage; there's no dialectic on the stage. Everything on the stage is rigged, because you've put it there or your fellow-artists did. The true dialectic happens between the audience you address and the play itself. (Hammond 1973: 26)

In line with this view, Brenton always keeps his interlocutor in mind, writing

> deliberately for the stage here, deliberately to the audience that comes to this theatre. And it's still the feeling that you write not only the words, but for the place where the words are said. And the actors who say the words and the minds to whom they are said. They are all the things that you write with. (Hammond 1973: 25)

This attitude, which the playwright first described rather early in his career, has characterized also his latest scene change. He meaningfully entitled an enthusiastic article commenting his first writing experience at Shakespeare's Globe *Playing to the Crowd*, thus immediately foregrounding the vast and heterogeneous audience of the reconstructed playhouse. In a passage at the core of the piece, he explains the reason for this choice:

> At the Globe, the audience is much more powerful than in a conventional theatre. You can see each other. People walk about and come and go, without affecting the performance. They are also much more vocal: laughs are quicker, responses seem sharper. Eye contact between performers and spectators builds a sense of shared undertaking … Everyone is held in a democratic space. (Brenton 2007)

Brenton has always been awake to the relevance of performing spaces (Hay and Roberts 1979: 146; Itzin and Trussler 1981: 91; Megson 2012: 217), and in this description he remarks some peculiarities of the relationship between the apron stage and the fully lit auditorium that outline the perfect conditions for a dialogue. Maybe this is why, in praising the Globe, he has chosen to compare it to a grand piano (Neill 2006: 9), recalling the image he used when a play of his was first produced on a performing stage:

> It's like getting hold of a Bechstein, hitting a really superb instrument, when all the time you have been shouting about a penny whistle, or a mouth-organ. You realize how powerful the instrument is, and varied, and how much fun. (Itzin and Trussler 1981: 91)

# Attracting the audience

'There's only one reason to go to the Globe, indeed to the theatre: pleasure' (Brenton 2007), and 'if there aren't other people to entertain or to deliver a play to then it doesn't exist' (Woddis 2010). In keeping with these principles, Howard Brenton has skilfully crafted his Globe plays so as to attract and maintain the attention of the audience; this care is obviously necessary for any production, but much more so amid the distractions of an open-air, equally lit theatre and with the opportunity for the spectators to leave, either momentarily or for good, at any time.

The most perspicuous feature of *In Extremis*, *Anne Boleyn* and *Doctor Scroggy's War* that makes them highly enjoyable and prevents the audience from ever getting bored, as nearly all press reviews have remarked, is the abundant presence of comic elements, usually interwoven in the serious scenes rather than alternated with grave passages, so as to exploit the fact that at the Globe 'knockabout laughs are easily won' (Brenton 2014a) without quite acquiescing to this inclination, rather 'pushing the comic and the tragic close together' (ibid.) to create a powerful balance. As a result, not only all dialogues are interspersed with witty replies, but even the potentially solemn religious debates show a lighter side, in spite of the weighty contents they convey. Abelard's condemnation in Sens, for instance, is advocated by Bernard with sober and passionate eloquence, but sanctioned by raucously drunken bishops (*IE* 79–81). Even more impressively, the arguments of the Puritan and Anglican representatives summoned by King James are explicitly purged of their slow parts when a spoken stage direction announces 'five hours later' and the participants immediately take an appropriately exhausted pose (*AB* 75–6), while the rest of their debates is constantly enlivened by the king's sense of humour and by the sudden changes of tone with which he keeps the divines under pressure (*AB* 73–80, 97–100). The utterly secular but unquestionably momentous dialogue between the British Commander-in-Chief and his French homologue on the eve of the Battle of Loos is also vivified by its comic side, based in this case on the linguistic obstacles the officers have to face (*DSW* 35–8). Although Brenton has wrought jokes in his works since the beginning of his career (see Itzin and Trussler 1981: 87–8; Dickson

2010), the funny aspects of these plays are not to be dismissed as a constant feature of his style because they clearly distinguish his plays for the Globe from the chronologically near and thematically similar *Paul* and *55 Days*, for instance, which display a much more sober atmosphere.

Another appealing trait of *In Extremis*, *Anne Boleyn* and *Doctor Scroggy's War* is, on the contrary, possibly exclusive to these three titles in Brenton's oeuvre: the presence of a romantic love interest at the heart of the plot. His previous plays featured several kinds of passion and desire, of course, but they were quite far from the archetypal couple embodied, as the playwright himself has extensively explained (Brenton 2006), by Abelard and Heloise. When asked about this novelty in his works for the Globe, Brenton suggests that it may be part of a desire 'to write of first and last things – love, death' (Brenton 2014a) – that comes with age. Although it is true that his latest output, while consistently engaged in social and political terms, is on average more concerned with great, universal themes than with the details of contemporary news, it must be remarked that none of his recent plays for other theatres (*Paul*, *Never So Good*, *55 Days*, *#aiww The Arrest of Ai Weiwei* [2013], *Drawing the Line* [2013], *Ransomed* [2015], *Lawrence after Arabia* [2016]) focus on a love story.

It may be argued that while Abelard and Heloise are among the best-known romantic couples, Anne's feelings for Henry are not as widely recognized; as a matter of fact, the rosiest interpretation of her behaviour may be Maxwell Anderson's, that shows her falling in love with the king only after their marriage (Anderson 1950). Yet this context makes Brenton's exception even more significant: his heroine never interacts with any other man except to discuss matters of politics or religion, in her dialogues with Henry she seems to be earnestly passionate about their life together (*AB* 35–9, 67–9, 105–6), and it is her who suggests, as soon as their marriage becomes possible, that they make love (*AB* 68–9), so that when she protests she loves him (*AB* 96), the audience is very likely to believe her. Furthermore, her final message to the 'demons of the future' is centred on love: 'be careful of love. No, don't be careful. Why not live for love? Why not live for a better world?' (*AB* 115). Even though they are ambiguous from the moral point of view, then, these characters captivate the audience's sympathetic participation because of their ill-fated romantic affections.

In spite of its war theme and military setting, *Doctor Scroggy's War* also features a love story, not quite at the heart of the play, but running through its whole narrative arc, intertwined with the development of its main themes. The upper-class, uninhibited and somewhat frivolous Penelope Wedgewood makes love to the 'temporary gentleman' Jack Twigg just before he leaves for France (*DSW* 29–32); later on, in her capacity as a voluntary nurse, she is part of the team who finds Jack wounded and sends him to Gillies's new hospital for the treatment of face injuries, but she does not realize it is him (*DSW* 60–1); when she sees him again, she is shocked (*DSW* 91), but, even though he cannot really believe she is in love with him (*DSW* 92), Penelope concludes that she 'is not going to give [him] up' (*DSW* 93); nevertheless, they eventually separate because she joins Sylvia Pankhurst's anti-war movement, while he intends to go back to the front (*DSW* 99–101). This short selective synopsis shows that Penelope and Jack's vicissitudes, although written in a far from sentimental tone, are those of a romantic love story. At the same time, these incidents are all deeply connected with the war, of which they help explore the consequences on gender and social relations.

An audience-attracting technique shared by most of the new plays written for Shakespeare's Globe that Brenton adopts on the contrary very sparsely is the foregrounding of music. In his works for the Elizabethan theatre there are five instances of vocal performances, one of which is doubtful: Anne sings a prayer with Tyndale and his followers (*AB* 50); Henry and Anne quote the lyrics of a song that expresses the wish to live happily secluded from all society (*AB* 37), but the script does not say or imply that they intone these lines;[5] the soldiers of Ralph's platoon march to the tune of *Goodbye Dolly Grey* (*DSW* 39, 41); some patients in Doctor Gillies's hospital sing while playing (*DSW* 63–4) and enact a vaudeville routine in drag (*DSW* 97–8). Besides the wounded men's exhibition, there are five more dance scenes: at the courts of Louis VI (*IE* 30) and of the lovesick Henry VIII (*AB* 29); more privately, between King James dressed in Anne's coronation dress and his favourite George Villiers (*AB* 70); at Field Marshal French's Ritz reception (*DSW* 23–4, 28); again at the Ritz, when Penelope only does a couple of turns alone (*DSW* 83). In all these instances, the music is undeniably diegetical, and the characters involved dance and sing in their fictional reality, not by virtue of a theatrical convention.

Nearly all these dances actually take place only briefly, as part of a scene change or in between other events, occasionally going on in the background of a dialogue. James's cross-dressed performance receives, on the contrary, special care from the playwright and presumably more attention from the audience;[6] the stage direction which opens the second act of *Anne Boleyn* says:

> Musicians playing. Enter JAMES wearing ANNE's coronation dress, hand in hand with GEORGE, who is not in drag. They dance as man and woman, beautifully, arms extended, whirling figures. The music stops, they embrace and kiss passionately. (*AB* 70)[7]

Besides drawing the spectators' attention back to the play after the interval, this action is charged with the task of helping the audience realize both the kind of relationship James is developing with George and, more importantly, the fact that he somehow identifies himself with Anne Boleyn, expressed by his wearing her coronation dress, since neither of these evolutions of the situation has been previously manifested.

All these choices are not exceptional in Howard Brenton's works, which feature hardly any songs but make use now and then of diegetical dances, either to establish a setting (most notably marking the passing of time in *Never So Good*)[8] or to express pithily a complex situation or concept (e.g. Charity's rendition of the transformation of Hess's old age and death into something unacceptably beautiful in *H.I.D.*, Brenton 1989: 15, 17–22). These are not coincidences: the playwright explains that he has 'always been wary of songs in plays' (Brenton 2014a) because 'they often don't drive the narrative forward, they can have the effect of stopping for a generalised gush of emotion that is meaningless' (ibid.), whereas 'dancing in plays … can have a mimelike power of story telling' (ibid.). These considerations hold for any theatre, but they have a particular urgency in an Elizabethan-style playhouse, because

> 'attention' at The Globe is crucial. 1,600 people are viewing the stage from a myriad of different angles, sightlines and 'hearing spots', some good some not. To keep them together, to get that 'collective imagination' going that can be so powerful in The Globe a play has to be clear, fast driven, there can be subplots and routines but everything must drive *one story* forward. The scope

can be vast – think of Shakespeare's *Antony and Cleopatra* – but every scene in that play is in the end about one thing – the affair. (Brenton 2014a)

Brenton is consequently careful in handling all alluring and potentially distracting devices in his Globe plays, from comic turns to musical performances. The same vigilance he maintains as regards direct audience address, which can engage the spectators by appealing directly to them.

> The rule is strict though: soliloquies and asides must come out of the immediate moment and press the action forward, if they are generalized they will dissipate the audience's attention. (Brenton 2014a)

Always abiding by this law, Brenton actually makes the most of the possible immediate connection between stage and auditorium, especially in *Anne Boleyn*, which was conceived for the Globe from the beginning and benefited from Brenton's previous experience there. Direct address will therefore be examined next, as a further step in the communication established by the play, acknowledging the audience's presence and role by breaking the fourth wall.

# Addressing the audience

There are basically two ways a play can point to the presence of its audience: by having characters (or performers, if out of their role) speak to actual spectators, or by staging onlookers that mirror their situation.

As for addressing the theatre's patrons directly, *In Extremis* does so only once, and in a silent way, but at a moment of paramount importance, with its very last image. Heloise 'holds the Penguin book out to Bernard, who stares at it, then out to the audience. Blackout. End of play' (*IE* 90). This way, the heroine almost hands down her heritage to the spectators, and implicitly asks for their informed judgement on the whole story. Moreover, this action was created specifically for the Globe: as both the production's prompt book and the author's testimony (Wu 2000: 33) show, the words 'then out to the audience' were not in the original stage direction, which goes to prove that the equally lit playhouse allows the audience to have a more prominent role, and that Brenton's fine ear for this instrument enabled him to seize this opportunity and integrate it in the text.

Anne Boleyn and Doctor Scroggy's War contain, on the contrary, several lines directed to the spectators. I have already mentioned the presence of 'spoken stage directions', passages in which a character sets the scene, not by means of descriptions or commentary on time and place, as many Shakespearean characters do, but by succinctly stating the kind of details that could make up the stage direction at the beginning of the scene, such as 'In Calais. Two years later' (AB 67), or 'France. saint-Omer. The Headquarters of Sir John French, Commander-in-Chief of the British Expeditionary Force. On the 24th of September, 1915' (DSW 35). The one quoted here is actually the only spoken stage direction proper in Doctor Scroggy's War. Penelope has a similar speech when she presents Fergal and provides the audience with some basic information concerning his past and the present situation (DSW 48–9), like stage directions sometimes do in order to prepare the entrance of a new character. The following passage, in which three nurses demonstrate the way Fergal is wounded (DSW 49–50), can be read in turn as embodying the description of a piece of stage business. Finally, in the last scene of Act 1, a soldier recites what might be a programme note on the casualties of the Battle of Loos (DSW 60). Howard Brenton's latest play for Shakespeare's Globe Theatre thus seems to feature an example of each possible sort of stage direction being delivered out loud (since voicing the indication of how a line should be spoken would be rather odd). It also contains a wide array of traditional asides and soliloquies, in the mouth not only of the principal characters (Jack, Gillies, Penelope, Ralph) but also of secondary (Fergal, French, Mr Twigg) and even frankly minor figures (Haig, Clancy). On two occasions Jack interacts with the audience even more explicitly, first by addressing them in the second person and putting into words their expectations ('You all know what is going to happen to me', DSW 60) and then by asking them to repeat the answer he has given in a previous scene ('What is it? Tell me, tell me! (Until he gets the response.) Yes! Yes! Flies on the dead!', DSW; cfr DSW 59).

In conclusion, Doctor Scroggy's War displays a remarkable variety of audience address modes, resulting in a fairly continuous but multifaceted communication between stage and auditorium. Conversely, in *Anne Boleyn* Howard Brenton establishes a rather determined, though hardly simple, relationship between the eponymous heroine and the spectators, which is instrumental to the definition of the character's complex status. The young woman appears as a figure out of time directly addressing the audience at the beginning and at the end of the script (*AB* 11–12, 115), as a person realistically living her life for most of the play, and as a spirit conjured up by James I in the scene when they finally meet and speak to each other (*AB* 113–15). The difference is essentially marked by whom she interacts with: the theatregoers, the other people in her own plot-line, or the protagonist of a parallel story, set in the following century, who has expressed the wish to establish such a dialogue (*AB* 16, 20–1, 82, 102). Howard Brenton stresses these shifts and grants further complexity to their pattern by briefly breaking their boundaries. At the end of the first act, Anne announces the interval as if it were some time she and Henry claim for themselves (*AB* 69), thus blurring the distinction between her 'direct address' and 'realistic' personas. Then, in the second act, Anne and James's encounter is anticipated by a moment in which she enters before he and some of his entourage leave the scene, and he reacts as if suddenly seeing a ghost (*AB* 101), while during the last part of her plot-line (2.8–10, *AB* 108–13) he remains lying on the stage, drunk and unconscious. These small breaches in the text's own conventions question them and draw the audience's attention to their significance; they are short or marginal enough not to prevent the spectators from empathizing with the characters' psychology, but shocking enough to remind them of the fictional nature of the theatre. Such an articulate situation provides some food for thought on the connection between stage and auditorium, but it also requires an almost exclusive rapport between Anne and the audience. It is consequently she who voices nearly all the spoken stage directions in the play.[9] She also introduces the second strand of the plot ('James the Sixth of Scotland, sixty-seven years after my – *(Gestures.)* come to rule you all. James the Sixth of Scotland. Now James the First of England', *AB* 12) and even announces the interval (*AB* 69). *Anne Boleyn* and *Doctor Scroggy's War* are not the only plays in which Howard Brenton has a character speak to the audience; *Never So Good*, for instance, has several passages of this kind and even three spoken stage directions (Brenton 2008: 56,

66, 91). But the two texts conceived for Shakespeare's Globe are unique in that they explicitly and specifically address the spectators in the second person (e.g. 'come to rule *you* all', *AB* 12, or '*You* all know what is going to happen to me', *DSW* 54, my emphases). What is more, in the case mentioned earlier of the break between the first and the second acts, Anne's words establish a correspondence between the characters' and the audience's time and even a causal connection between their actions, because they suggest that the performance will be interrupted and the spectators will take a pause in consequence of the royal couple's desire for some privacy.

The direct relationship between the protagonist and the audience is established even more powerfully by means of the monologues that open and close *Anne Boleyn*. In the first lines of the play, she interrogates and teases the audience, as if doubting whether to kick-start the performance or not (*AB* 11), and in the last ones she acknowledges the end of their communication and blesses the 'demons of the future' ('oh, I can't see you any more. And now you can't see me. Goodbye, demons. God bless you all', *AB* 115), thus framing the whole stage action as a long conversation between her and the spectators. Anne's final gesture, just like Heloise's, was changed in a way that emphasizes her interaction with the audience: while the original stage direction in the prompt book said 'she smiles and turns away',[10] the play-text ends with 'she blows the audience a kiss' (*AB* 115).[11] This intervention is not as relevant but quite consistent with the modified closing image of *In Extremis*, in that both foreground the relationship between stage and auditorium, and both testify to how fruitfully Howard Brenton worked in close collaboration with the director and the actors.

The kind of set-up outlined here tends to inscribe the spectators' reactions in the text, assuming, for instance, that they will give a positive answer (though possibly a silent one) to Anne's question if they want to see 'it' (*AB* 11), thus prompting her to add 'I'll show you then'.[12] Although, as Brenton pointed out, the viewers' contribution is the only thing in a performance that is not fixed by its creative team (Hammond 1973: 26), texts and productions actually tend to predict it, at least in order to provide for it. Usually, the more an audience is implicated in stage action, its input foreseen by the script, the less its involvement is free, as Susan Bennett has effectively shown in the case of Piscator's theatre (Bennett 1997: 24–6). In his Globe plays, Howard Brenton operates so as to highlight the spectators' role while assuming only something which can almost be taken for granted: their curiosity. If they were not interested, they would probably be somewhere else, or they would not be paying attention, so the performance can rather safely presume they will be eager to hear and to see, and that is what the beginning of *Anne Boleyn* is based on.

The same observation concerning the audience's nature is the premise of another way the play speaks of, and therefore to, the spectators: by mirroring their somewhat nosey attitude. From this point of view, James I embodies their curiosity, partly morbid, partly serious, for Anne Boleyn's life (*AB* 14–16, 20–1, 98–102, 113–15), and the heroine is right, in the last scene, to consider him a representative of the 'demons of the future', who 'are so strange to [her], as [she] must be strange to [them]' (*AB* 115). But the Stuart king is not the only audience figure in the text. On the contrary, lots of characters are more or less explicitly described as 'hovering', 'lurking' or 'sneaking back' on the stage in order to eavesdrop supposedly private conversations, just like the people in the auditorium (*AB* 12, 18, 24, 26, 29, 33, 39, 57, 60, 63, 67, 79, 108). This recurring image is certainly connected to the atmosphere of treachery that pervades the court, but its frequency is significantly higher here than in other Brenton plays with a similar theme: there are only two eavesdroppers in *55 Days*, for instance,[13] and hardly any in *Never So Good*, in spite of a character explicitly asking, 'why do you all spy on each other?' (Brenton 2008: 64).[14] It seems thus fair to suppose the specific pattern of one or more figures lurking upstage to be connected with the visible presence of its counterpart in the Globe's yard and galleries.

*In Extremis* features another portrayal of the audience: the three young nuns that snoop on the lovers. In 2.3, Abelard and Heloise take refuge in the convent of St Marie Argenteuil, where after a while they secretly meet in the chapel; one of the nuns, Berthode, tells her two friends she has observed the couple's encounter (just like the spectators have), and the others, Marie and Francine, try to display the actions she describes, so that they produce a rudimentary dramatic performance; then the three of them go to the chapel and watch the sleeping lovers, thus becoming onlookers of the same spectacle the audience is seeing (*IE* 61–2).

The role of the eavesdropper has been insightfully analysed by Freddie Rokem (2000: 202–7), who calls 'screen scenes' those in which 'one of the fictional characters is secretly spying on one or several of the other characters' (ibid.: 203). Just like the onlookers described here, those scrutinized by Rokem take a position outside the direct action and thus 'serve as a model for spectatorship in the theatre' (ibid.: 204). But in traditional drama, according to Rokem, most of these screen scenes end when the eavesdropper is 'suddenly and unwillingly drawn back into the action again' (ibid.) and this way victimized; in theatre about historical events, on the contrary, 'instead of an eavesdropper who is "punished" for secretly watching the action on the stage, ... the witness is already a victim who is giving some form of testimony within the framework of the performance of what he or she has seen' (ibid.: 205). Neither description fits the fictional spectators of Brenton's Globe plays, who are and remain on the edges of the story (with the partial exception of James, a protagonist in his own strand of the plot but a distant onlooker from Anne's point of view).

It can be argued that while the eavesdroppers analysed by Rokem are sacrificed as scapegoats to atone for the spectators' spying and to ensure their catharsis (2000), Brenton's onlookers are not punished because they are, at least in part, a role model for the audience to follow. Both *Anne Boleyn*'s James I and the nuns of *In Extremis* are initially spurred by a morbid curiosity, but then they learn to see something deeper in the object of their gaze. When James finds the books, he evidently starts to think of Anne not only as a sensual enchantress but also as a person who was instrumental to the establishment of the Church of England; studying her acts, he discovers a possible alternative explanation of her downfall (*AB* 114) and he even addresses some profound religious questions (*AB* 114). The case of the three nuns is less clear, but their action at the end of the scene, when they silently kneel in front of the altar where the lovers are sleeping (*IE* 62), seems to insinuate that prurient gossip and scandal have been replaced by the peaceful and perhaps thoughtful contemplation of an image of love.

# Admonishing the audience

Howard Brenton's inscription of the audience in his plays for Shakespeare's Globe is not only a fascinating formal feature that doubles and emphasizes the spectators' visibility; it is also a way to foster a reflection on a questionable trait of our society. James and the nuns show that a morbid nosiness may evolve into an earnest desire to know and thus lead to a deeper understanding – and questioning – of the world, but the fact that the spectators can easily recognize themselves in these characters' initial prurient curiosity for the sordid details of the protagonists' love affairs is certainly not flattering.

The importance of this theme is supported by the playwright's long-standing interest for the situationist reading of contemporary society (Itzin and Trussler 1981: 96–7; Wu 2000: 20–3; Megson 2012: 213–14).[15] Today, Brenton still thinks 'as strongly as [he] ever did that we are enslaved by a delusion' (Brenton 2014a). In Guy Debord's words, 'the whole life of those societies in which modern conditions of production prevail presents itself as an immense accumulation of *spectacles*. All that once was directly lived has become mere representation' (Debord 1994: 12),[16] where 'the spectacle is not a collection of images; rather, it is a social relationship between people that is mediated by images' (ibid.).[17] This general condition may well be represented by the way theatregoers are guided by received images of such characters as Anne Boleyn or Abelard and Heloise to look not for the essence and causes of their predicaments but for more depictions of the same kind.

If Debord states that the spectacle 'is the omnipresent celebration of a choice already made in the sphere of production, and the consummate result of that choice' (Debord 1994: 13),[18] though, Brenton's Globe plays seem to foreground the spectators (as theatregoers in the auditorium, but not only, since everyone is constantly an audience member in relation to the spectacle of society). They are shown to be themselves at least partly responsible for this condition and they have the power to transform it, on the model of James and the three nuns, by changing their own way of looking at things, by trying to go beyond the spectacle instead of eagerly seeking it.

The relevance of this interpretation emerges distinctly in the beginning of *Anne Boleyn* (*AB* 11). For ten lines the heroine teases the audience by alternately offering and refusing to show an undefined 'it', then – 'Ready? Look!' – she takes out of her capacious bag a little book, her Bible. 'Why? Don't you realise? This killed me! This book!' she adds, apparently replying to the spectators' disappointed expressions. After a short recollection of the moment of her death, Anne puts the volume back in its place and interrogates the audience once again: 'what you think I was going to show you? This?' This time, without any ceremony or delay, she produces her severed head, and immediately she dismisses it as a 'heavy little cabbage', 'smaller than you think'. The only thing she wishes to tell regarding her death is that she closed her eyes herself, after being beheaded, a detail that symbolizes her strong will and independent mind.

This scene benignly rebukes the audience's thirst for sensation and tries to direct attention towards the proper object of the piece (the way Anne worked to bring the Reformation to England) before satisfying their wish to see something dreadful. Then, even while he humours the spectators' curiosity, Brenton provides them with a reminder of his serious theme, the absurd image of a person with two heads – one on her shoulders, the other a macabre memento in her hands. Such a figure recalls the traditional depiction of martyrs carrying on a plate the body parts they were deprived of, so the heroine showing her severed head establishes an implicit connection with her statement that she was killed because of the Bible.

Most reviewers have overlooked the way Brenton starts by playing on the audience's expectations, even though several remarked the fact that the protagonist carries her own head in a bag (see e.g. Gore-Langton 2010; Marlowe 2010a; Shore 2010). Two even gave evidence of horror's charm by relating the episode as if there were no 'double take' but the immediate display of the anticipated bloody object:

'Do you want to see it?' she asks us with a teasing smile, reaching in for the expected, severed head. (Bassett 2010)

The crowd of groundlings grin and nod when Anne Boleyn teasingly asks: 'Do you want to see it?' She's referring to her decapitated head – the head she lost to Henry VIII after losing her heart to him. (Szalwinska 2010)

The second example is especially interesting because it summarizes the sensational expectations the play's title may evoke: a woman's passion followed by her violent death, both caused by the same powerful man. Such an effective blurb suggests that the 'slip' may be intentional, a result of the choice to present *Anne Boleyn*'s most appealing side. On the other hand, at least one critic chose to emphasize the first scene's 'teasingly intelligent style' (Gardner 2011) that sets the tone for the whole play:

> Miranda Raison's Anne walks on the stage with her own decapitated head in a bag and plays shamelessly to the gallery and our predilection for the gory bits of history. (ibid.)

This variety of readings and interpretations can be considered representative of the wide, heterogeneous audience Howard Brenton wrote the play for, providing them with a complex stage narrative that intermingles entertainment and food for thought, offering them a chance to reflect on their own role but without fixing their position. After all, 'you don't write to convert. More – to stir things up. For people to make what they wish of it' (Itzin and Trussler 1981: 97).

# Conclusions

The new plays produced by the reconstructed Globe Theatre constitute an interesting corpus to analyse because they have been written or at least adapted for a very peculiar venue. This unique situation provides a valuable opportunity, in particular, to focus on the specific work of the playwright, i.e. on the creation of a literary text that is expressly intended for performance and therefore neither ignores nor prescribes its staging but envisages it as an array of possibilities. They also offer a chance to mark out the influence of the playhouse itself on dramaturgy, because the architectural and general ambience is the only ingredient they share, while authors, genres and creative teams vary. So the features that keep recurring in these scripts can be ascribed to Shakespeare's Globe itself and to how writers have responded to its characteristics. In this perspective the plays have been discussed here not individually, highlighting their singular traits and achievements, but as a group, heterogeneous in many respects but unified by the context in which it was produced. The detailed case study of Howard Brenton's texts for the Globe complements this analysis by providing an example of how the relation between playwright and theatre can work.

Built with materials, designs and even techniques that could have been used in the late sixteenth century, the playhouse is in itself unique, today, especially for the visibility it gives to the spectators surrounding the stage, who are in full light just like the performers; furthermore, it is bound to evoke a multiplicity of epochs, so that the traditional opposition between fictional time and real time of the performance is enriched by the constant presence of the building's Elizabethan appearance and possibly even by the splendour of antiquity its décor would have echoed four hundred years ago;

finally, these peculiarities attract an impressively varied audience, including tourists, school groups and Shakespeare enthusiasts.

Scripts intended to be performed in such unique conditions must address the difficulties they entail, while making the most of the opportunities they offer too. A close investigation of the twenty-seven new texts staged by Shakespeare's Globe under its first two artistic directors – Mark Rylance (1995–2005) and Dominic Dromgoole (2006–15) – leads to observe some recurring features that almost outline a very broad dramatic genre, obviously in the descriptive sense of the term. To dispel any possible misunderstanding concerning the existence of a recipe for the Globe well-made play, suffice it to say that not only the presence of all these features does not guarantee success, either in performance or in retrospective consideration, but some of the most popularly and critically acclaimed among these scripts do not follow all the trends traced here, a case in point being the very sparse presence of song and dance in Howard Brenton's *In Extremis* and *Anne Boleyn*.

On the one hand, most of the traits many of these plays share dovetail with the main problem the venue poses, i.e. the necessity to capture the attention of an audience that is extremely heterogeneous, physically uncomfortable and subject to all sorts of disturbances: engaging plots and themes, shocking moments, comic elements and musical performances are all valuable assets from this point of view. On the other hand, the spectators' constantly visible and audible presence can be put to good use, so as to involve them in the performance, both as interlocutors of the characters and as masses of unpaid extras in crowd scenes, or even in order to question the role and the responsibilities of the public they represent.

All these characteristics are directly linked to the theatre's structure and to the way it works. Even though the twenty-first-century Globe texts share most of them with Shakespeare's drama, the reason for these similarities appears to be the analogous operating conditions rather than a desire to emulate the illustrious predecessor. As a matter of fact, they all find convincing explanations in the context for which they are meant, whereas they sometimes depart clearly from the Elizabethan model (e.g. in the absence of fool figures among their comic elements). Even those aspects of these plays that tend to establish a continuity with the repertoire of the first Globe do not closely follow a Shakespearean pattern but rather refer back to it, by quoting lines and situations or by addressing the questions of history and identity the reconstructed theatre also symbolizes. Verse plays may look like a homage to the Bard's poetry, but once again his masterpieces have provided valuable examples of what *can* be done in this exceptional space, rather than a blueprint of what *must* be done; so much so that the verse forms chosen by the Globe's third-millennium playwrights are often not Elizabethan, and that the majority of these new authors have actually preferred to search for a suitably heightened and linguistically rich prose.

One quality all of these scripts appear in conclusion to share is a considerable 'openness', in the sense expounded by Marco DeMarinis (1982: 191–4; 1987: 103–4) that they allow for a very wide range of interpretation levels (from freewheeling entertainment to complex metatheatrically prompted self-examination), so as to cater to an audience whose background, knowledge, interests and ideas are conspicuously varied. They seem even more apt to be read on several planes in the form in which they have been studied here, i.e. as literary texts meant for performance, because the creative process of production is likely to privilege some of the possible reception levels over others; yet, the staging also implies the involvement of several codes that are necessarily absent from the written page, thus providing yet more planes on which performances can be appreciated.[1]

Howard Brenton's scripts for Shakespeare's Globe are a valuable opportunity for the case study of a success story, because they testify to the fruitfulness of this artistic combination of playwright and theatre. The text of *In Extremis* (2006) was chosen, ready-made, by Dominic Dromgoole for his first season as artistic director of the Globe and underwent only some minor adjustments on the writer's part, while *Anne Boleyn* (2010) and *Doctor Scroggy's War* (2014) were specially commissioned for the reconstructed Elizabethan playhouse; their different origin notwithstanding,[2] they share some relevant features that bespeak the connections between Brenton's stylistic and thematic hallmarks and the Globe's specificities, in spite of the distance that may apparently separate a forward-looking engaged playwright and the working replica of a sixteenth-century theatre.

All three plays belong to the historical genre but display a perspicuous relevance for the moment in which they were written. This interconnection of different chronological planes characterizes many of Brenton's works, because the playwright often chooses to address contemporary issues by depicting historical events or epochs that contributed to their development or by representing similar situations in faraway times, so as to foster a clear-minded reflection on the subject. This kind of perspective is matched by the Globe's Foucauldian heterochronia, in which the spectators' present, the age in which the performance is set, the Elizabethan architecture of the playhouse and its allusions to antiquity are all joined in one complex spectacle. Moreover, the visible juxtaposition of different time frames – actual, reconstructed and fictional – is congenial to the dramatist's concern for historiography and its mythologizing potential, which is exposed cursorily by *Doctor Scroggy's War*, in an extended yet implicit manner by *Anne Boleyn* and openly by *In Extremis*.

These observations highlight the consonance between Howard Brenton's poetics and the peculiarities of Shakespeare's Globe, but the productivity of their combination is based also on the playwright's ability to write specifically for this context and respond to its uniqueness. This aspect of his work is more evident in the case of the other distinguishing trait of the reconstructed Elizabethan playhouse, the visibility of a sunlit heterogeneous audience that surrounds the stage. These performance conditions are quite in tune with Brenton's sensibility for the spectators and for their active role in the theatre, but that is not all. On the one hand, they require a particularly careful handling of the playgoers' attention. On the other, they enable the dramatist not only to present his thought-provoking creations to a wide variety of people, and thus to establish a productive dialogue between the authors and the receivers of the performance, but also to foreground and question the attitude of the audience in a way that would be impossible, or at least not as successful, elsewhere. Thrown into relief by the structure of the playhouse, spectators are addressed directly in all three plays, but they are even more central to *In Extremis* and *Anne Boleyn*, in which they are also mirrored by on-stage eavesdroppers. In these two texts their possibly superficial and morbid curiosity is gently mocked so as to encourage them to follow the lead of their fictional counterparts and dig deeper into the objects of their gaze.

Howard Brenton's plays produced by Shakespeare's Globe thus prove that the reconstructed Elizabethan playhouse is also an important working theatre of the twenty-first century and a wonderful 'instrument', the peculiarities of which enable writers with a sensitive 'ear' and an open mind to create new drama that is relevant to the present in form as well as in content.

# NOTES

## Introduction

1   1995 is the year of the 'Workshop'; in 1996, the 'Prologue' consisted of only one production, *The Two Gentlemen of Verona* directed by Jack Shepherd; 1997 saw the official opening by Queen Elizabeth II and the first full season, billing four different titles.
2   This is how Shakespeare's Globe is defined in the collection of essays investigating its first ten years edited by Christie Carson and Farah Karim-Cooper, *Shakespeare's Globe. A Theatrical Experiment* (2008).
3   A promising exception is Catriona Fallow's 'The Plays of Peter Oswald: New Writing at Shakespeare's Globe 1998–2005' (2014).

## Chapter 1

1   For detailed accounts of the reconstruction process, see Mulryne and Shewring (1997). A storyline of Sam Wanamaker's project and its realization can be found on the theatre's website: http://www .shakespearesglobe.com/about-us/history-of-the-globe/rebuilding -the-globe (accessed 9 July 2013).
2   Examples of the Globe Theatre's ongoing improvements are extensively related in Mulryne and Shewring (1997), and frequently referred to in Carson and Karim-Cooper (2008). The theatre's website provides a very brief outline of the Architecture Research Group's current work: http://www.shakespearesglobe.com/education/ library-research/architectural-research-group (accessed 9 July 2013).
3   Because the Globe is still first of all an ongoing experiment, major adjustments are nevertheless not impossible, in spite of the obvious practical obstacles; they are actually hypothesized by Franklin J. Hildy (2008: 14), and even advocated by Mark Rylance (2008: 113).

4    The EOSIs are not published, but they are filed in the archives of
     Shakespeare's Globe, so as to be available to both the theatre's staff
     and external researchers.

5    The *Nara Document on Authenticity* was drafted by the participants
     at the Nara Conference on Authenticity in Relation to the World
     Heritage Convention (Nara, Japan, 1–6 November 1993) and edited
     by its general rapporteurs, Raymond Lemaire and Herb Stovel. The
     conference had been organized by the Agency for Cultural Affairs
     (Government of Japan) in cooperation with UNESCO, ICCROM
     and ICOMOS. The document has been annexed to all versions
     of the *Operational Guidelines for the Implementation of the
     World Heritage Convention* since 2005 (http://whc.unesco.org/en/
     guidelines/, accessed 3 June 2014).

6    Although it is possibly the most correct term for the kind of
     reconstruction exemplified by Shakespeare's Globe, the word 'model'
     is very seldom used to define it, a significant exception being the
     extremely precise phrase 'a working model of the Globe' employed
     by Mark Rylance (2008: 105). It will appear only sparsely in this
     text too, because of the ambiguity its several meanings can entail:
     since 'model' most commonly designates the original from which
     copies are made and, as an adjective, an ideal, exemplary member
     of a certain class, its more technical acceptation is easily overlooked
     and cannot be used except when misunderstanding is impossible.

7    The whole documentation concerning the inclusion of Villa Adriana in
     the World Heritage List (1999) can be found on the UNESCO website
     (http://whc.unesco.org/en/list/907/documents/, accessed 9 June 2014).

8    See, for instance, Barassi (2007) and Cooper (2007), that employ
     Riegl's categories to discuss the use of copies in museums and
     exhibitions; Perniola (1994), that refers to his analysis in order
     to explain several possible attitudes towards the conservation of
     historical town centres; or von der Goltz (2010), that considers the
     Rieglian 'values' in the case of contemporary art.

9    It may be interesting to note that Riegl repeatedly stresses the
     scholarly basis of 'historical value', which he contrasts with the claim
     that 'age value' can be appreciated by anyone (1903: 7–9, 22). His
     theory thus indirectly supports the reconstructed Globe's aim to be
     an educational and research tool, from the basic level of spectators
     getting in touch with Elizabethan theatre practices to the specialized
     investigations and experiments of academics and practitioners,
     rather than a tourist attraction, such as ancient monuments, in
     Riegl's view, naturally are.

10   '[E]in unlösbarer Konflikt mit dem Alterswert…, wenn die Kopie nicht
     gewissermaßen als Hülfsapparat für die wissenschaftliche Forschung,

sondern als vollwertiger Ersatz für das Original mit Anspruch historisch-ästhetische Würdigung auftritt' (my translation).

11   The assumption that Elizabethan stagecraft may be a fruitful example for twenty-first-century artists seems to underlie all the Globe's EOSIs in such a powerful way that no one feels the need to state it explicitly. Indirect expressions of the continuity between Shakespeare's theatre and the present are on the contrary numerous; two examples may be actor Peter Hamilton Dyer's assertion in his 2006 EOSI that Elizabethan performers anticipated the relationship with the audience of today's rock stars and composer Claire van Kampen's observation on the first Globe audiences 'that the 'Globe experience' resonated deeply with a theatre practice which, though long forgotten, was tantalisingly being remembered' (2008a: 79).

The importance of this feeling of proximity to the project of the reconstructed Globe is also indirectly confirmed by Dennis Kennedy, who forcefully stresses Shakespeare's otherness as part of his argument that the Elizabethan-like playhouse is essentially a tourist attraction (1998: 187).

12   The importance of avoiding this danger when a copy is on display has been emphasized in his 'Rieglian analysis' by Sebastiano Barassi (2007).

13   See paragraph 82 of the 2013 *Operational Guidelines* (2013: 22). It may be interesting to notice that its creators' focus on this theme resulted in the reconstructed Globe's qualifying as essentially 'authentic' from nearly all the proposed points of view: 'form and design; materials and substance; use and function; traditions, techniques and management systems; location and setting; language, and other forms of intangible heritage; spirit and feeling; and other internal and external factors' (ibid.). A substantial exception is of course the 'internal factor' that it has been built four centuries after the time to which it refers.

14   The reference is obviously to Horatio's hint at his intention to commit suicide, 'I am more an antique Roman than a Dane' (*Hamlet* 5.2.293).

When quoting specific passages of Shakespeare's plays, I will always indicate act, scene and – when appropriate – lines with Arabic numerals separated by periods. In the case of twenty-first-century plays, which do not have numbered lines and are often undivided, I will instead use page numbers; only when the reference is to a whole scene which is identified as such in the script I will indicate the act and scene with Arabic numerals separated by a period. Any exception to these usages will be written in full.

15    Most of the time, prompt books only carry the marks of changes, but sometimes a rehearsal note or some kind of record will make the writer's contribution explicit. A very complete document is for instance Peter Oswald's list of cuts and alterations included in the *Golden Ass* bible (Shakespeare's Globe Library and Archives ref. GB 3316 SGT/THTR/SM/1/2002/GA). In her 2010 EOSI, Nell Leyshon gave a description of the process *Bedlam* went through, explaining that the text was modified when she attended rehearsals, at the very beginning, for the first run at the end of week two, and then again 'when it needed a better run'.

16    This and all quotations from Jessica Swale's interview are printed here by kind permission of the playwright.

17    The stage direction at the beginning of the scene in the published script is 'Mr Peck is pulling the cart along. Inside it, Carolyn is hiding under the blanket' (*BS* 81). In the Globe production, Christopher Logan doubled as Mr Peck and Collins and had a rather quick change between 2.1 and this scene, which made it impossible for him to come back on stage with a cart. In order to replace this device with a completely different way of smuggling Carolyn out of the college, Swale had to rewrite the scene. She decided to keep the original version in the published text, because it represented the way she had actually conceived that moment. Nevertheless, she has allowed the other companies that have staged *Blue Stockings* to choose between the book's 2.4 and the 'Globe version' recorded in the prompt book; up to now, all productions have featured the latter, either because the actors playing Mr Peck had the same doubling problem or due to the practical difficulties of bringing a cart on stage. Jessica Swale told me the episode in the course of a telephone interview on 11 September 2014.

Unless otherwise stated, the productions referred to here are always those of Shakespeare's Globe Theatre, the year and director of which are included in the list of the plays.

18    *A New World* is unpublished, probably because of the pre-existing screenplay; therefore, in the present study I will refer whenever possible to the corresponding pages in the printed version and point out the differences between that text and the prompt book's.

19    Evidence of the episode can be found in the prompt book (Shakespeare's Globe Library and Archives ref. GB 3316 SGT/THTR/SM/1/2010/AB), in the notes to the rehearsal of 17 June 2010.

20    'Mr Walker is working on writing in a pre-show announcement about phones, photography and smoking!' (rehearsal notes, no 17, 20 June 2008, Shakespeare's Globe Library and Archives ref. GB

3316 SGT/THTR/SM/1/2009/Front, printed here by kind permission of Shakespeare's Globe's Library and Archives). The result was a rap piece performed by two members of the cast and it effectively attracted attention, to the point of being explicitly mentioned in reviews (Gregory 2008; Shuttleworth 2008).

21 Quotations from Ché Walker's EOSI are printed here by kind permission of the playwright.

22 Quotations from Nell Leyshon's EOSI are printed here by kind permission of the playwright.

EOSIs are transcribed literally from audio recordings and so they reproduce the irregularities of speech; in order to maintain their validity in full, they are quoted here without further revision.

23 Research bulletins documenting the rehearsals were realized for most productions between 1997 and 2002. The report on *The Golden Ass* – the only one concerning a new play – is available on the Globe's website (http://www.shakespearesglobe.com/uploads/ffiles/2012/03/545849.pdf, accessed 25 November 2014).

# Chapter 2

1 '[D]es "uchronies", non pas hors l'histoire, … mais pris dans trop d'histoires différentes (souvenirs de l'auteur, du narrateur, chronologie du héros, références historiques générales et datées) pour ne pas être à la fois passés, présents et à venir' (my translation).

2 It is important to remark that the Friends of Shakespeare's Globe can join in activities that go beyond the priority booking of tickets or the exclusive events offered by most theatres to their supporters. From 1991 (before the theatre was even built, that is) to 2013, for instance, some Friends have met on Sunday afternoons to read aloud Shakespeare's plays, the roles being drawn 'Out of a Hat', as the gatherings were called (Rowley 2013).

3 There were over 500 volunteer stewards for the 2013 season according to Shakespeare's Globe Annual Review 2013, available online (http://www.shakespearesglobe.com/about-us/todays-globe/annual-review, accessed 31 October 2014), p. 43.

4 'Espaces, en quelque sorte, qui sont en liaison avec tous les autres, qui contredisent pourtant tous les autres emplacements' (Foucault [1967] 1994a: 755).

5 'Des lieux réels, des lieux effectifs, des lieux qui sont dessinés dans l'institution même de la société, et qui sont des sortes de contre-emplacements, sortes d'utopies effectivement réalisées dans lesquelles

les emplacements réels, tous les autres emplacements réels que l'on peut trouver à l'intérieur de la culture sont à la fois représentés, contestés et inversés, des sortes de lieux qui sont hors de tous les lieux, bien que pourtant ils soient effectivement localisables' (Foucault [1967] 1994a: 755–6).

6  'En un sens parentes des bibliothèques et des musées, car, en retrouvant la vie polynésienne, on abolit le temps, mais c'est tout aussi bien le temps qui se retrouve, c'est toute l'histoire de l'humanité qui remonte jusqu'à sa source comme dans une sorte de grand savoir immédiat' (Foucault [1967] 1994a: 760).

7  The proximity of the two 'hybrid' heterochronias may yet have a bearing on the frequency with which reviewers complain about the behaviour of 'tourist spectators'. Especially since these negative reactions seem to be mainly directed at American visitors (Prescott 2008), the British critics' indignation may be somewhat fuelled by the perception of the economic superpower's holiday invasion as the menacing approach of a potential 'soft' coloniser. This reading would draw the reconstructed Elizabethan theatre nearer to the Polynesian villages of Foucault's example, at least in perspective. Nevertheless, this possible similitude from the point of view of economics is forcefully contradicted by the opposite cultural relation between traveller and destination: tourists at Shakespeare's Globe expect to learn something about great poetry and drama, or maybe to question a staple of received literary values, but not to look down on pristine conditions from which they have been distanced by historical progress.

8  Although in the past tourists have been encouraged to witness exotic peoples' genuine daily life, and unfortunately instances of these 'anthropological safaris' still exist, as a rule traditional customs are displayed by actors, who may actually be native to the area, but nonetheless impersonate a character in a more or less realistic performance: the main goal of basket-makers, for instance, is not to provide their community with the containers they need, but to show the visitors techniques and peculiarities of their handicraft.

9  An impressive example is *The Rocky Horror Show*, attended worldwide by audiences dressed up like its characters, even though that may result in embarrassing or potentially offensive appearances; this has become a regular practice to the point that the official website of the musical's latest UK tour explains the etiquette of costumed spectatorship (http://rockyhorror.co.uk/about-the-show/virgins-guide, accessed 9 September 2013). A smaller-scale but equally relevant case may be the Playhouse Theatre in London promising free entry to anyone who wore appropriate medieval clothes at *Spamalot* performances (http://www.moneysavingexpert

.com/deals/spamalot, accessed 9 September 2013; the offer was not mentioned in the production's official website, but its terms were fully stated on a billboard in the venue's box office).

10  For this and all quotations from Simon Bent's *Under the Black Flag*: *Under the Black Flag* © Simon Bent 2006 by kind permission of Oberon Books Ltd.

11  This and all quotations from Chris Hannan's *The God of Soho* are printed here by kind permission of Nick Hern Books.

12  The reference to *King Lear* 1.1.87–90 may be bland, since the subject of the conversation and the relationship between the two speakers are quite different, but it is unavoidable and it actually makes the dialogue funnier and more meaningful, because Natty suggests Baz should have borrowed his answer from Shakespeare and provides two examples that are completely wrong, while he has actually quoted Cordelia's well-known 'nothing'.

13  This and all quotations from the Globe's application for the Resident Dramatist Attachment Award are printed here by kind permission of Mark Rylance.

14  Printed here by kind permission of Peter Oswald.

15  This and all quotations from Chris Hannan's interview are printed here by kind permission of the playwright.

16  Printed here by kind permission of Peter Oswald.

17  Unfortunately no prompt book of *Man Falling Down* is held by Shakespeare's Globe Library and Archives, because the play did not undergo the usual rehearsal process but was written and directed by Jack Shepherd and Oliver Cotton as it developed in a workshop exploring the theatrical use of masks. The only sources of information available are a performance's video recording and the very few articles published on this subject.

18  For this and all quotations from Peter Oswald's *The Storm*: *The Storm (after Plautus)* © Peter Oswald 2005 by kind permission of Oberon Books Ltd.

19  For the sake of completeness, I will point out that Palaestra has an earlier monologue in verse, when she shows Daemones how as a prostitute she allures customers by playing the role of chaste Diana (*S* 69–70). But at that moment the girl is not speaking for herself, she is acting the part of a goddess in what moreover looks like a set piece. Therefore the passage does not seem to contradict the general restriction in the use of verse outlined here.

20  For the description of the two pairs of characters as comic double-acts, see Boon (1991: 207).

21    Sceparnio's first monologue is preceded only by the prologue (S 7–9) and his conclusion is followed by a choir (S 91–2) and the epilogue (S 92).

22    Of course, the grating effect of anachronisms depends on the listeners' ears. It is difficult to say, for instance, how many spectators realized that the shock value of Bertha's 'bugger the monks!' (AO 49) was partly due to the fact that the exclamation jars not only with the queen's dignity but also with her times.

23    Since the Globe script has not been published I will refer here to Tony Harrison's previous text of The Mysteries ('M'), pointing out the differences when useful.

24    It may be useful to note that even though the setting indicated at the beginning of the script is simply 'ancient Greece' (S 5), towards the end of the play Charmides brings the news that 'Rome has been captured by the Goths' (S 80), so the action appears to take place in the fifth century AD.

25    The production's programme features two poems on prostitution by Peter Oswald (p. 27), showing the prominence this aspect of the play has in the eyes of the author and of the theatre's management.

26    For this and all quotations from Nell Leyshon's Bedlam: Bedlam © Nell Leyshon 2010 by kind permission of Oberon Books Ltd.

27    Printed here by kind permission of Eric Schlosser.

28    The term 'myth' is used throughout this paragraph to indicate a foundational narrative, usually endowed with symbolical or allegorical import, regardless of its being currently believed at least by some people to be literally true or generally regarded as fictional; its alternative meaning, denoting a widespread but false story or explanation, is not in any way implied.

29    The importance Simon Bent attributed to the historical aspect of the play is nevertheless manifest in his decision to forgo chronological consistency with Treasure Island in order to set Long John Silver's adventures in the time he wished to depict.

30    Another character of Under the Black Flag, General Harrison (UBF 70–5, 117–18, 132–7), bears the name and title of a historical figure (Major-General Thomas Harrison, 1606–60), but their biographies differ in a crucial way: the fictional one is killed by Captain Mission because he refuses to attack the pirates that have surrendered (UBF 137), while the factual one was executed after the Restoration. Since Bent's Harrison does not do much more, there appears to be very little ground to identify him with his real-life namesake.

31    It is probably just a coincidence, but these British histories are actually almost entirely English, with a reasonably proportionate Welsh presence consisting in the Britons of Augustine's Oak, Under the Black

*Flag*'s Frederick, *Holding Fire*'s Eli Morgan and the Newport episode (*HF* 96–106). There are a few Irish characters (Edward in *Under the Black Flag*, Feargus O'Connor in *Holding Fire*, Burke and his parrot in *A New World*, Seamus in *The Frontline*, Fergal O'Hannagan in *Doctor Scroggy's War*, possibly Maeve Sullivan and her brother in *Blue Stockings*), while Scottish people are represented only by *Anne Boleyn*'s King James, who occasionally recalls his background (*AB* 12–14, 78–9) or uses a Scots word (e.g. 'bairn', *AB* 76), by the caricatural Dr Scroggy and by *Pitcairn*'s William McCoy. Up to now, there have been no scenes set in Scotland.

32   It may be argued that *Anne Boleyn* is fairly focused on its title character, but the role of King James and its importance in the play cannot be dismissed. Anyway, it must be noticed that Howard Brenton's play is the one with the least linear structure, so even if it should be considered a single-protagonist history it would not invalidate the general idea that these plays tend to balance their complexities with more traditional and simplifying features.

33   *Gabriel*'s metaphorical protagonist is certainly the natural trumpet, but this musical instrument is not a character, so it cannot be the main one. Similarly, Henry Purcell cannot be considered the play's protagonist, despite his centrality in absentia (Halliburton 2013; Hemming 2013; Taylor 2013), because even though he is constantly present through his music, he never actually appears in person.

34   Hearing and seeing fellow audience members laugh at what seems to be an inappropriate moment, for instance, is an experience that all Globe spectators are likely to know first-hand; it is analysed in its awareness-inducing power by Penelope Woods (2012: 125, 302–6).

35   This and all quotations from the unpublished script of *A New World* are printed here by kind permission of Trevor Griffiths.

36   It may be useful to remark that when, as in the case of Shakespeare's Globe Theatre, playwrights collaborate with the production's cast and creative team, the prompt book's text is usually the ultimate one, because the published version necessarily goes to press while rehearsals are still in progress in order to be available for sale when the show opens. Therefore both the published script and the prompt book represent choices approved by the author, but unless there is evidence to the contrary, the performed text, when available, represents a later stage in the creative process and thus the writer's (temporarily) last word on the subject.

37   Shakespeare's Globe Library and Archives ref. GB 3316 SGT/THTR/ SM/1/2007/HF.

# Chapter 3

1    Shakespeare's Globe is specifically discussed in the paragraphs
     entitled 'Making a Globe' (Kennedy 2009: 105–9) and 'Shax™'
     (ibid.: 109–14).
2    On attempts (or lack thereof) at charting theatre audiences see, for
     instance, Ursula Canton's reflections in *Biographical Theatre: Re-
     Presenting Real People?* (2011: 125–6).
3    This interested attitude is even more forcibly prescribed by a
     monument, and such is Shakespeare's Globe, according to the
     arguments presented earlier. Since its status is still debated, though,
     I prefer here to stress that as a Bankside landmark (which such
     a conspicuous building undoubtedly is) the reconstructed Globe
     commands that sort of attention anyway.
4    A similar definition is the one employed by Dennis Kennedy in the
     chapter 'The spectator as tourist' (Kennedy 2009: 94–114), in which
     nearly all punters of Shakespeare's Globe are consequently set down
     as tourists.
5    Quotation printed here by kind permission of Penelope Woods.
6    A copy of the document compiled by the theatre's staff for each
     performance is held by Shakespeare's Globe Library and Archives.
     It relates the main facts and figures concerning the event, such
     as tickets sold, weather conditions, starting and ending time,
     unexpected happenings.
7    The term 'groundlings', designating the spectators that stand in
     the yard, appears for the first time in *Hamlet* 3.2.11. Although for
     centuries it has implied a certain disdain for this part of the audience,
     whose lower position on the social ladder presumably entailed a
     gross, uneducated taste, nowadays it is rather proudly employed
     by the groundlings themselves as a badge of connoisseurship:
     besides being a Shakespearean word, it stresses their choice of stage
     proximity over comfort.
8    See, for instance, this extract from actor Ben Deery's 2010 EOSI:
     '*What's your impression of the Globe audience?* They're really
     bright! That's the most noticeable thing. I don't know if it's to do
     with the space, as well, that encourages that. There are so many
     little gags that I can imagine doing in any other theatre that just
     wouldn't get a laugh, but here it does. Like a joke about a sixteenth-
     century Prespertarian, gets a laugh. It doesn't happen in other places'
     (quotation printed here by kind permission of Ben Deery).
9    Examples can be found even in reviews that censure the play and
     so do not share the interested audience's taste; an unsatisfied critic
     points out, for instance, that 'the Globe's indefatigable tribesmen

and women, standing down in the pit in the drizzle, lapped up every word' (Walker 2007).

10   To name but a few, whose positions have been sanctioned by their inclusion in the Globe's main theoretical publication to date, i.e. *Shakespeare's Globe. A Theatrical Experiment*, edited by Christie Carson and Farah Karim-Cooper (2008): Alan C. Dessen, David Lindley, Martin White and Gordon McMullan.

11   The phrase 'original practices' is usually employed by the Globe's artists to qualify productions that explore techniques of Shakespeare's time; it is meant to imply that such stagings cannot be properly 'authentic' and that they take up only some aspects of Elizabethan stagecraft. Some insightful reflections on this subject can be found in Jenny Tiramani, *Exploring Early Modern Stage and Costume Design* (2008: 58).

12   The anti-spectators prejudice seems to lurk once again behind these scholars' well-argued perplexities in that they never mention the same problems arising in the artists' minds. In EOSIs performers appear on the contrary to be conscious of the fact that even if they study Elizabethan and Jacobean acting styles they cannot delete the heritage of Stanislavskij and Brecht or the influence of cinema and television, for instance. Mark Rylance delineates the same situation on stage and in the auditorium when he observes that 'the audience was learning how to be in the Globe just as we actors were learning' (Rylance 2008: 113).

13   This and all quotations from Howard Brenton's interview are printed here by kind permission of the playwright.

14   Two meaningful exceptions to these plays' embracing supernatural events as an attractor of the audience's attention are *The God of Soho* and *The Last Days of Troy*. In spite of being partly set in Heaven and populated with deities, Chris Hannan's script features no spectacular miracle, in accordance with the fact that its gods do not seem to wield any power. They are depicted as personifications of certain aspects of the world, so that for instance 'a lack of loveliness in the world' (*GS* 9) accompanies the Goddess of Love's suffering (*GS* 9–15), and a general crisis parallels Big God's losing his mind (*GS* 27–30, 34–5, 44–5, 80–2), but when Big God and Mrs God descend on earth, they are just 'taller and larger than life' (*GS* 34), looking 'like extended slightly cartoonish versions of themselves' (*GS* 34) and they can hardly interact with the world (*GS* 34–5, 63–5). As the chief divinity humorously suggests, he is just 'a voice in a mental person's head' (*GS* 64), so it is quite appropriate that these disempowered gods should not be enshrouded in an atmosphere of magic or mystery. Actually, the most extraordinary thing they

do is to disappear: when the Goddess of Love and the New God
are finally reconciled, they do not surface from the pool in which
they have plunged (*GS* 84), and the audience can imagine that in
the restored harmony symbolized also by Natty and Baz's kiss (*GS*
85) the divine lovers have returned to a higher, possibly enchanting,
dimension.

The loss of power these gods may have gone through is represented
in *The Last Days of Troy*, which features a double version of Zeus
and Hera. At the time of the Trojan War, they have the prerogatives of
ancient divinities, somewhat human in their jealousies and affections
but actually mighty, as minimally but effectively signalled by the
roll of thunder accompanying Zeus' nod (*LDT* 25). In the twenty-
first-century scenes, on the contrary, they are just a poor old couple,
providing a series of comical moments based precisely on their
conspicuous lack of dignity and command. The contrast between past
and present of the divine king and queen is not only a source of light-
hearted fun, though, because in their last dialogue (Scene 12, *LDT*
128–31) they reflect on the change they have undergone and identify
the conclusion of the Trojan War as a crucial point in their decline,
thus offering a possible reading of the whole play.

15   Agave's transformation into a snake, on the contrary, seems to
     call essentially for a piece of virtuoso acting by stressing that 'the
     transformation is hideous and she fights it every step. But once
     it's complete, she slithers off' (*LC* 55). In Matthew Dunster's
     production, Finty Williams's performance was complemented
     by the Maenads slipping her into a cylindrical spandex snake
     costume.

16   More information concerning Pinner's contribution to the staging
     of *The Globe Mysteries* can be found in the production's rehearsal
     notes, that record what he was called to help realize and how he
     collaborated with cast and crew.

17   Quotation printed here by kind permission of Dominic Dromgoole.

18   Speaking characters, as listed in the script. In the case of *Man
     Falling Down*, for which no promptbook is available, because
     it was the issue of a workshop, I have counted the characters
     named in the production's page of the Globe's website, http://
     www.shakespearesglobe.com/education/discovery-space/previous
     -productions/man-falling-down (accessed 7 December 2014).
     Undefined groups (e.g. 'crowd' or 'courtiers') have been counted as
     one character, while 'numbered' characters (e.g. 'courtier 1') have
     been considered as separate individuals.

19   As listed in the published playtext, when available, or on the
     Globe's website, in the 'previous productions' section, http://

www.shakespearesglobe.com/education/discovery-space/previous
-productions (accessed 29 November 2016). This figure gives an
idea of how much doubling the play allows, because Shakespeare's
Globe, like any other theatre, tries to keep the costs low by
not hiring unnecessary actors, but production choices can vary
significantly.

20  In *Helen* there are more performers than characters because of the
chorus, which is made up of six people speaking as one.

21  *The Oresteia* also features a chorus whose lines were divided in the
prompt book but not in the published text, yet the players are not
more than the characters because several performers had double
roles.

22  The management of Shakespeare's Globe consciously fostered this
technique: in a radical reversal of contemporary customs, 'from 1997
to 2005, Globe productions were budgeted … with costume budgets
exceeding those for set design, in the hope that this would encourage
directors and designers to concentrate their storytelling choices on
the dress of the performers, just as the players of the late sixteenth
century did' (Tiramani 2008: 60).

23  Contrariwise, a play that does not promise anything of the kind,
*A New World*, features a representation of the night in which
Paine and Carnet conceive their child. Trevor Griffiths's screenplay
required 'oblique tendrils of lovemaking through the night: fierce,
direct, honest' (*TAT* 172); the prompt book carries a note from the
playwright to director Dominic Dromgoole, asking him to do what
is possible and if necessary cut the scene. The production is granted
a degree of freedom by the fact that the two characters start to make
love at the end of a sequence, just before a song and a change of
setting (*NW* 147).

24  Rivka Jacobson is to my knowledge the only reviewer who seems
to imply the seriousness of the scene in which Natty and Baz
make love without taking any pleasure in it (*GS* 67–9). It exposes,
she writes, 'loveless, mechanical sex which is also devoid of any
eroticism' (Jacobson 2011). So in her view, too, it does not satisfy
any voyeuristic impulse.

25  The protest is expressed with force by Caroline McGinn (2007);
others imply the same critique (Cavendish 2006; Shore 2006b). The
one reviewer that seems to consider the scene potentially disturbing
(but not too much) is Peter Brown, who writes that 'sensitive
theatregoers need not be too alarmed, because there won't be quite
so much controversy surrounding this play, though it certainly has
an earthy dose of sex, and there's a castration scene which might
send shivers down a few spines' (Brown 2006).

26   John Dove's production made the scene more stylized by doing away
     with the blood entirely.

27   Actually the play contains another very violent episode, the
     'Slaughter of the Innocents' (number 11 in the prompt copy, *M*
     82–3). The interpretation expounded by Beadle may well stand also
     in the case of this scene, which somehow foreshadows how the still
     innocent Jesus will be persecuted again. Yet it is interesting to note
     that while in the published 1985 version only a short lamentation
     follows the silent murder of the babies, the prompt book of *The
     Globe Mysteries* presents a perceptibly longer piece: it begins with
     the 'Song of the Mothers', a wailing rendering of the 'Coventry
     Carol' that in the Globe was sung by an increasingly agitated group
     of women dispersed among the groundlings; gory actions and
     excruciatingly painful dialogues follow, with the mothers trying
     to protect their sons either physically or by lying; finally, Herod
     dances to the same melody, but with a lively rhythm, on a pile of
     bloody little corpses. The gruesomeness of the stage business is due
     to production choices, but undoubtedly Tony Harrison decided to
     expand this episode, from less than one printed page to a collection
     of dialogues between mothers and soldiers that make the massacre
     even more harrowing. The importance thus acquired by this scene is
     even more in the light of the fact that the transition from the 1985
     *Mysteries* to *The Globe Mysteries* was mainly characterized by cuts
     and abridgements in order to compress a trilogy of plays into a
     single piece.

28   As for the images that accompany these words, the stage direction
     at the beginning of this scene only reads: 'a TV studio' (*LC* 61), but
     it is difficult to suppose the monologue could be played without
     any sign of the dead deer it is centred on. In Matthew Dunster's
     production, the animal was represented by the same carcass that
     had stood in for Pentheus's corpse 'left hanging from a butcher's
     hook in the centre, slowly dripping blood' (*LC* 52). Even if no
     gory representation should accompany Antonia's monologue,
     the memory of previous violent scenes would certainly be on the
     spectators' minds. Among these, the most visually impressive is
     surely Pentheus being torn apart by the Maenads (*LC* 52), but
     almost as horrible, maybe even more because of its contemporary
     realistic setting, is Antonia herself smashing violinist Louisa's hands
     with a hammer (*LC* 50). By the way, this atrocious outburst follows
     the attacker's watching a 'nature programme about lions' (*LC* 47)
     that actually chronicles in detail the fight between Hercules and the
     Nemean lion, at the end of which the man dons the beast's hide (*LC*

48), so the connection between violence and television had already been established in the play.

29 The ballad was successively changed, as the production's prompt book shows, but without altering its tone.

30 A Narrator is listed among the dramatis personae of *Bedlam*, but this definition does not quite fit Tom o'Bedlam, who presents himself and his story (*B* 13, 70–2, 105) and occasionally comments on the action (*B* 35), but always does so in the character of an eighteenth-century street entertainer and former inmate of the asylum on which the plot pivots.

31 See the first 'Costumes' note in the Production Meeting Minutes of 29 July 2009, from which all the quotations in this period are taken. Quotations from this prompt book (Shakespeare's Globe's Library and Archives ref. GB 3316 SGT/THTR/SM/1/2009/NW) are printed here by kind permission of Shakespeare's Globe's Library and Archives.

32 For example, a very interesting and funny double quotation from the future marks once again a self-reflexive comment: 'Do we know, could we know, any of this? But I go with Marx on this one: Forget the facts. Just give me the truth. That's Groucho by the way. The People's Marx' (*NW* 41).

33 In the prompt book these two dialogues are slightly different from the ones in the published version, but the result from the point of view of the present observations is quite the same.

34 It may perhaps be useful to point out that at Shakespeare's Globe the interval is often announced one way or another because its beginning cannot be marked by the lights going up in the open-air, fully lit auditorium.

35 The prompt book presents a slightly different and longer version of this piece, but to the same effect.

36 The evolution from the published version to the more extended one in the prompt book seems to suggest the perception that the audience might on average need a little more time to realize what is going on and then decide to collaborate.

37 It must nevertheless be noted that both in the example of Anne's initial question and everywhere else in the text, the following lines would not sound absurd if the audience should give the 'wrong' answer, but the relationship between the character and the spectators would not be as harmonious; in this case, for instance, the play would start with an act of defiance (Anne showing them something they do not want to see). Anyway, the fact that this 'accident' would not result in an incoherent speech proves the playwright's open attitude towards his interlocutors in the auditorium.

38   Deborah Bruce's production made the most of this scene. All
     available cast members were placed in the yard, some in recognizable
     costumes but others in plain clothes, so as to look like theatregoers;
     more interestingly, Gabriel divided the crowd in good and bad
     souls and placed some trestles in between. The fact that the angel
     was wearing the Globe stewards' tabard over his costume made the
     action funny, but sometimes the worried or unhappy expressions
     of groundlings separated from their family or friends made it
     moving too.

39   The royal box action actually took place in the upper stage/
     musicians' gallery in Christopher Luscombe's production. This
     choice probably gave it a better visibility and certainly avoided
     belying the uniqueness of the king's position, since there are two
     lords' rooms on the sides of the central, slightly jutting upper stage.
     On the other hand, besides renouncing the possibility of placing the
     fictional royal spectator in an area actually dedicated to audience
     members, this decision entailed some adjustments, because for the
     duration of those two scenes the musicians and their instruments had
     to be removed from their habitual location, where they performed
     most of their parts.

40   In Matthew Dunster's production the audience's involvement and
     the disturbing similarity between the offers of spiritual and sensual
     experiences were stressed by the fact that Beth and her Christian
     group handed the spectators religious-themed flyers while Violet
     gave out business cards of the club where she works.

41   At least sometimes the three actors actually managed to guide the
     spectators' reactions, eliciting in particular roaring approvals for the
     cry 'more beer' (*UBF* 16), as attested by the video recordings and by
     Sheila Connor's review (2006).

42   Philippe is actually acquitted, or possibly granted a pardon thanks to
     the Thermidor, but the audience will discover this only later (*L* 119);
     for the time being he seems to be doomed just like the others.

43   It is probably because of this structure, together with the lively
     depiction of a diverse society, that *The Frontline* has been
     compared more than once to Ben Jonson's *Bartholomew Fair* (see
     e.g. Billington 2008; Edwardes 2008; Fricker 2008; Lichtig 2008;
     Tanitch 2008; Taylor 2008). Ché Walker explicitly stated he did
     not know this Jacobean precedent (Curtis 2009), but probably the
     first person to trace the similarity was artistic director Dominic
     Dromgoole, who considered it a promising resemblance for a play
     commissioned by Shakespeare's Globe (Allfree 2008; Whalen 2008).

44   It may be argued that Seamus is actually responding to Donna's
     previous statement. The text does not give any definitive evidence in
     favour of one interpretation or the other, but the order in which the

lines are written suggests that Seamus's must at least sound as a reply to Mordechai Thurrock's, even if it is not.

45 Shakespeare's Globe Library and Archives ref. GB 3316 SGT/THTR/ SM/1/2006/UBF. Printed here by kind permission of Shakespeare's Globe Library and Archives.

46 In this specific instance, the whole scene consists of Evariste's monologue and there are no stage directions to determine unquestionably whether he is rehearsing or delivering the speech. What makes it look like a run-through more than a performance, besides the precedent and subsequent occurrences of similar situations, is the lack of any fictional audience or context.

47 The published text has the second act begin with a 'prelude' (*HF* 54), but this short scene was cut in the Globe production. Since such choices are agreed with the playwrights, it seems fair to consider the version performed with the writer's consent.

48 The prompt book carries a somewhat different version of this speech, though essentially to the same effect. The main changes are that Clytus reads a little more of the original text before translating it and that there are no fabricated phrases like 'rubberaria' and 'piecus preposterosus'; the Latin words are all Apuleius's.

49 The prompt book's version of this monologue is different from the printed one, it features other images, but the definition 'human lions' and the sad avowal that he was once one of them are significantly left unchanged.

50 To the best of my knowledge, no critic mentioned this mise en abyme of the audience's morbid curiosity in the reviews of the Globe's production, but it must be remarked that the staging can considerably foster or impair the emergence of this theme. The accounts of rehearsals show how director Tim Carroll and actor Mark Rylance chose to focus on the ass's new consciousness rather than on its implications for the spectators (see the research bulletin for *The Golden Ass*, 75–6), opting for an introverted rendering of his soliloquy's beginning (*GA* 95–6). Since his address to all present (*GA* 95) takes place in the middle of some fairly convulse stage business and is immediately followed by the overwhelming action of the lions' foray and the Ringmaster's death, it is rather difficult to drive home the analogy between Lucius and the audience without referring back to the spectators at this quieter moment. Other productions may give more relevance to the metatheatrical aspect of the curiosity theme.

51 The two remaining characters on stage – Teresa and Stan – occupy an intermediate, or rather wavering, position, because they intervene here and there in the main dialogue, especially towards the beginning and the end. They may be interpreted as belonging to Natty and

Baz's plane, though in minor roles, or swinging between the couple's level and that of first grade observers, of which Clem is a constant representative. At any rate, they do not add another dimension to the scheme.

# Chapter 4

1   See also the playwright's note to the printed text (*IE*, unnumbered initial page). The fact that the first version of *In Extremis* was written in the context of a university workshop, in which the author collaborated with young promising actors, attests to Brenton's continuing open-minded attitude towards new ideas and situations and the importance he attaches to dialogue among theatre artists and shared experiences in the development of texts.

2   'The director, John Dove, and his company found the building helped the play in all kinds of ways. Actors can go round a pillar and begin the next scene 10 hours or even two years later. One of the biggest surprises was how strong "word painting" can be. Tell the audience you are beside Notre Dame in Paris and the cathedral miraculously seems to appear. Why this should be in a theatre with such an overwhelming, colourful presence I don't know, but the effect is very marked. ... Scenes in my plays often vary in style – the principle is to write a scene in the way that dramatises its action best; if it comes out farcical, or as a serious argument, so be it. I've taken some stick for this "unevenness". But the Globe seemed to welcome this aberration – or experimentation – of mine' (Brenton 2007). 'And this stage presents unique opportunities. Storytelling plays can be difficult in enclosed, dark conventional theatres with the audiences virtually strapped in their seats. But the Globe, with its relaxed atmosphere, makes dramatic storytelling sing' (Neill 2006: 9).

3   Howard Brenton has repeatedly stated he was planning to have one actor play all the Tudor monarchs, from Henry VII to Elizabeth I (see, for instance, Brenton 2011; Woddis 2010). A faint trace of this idea – though connecting the first Stuart king to a Tudor queen – may perhaps be recognized in the beginning of Act 2, when James I wears Anne's coronation dress (*AB* 70–1).

4   Two other plays, Glyn Maxwell's *Liberty* and the opera version of Seamus Heaney's *The Burial at Thebes*, co-produced by Shakespeare's Globe respectively with Lifeblood Theatre Company and with the Manning Camerata and the Onassis Foundation, were from the beginning intended for a tour that started with their run at Shakespeare's Globe Theatre.

It may be interesting to add that in 2014 the Globe, in partnership with the English Touring Theatre, also toured a revival of Howard Brenton's *In Extremis* (although with a different, much more marketable title, *Eternal Love*): see the ETT's website, www.ett .org.uk, and more specifically the page dedicated to *Eternal Love*, http://www.ett.org.uk/productions/78/eternal-love (last accessed 24 January 2015).

5    Shortly before *Anne Boleyn* opened, to an interviewer who asked him if he still professed to be Marxist Brenton answered, 'I wish I wasn't, but once you've seen the bare bones of the world in that way, there's no going back' (Dickson 2010).

6    On subsidized and commercial theatres in the United Kingdom, with a specific focus on Shakespeare's Globe, see Rose (2011).

7    Bernard of Clairvaux, Abelard's main opponent in Brenton's play.

8    Similar statements can be found elsewhere, e.g. Brenton 2006; Wilkinson 2006.

9    In Paul Hernadi's words, 'dramatic works need an air of plausibility, and what better indication that a series of events is possible than the fact that it actually occurred?' (Hernadi 1976: 45).

10   Similar statements can also be found in Reinelt 1985 and Reinelt 1992. Other scholars have also identified Brenton as one of the main heirs of Brecht. See, for instance, Schechter 1983.

11   All the following quotations from this interview will refer to the version published with some changes in *New Theatre Voices of the Seventies: Sixteen Interviews from Theatre Quarterly, 1970–1980* (Trussler 1981), but these words were significantly omitted from the text edited in 1980, when Brenton's attitude towards Brecht had already started changing.

12   Howard Brenton worked on a text by Bertolt Brecht again in 1982, when he adapted *Gedichte im Exil* for the stage (*Conversations in Exile*, 1983).

13   'But then the notion of a form in the theatre being pure I view with great suspicion', he added (Hay and Roberts 1979: 139). By the way, the definition of 'the Brechtian, *received* idea of an epic' (my emphasis) may suggest he already sensed what was perceived as Brechtian at the time might not be quite the real thing.

14   Compare Hay and Roberts 1979: 138–9, with Reinelt 1992: 44–5.

15   Breton himself described his idea of human nature as a 'Sartrean view', though quoting as another possible reference a teaching in the Gospels, 'by their deeds you will know them' (Wu 2000: 30).

16   It may be worth noting that *Leben des Galilei* and *Mutter Courage und ihre Kinder* are, together with *Die Mutter*, the plays Brenton

mentions when he speaks of Brecht in positive terms. See e.g. Brenton 1986a: 5, 6; Mitchell 1987: 199–200; Reinelt 1992: 40.

17 In the present study, a 'spoken stage direction' is an aside that defines the time, place or situation in which the scene takes place.

18 Speaking of *55 Days*, Howard Brenton stated, 'it's my last religious play' (Hemming 2012).

19 Brenton is here referring to the protagonist of his play *Scott of the Antarctic* (1971), explorer Robert Falcon Scott. John Wesley was the main character in another of his works, *Wesley* (1970).

20 *Paul* thus presents a sort of reversal of the problem enucleated by Wu: instead of a morally inconsistent person striving to realize a rightful project, this play depicts a man whose life is perfectly coherent with a potentially untrue world view. In Janelle Reinelt's words, here Brenton poses 'the open question of the value of Paul's mission to the Gentiles if the historical underpinnings of his claims are false – if Paul's great preachment on love and ideas about grace and universal salvation were based on a misunderstanding of the nature of his own experience and of Yeshua's corporeal status' (Reinelt 2007: 169). This way, the play offers another perspective on the problem of what can warrant or undermine the validity of an ideal or its success.

21 See, for instance, this extract from Emma John's review: 'Strangely, while Brenton uses the play to endorse Abelard's progressive doctrines, ... this production left me with rather ambivalent feelings toward the pair' (John 2007). Others observe in a less bewildered but still somewhat surprised tone that the play's best lines are often Bernard's (e.g. Sierz 2006).

22 Howard Brenton has also hypothesized that Brecht's theory of detached acting may have been triggered by the wish to make the German actors of the time more 'English' (Reinelt 1992: 49).

23 This is a recurrent theme in Howard Brenton's statements. See e.g. Hayman 1976: 57–8; Hay and Roberts 1979: 139–40; Woddis 2010.

24 For some earlier thoughts, less theoretically conscious but quite consistent with these, concerning this kind of characters, see Itzin and Trussler 1981: 95.

25 Feldman himself acknowledges that the wording 'historiographic metatheatre' was modelled on the phrase 'historiographic metafiction' coined by Linda Hutcheon (1988: 105–23), whose work he sees as a relevant precedent of his; nevertheless, since he conceives of the two genres as 'half siblings' (Feldman 2013: xv), he does not base his argument on hers.

26 The subject of history appears to be specifically linked with the figure of Sir John French, in whose conversations with Jack it is

repeatedly, though briefly, brought up. It is by quoting the cavalry's role in the battle of Elandsaagte and then setting straight two misconceptions regarding the victories of Agincourt and Waterloo that the young man first makes a good impression on the field marshal (*DSW* 26–8). After the massacre of Loos, the commander challenges the captain's faith in the romanticizing view of military history: 'Where are the glorious cavalry charges now? Lances to the fore?' (*DSW* 56). Again, when they meet at Gillies's hospital, Jack, though horribly wounded, repeats his assertion, 'the British cavalry are immortal' (*DSW* 93; cfr. *DSW* 27); French, who is unharmed but feels the weight of his responsibilities, answers 'In memory, perhaps' (*DSW* 93). These vague hints at how historical events may be misrepresented or mythologized by memory and tradition, resulting in mistaken convictions that concern the present as well as the past, acquire a different relevance in the light of the field marshal's reflections on his own historiographical destiny. In a short soliloquy he expresses his disillusionment (to say the least) with warfare, concluding 'And no one will ever believe that that is what the Commander-in-Chief thought, the day before the Battle of Loos' (*DSW* 47). This brief comment applies the general idea of history's fallibility to the specific case of the First World War, and more precisely stresses that the widespread idea of its commanders' callousness with regard to their troops' enormous losses may be only apparently correct. So the theme of historiography's (un)reliability appears in *Doctor Scroggy's War* too, although in a far less central position than the one it occupies in *Anne Boleyn* or *In Extremis*.

27 The distinction I am suggesting to adopt is the one posited by Ursula Canton in the case of biographical theatre: meta-biography can be explicit, she explains, when it features a biographer among its characters, but it can also be implicit, when other self-reflexive elements characterize the script or the performance (Canton 2011: 98–102).

28 This and all quotations from Howard Brenton's *In Extremis* are printed here by kind permission of Nick Hern Books.

29 The article deals mainly with *Anne Boleyn* and David Edgar's play on approximately the same subject, *Written on the Heart* (2011), but only his analysis of Brenton's work is relevant for the present discussion, and I will therefore keep to that part of Bull's argument.

30 In these two plays, the consequences of Gutenberg's invention are not addressed. Neither the stabilization of texts nor their wider circulation is directly represented. The increased availability of books was of course fundamental in the birth and spread of Protestantism, but this connection remains implicit in two stories set in culturally privileged environments, and the paperback exhibited by Heloise

is not tacitly contrasted with illuminated manuscripts but with Bernard's printed yet unread oeuvre. In *Anne Boleyn* the small size of a prohibited book is linked to the possibility of smuggling it (*AB* 16), but there is no comparison with the bulkier manuscripts of previous ages, so the reference to the advantages of printed texts is once again unspoken.

31   Howard Brenton's admiration for this scene is also expressed in Brenton 1986a: 5–6.

32   This image may perhaps refer to a metaphor in Maxwell Anderson's *Anne of the Thousand Days*, the best-known previous play on Anne Boleyn. There, in a soliloquy expressing his sense of guilt, Henry sees the queen's head as a weight in the bag of his memories and deeds: 'Open the bag you lug behind you, Henry./Put in Nan's head./Nan's head./And her eyes, and the lips you kissed./Wherever you go they'll follow after you now' (Anderson 1950: 73–4). Here, Anne's bag holds what may be interpreted as the symbols of her best success (establishing the Reformation in England) and of her worst failure (losing Henry's love, the crown and even her life).

33   This qualification is required by the presence in 3.3 (the Council of Sens) of several books, carried and then thrown on the floor by Abelard (*IE* 79 and 82): they are very likely to be philosophical treatises, but while the other volumes discussed here are read and talked about on stage, these can only be a matter for conjecture, and could even be easily omitted in performance.

# Chapter 5

1   Howard Brenton's best-known early plays are published in a collection significantly entitled *Plays for the Poor Theatre* (1980).

2   *Gum and Goo* (1969), *Wesley* (1970) and *Scott of the Antarctic* (1971) are meaningfully collected under the title *Plays for Public Places* (1972).

3   *A Short Sharp Shock* (1980), *The Genius* (1983), *Greenland* (1988), *Iranian Nights* (with Tariq Ali, 1989) and *Berlin Bertie* (1992) were first produced by the Royal Court, *Thirteenth Night* (1981), *H.I.D. (Hess Is Dead)* (1989) and *Moscow Gold* (with Tariq Aii, 1990) by the Royal Shakespeare Company, and *The Life of Galileo* (translated from Bertolt Brecht's *Leben des Galilei*, 1980), *The Romans in Britain* (1980), *Danton's Death* (translated from Georg Büchner's *Dantons Tod*, 1982) and *Pravda* (with David Hare, 1985) by the National Theatre. The main exceptions were Brenton's collaborations with the company Foco Novo, *Conversations in Exile*

(adapted from Bertolt Brecht's poems, 1982), *Sleeping Policeman* (with Tunde Ikoli, 1983) and *Bloody Poetry* (1984), the last two of which were revived at the Royal Court shortly after their première.

4     The best-known aspect of the scandal is that Mary Whitehouse, founder and leader of the National Viewers' and Listeners' Association, privately sued director Michael Bogdanov (whom she accused of procuring an act of gross indecency by staging an attempted homosexual rape) when she learnt the production could not be prosecuted under the 1968 Theatres Act. More relevant to my argument is the fact that Sir Horace Cutler, leader of the Greater London Council (GLC), threateningly connected disapproval of *The Romans in Britain* with the GLC's funding of the National Theatre; the grant was actually not cancelled, but this menacing skirmish could well have discouraged subsidized theatres from commissioning or producing other plays by Howard Brenton, while the continuous collaboration between the playwright and those institutions seems to go quite beyond mere gestures of solidarity. For a meaningful account of the whole episode see Roberts (1992).

5     In John Dove's production, Miranda Raison and Anthony Howell actually recited the lyrics without singing them.

6     The relevance this moment was given also in production at the Globe is attested by choreographer Sian Williams's accurate description of how she worked on it, recorded in her 2011 End of Season Interview.

7     This and all quotations from Howard Brenton's *Anne Boleyn* are printed here by kind permission of Nick Hern Books.

8     Appearing mainly between scenes, in *Never So Good* the dancers at the Ritz go from 'a ballroom tango' to 'a quickstep', 'the jitterbug', a 'jive to Elvis Presley's "Hound Dog"' and finally a performance on 'John Lennon's recording of "Twist and Shout"' (Brenton 2008: 16, 36, 46, 62 and 94, respectively).

9     The only 'spoken stage direction' that is not delivered by Anne is actually located in the middle of a scene she does not take part in (*AB* 75), so that it could not be assigned to her without some major structural changes.

10    Shakespeare's Globe Library and Archives ref. GB 3316 SGT/THTR/ SM/1/2010/AB. Printed here by kind permission of Shakespeare's Globe Library and Archives.

11    This situation is anomalous, because the final version of the script is usually the prompt book's. It is nevertheless quite clear that in this case the printed version is the latest, because it describes the action that Miranda Raison actually performed as attested by video recordings. Since all changes to the text were made by the playwright himself during rehearsals (Brenton 2014a), the kiss was probably

introduced at this stage of the creative process and marked down
by the writer and the actress, but not by the prompter, presumably
a member of stage management, who attached little importance to a
small final gesture that does not cue any further event.

12   A distinction must be made here: if spectators were not to behave
as expected in this scene, the dialogue would not lose its meaning,
but its relevance. In other words, Anne's speech would not become
inconsistent, but her relationship with the audience would change,
because instead of satisfying their curiosity, she would be pressing
on them an undesired spectacle; therefore, there would be no
denunciation of their voyeurism, but neither would there be any
point in exposing an attitude they do not have. So the meaning
of this scene, and possibly of the whole performance, would be
subverted, not destroyed, which goes to prove both the spectators'
power and the fact that the playwright actually recognizes their role
and sets out consciously to play with them, without cheating.

13   What is more, in both instances, the supposed eavesdropper is not
properly snooping. In 1.3, although Richmond asks, 'will you forever
snoop and pry and stand in His Majesty's hearing?' (Brenton 2012:
23), Hammond is hovering not in order to spy but because he has
something more to relate to the king (ibid.: 24–6); in 2.1, Mary is
concerned with her husband's safety and willing to share his fate
(ibid.: 60–2).

14   Two characters overhear a colleague practising the speech he is going
to deliver, to be precise (Brenton 2008: 37, 89–90), but both do so
apparently by chance and then address the person they listened to,
avowing they have heard the rehearsal, so that the scenes appear to
be quite different from those in *Anne Boleyn*. The same can be said
of the phone calls between Macmillan and Eisenhower, that feature
staff members on telephone extensions on both sides (ibid.: 66–8,
75–7).

15   The influence of situationism in Brenton's works is analysed by: Bull
1984: 17–25; Boon 1990: 138–50; Boon 1991: 55–8; O'Connor
2001: 86–94.

16   'Toute la vie des sociétés dans lesquelles règnent les conditions
modernes de production s'annonce comme une immense
accumulation de *spectacles*. Tout ce qui était directement vécu s'est
éloigné dans une représentation' (Debord 1992: 10).

17   'Le spectacle n'est pas un ensemble d'images, mais un rapport social
entre des personnes, médiatisé par des images' (Debord 1992: 10).

18   'Est l'affirmation omniprésente du choix *déjà fait* dans la production,
et sa consommation corollaire' (Debord 1992: 11).

# Conclusions

1   See De Marinis's observation that all performances are actually 'open' because the simultaneous utilization of several codes allows artists and spectators to communicate on very different levels according to their knowledge and understanding of those codes (De Marinis 1982: 284).

2   An interesting difference may nevertheless be remarked in the fact that *Anne Boleyn* and *Doctor Scroggy's War* make ample use of audience address, while *In Extremis* features only one example of such direct communication between stage and auditorium, which was added during the rehearsal process. This specific device, though not completely absent from the rest of Brenton's works, has evidently struck him as especially suited to the structure of Shakespeare's Globe.

# REFERENCES

Akbar, Arifa (2010), 'Globe Stages First Play Written by a Woman', *The Independent*, 16 February 2010: 15.

Allfree, Claire (2008), 'From Streets to Globe', *Metro – London*, 8 July 2008: 27.

Allum, Gina (2010), 'Sheer Bedlam', *New Statesman*, 22 September 2010. Available online: http://www.newstatesman.com/blogs/cultural -capital/2010/09/18th-century-bedlamplay-mad (accessed 22 December 2014).

Amer, Matthew (2013), 'Jessica Swale: An Education', *Official London Theatre*, 22 August 2013. Available online: http://www .officiallondontheatre.co.uk/news/backstagepass/features/article/ item195227/jessica-swale-an-education/ (accessed 7 April 2014).

Anderson, Maxwell (1950), *Anne of the Thousand Days*, New York: Dramatists Play Service.

Ansorge, Peter (1973), 'Disrupting the Spectacle: Howard Brenton Talks to Peter Ansorge', *Plays and Players*, 20(10): 22–3.

Armitage, Simon (2014), 'Introduction', in Simon Armitage, *The Last Days of Troy*, London: Faber and Faber: v–viii.

Augé, Marc (1989), *Domaines et châteaux*, Paris: Éditions du Seuil.

Augé, Marc (1992), *Non-lieux. Introduction à une anthropologie de la surmodernité*, Paris: Éditions du Seuil.

Augé, Marc (1997), *L'impossible voyage. Le tourisme et ses images*, Paris: Éditions Payot & Rivages.

Barassi, Sebastiano (2007), 'The Modern Cult of Replicas: A Rieglian Analysis of Values in Replication', *Tate Papers*, no. 8. Available online: http://www.tate.org.uk/research/publications/tatepapers/modern-cult -replicas-rieglian-analysis-values-replication (accessed 12 June 2014).

Bassett, Kate (2010), 'Boleyn's Is a Bloody Tale, But Oh, What a Spring in Its Step', *The Independent on Sunday*, 1 August 2010, then *Theatre Record*, 30(15): 841.

Beadle, Richard (2011), 'From Beginning to End', in the programme for *The Globe Mysteries*, London: Shakespeare's Globe Theatre: 2–5.

Beckerman, Bernard ([1970] 1979), *Dynamics of Drama. Theory and Method of Analysis*, New York: Drama Book Specialists.

Benjamin, Walter (1936), 'L'oeuvre d'art à l'époque de sa reproduction mécanisée', French translation by Pierre Klossowski, *Zeitschrift für Sozialforschung*, 5: 40–68; first published in German in *Schriften* (1955), Band I, Frankfurt am Main: Suhrkamp: 366–405.

Bennett, Susan (1997), *Theatre Audiences: A Theory of Production and Reception*, second edition, London: Routledge.

Bennett, Susan (2005), 'Theatre Tourism', *Theatre Journal*, 57(3): 407–28.

Bennett, Susan (2008), 'Shakespeare on Vacation', in Barbara Hodgdon and W. B. Worthen (eds), *A Companion to Shakespeare and Performance*, Chichester: Wiley-Blackwell: 494–508.

Billington, Michael (2006a), 'Globe's Ramshackle Pirate Panto Misfires', *The Guardian*, 20 July 2006: 38, then *Theatre Record*, 26(15): 840.

Billington, Michael (2006b), 'Brenton Offers Up His Soul to the Devil', *The Guardian*, 4 September 2006: 36.

Billington, Michael (2008), 'Madness Is the Method as Babylon Comes to Camden Town', *The Guardian*, 11 July 2008: 36, then *Theatre Record*, 28(14): 814–15.

Billington, Michael (2009), 'A Greek Comedy, But Helen's Jokiness Misses the Point', *The Guardian*, 6 August 2009: 32.

Billington, Michael (2014), 'Howard Brenton Explores Horror of Combat', *The Guardian*, 18 September 2014. Available online: http://www.theguardian.com/stage/2014/sep/18/doctor-scroggys-war-review-howardbrenton-shakespeares-globe-london-first-world-war (accessed 24 January 2015).

Bold, Alan (1979), *The Ballad*, London: Methuen.

Boon, Richard (1990), 'Politics and Terror in the Plays of Howard Brenton', in John Orr and Dragan Klaić (eds), *Terrorism and Modern Drama*, Edinburgh: Edinburgh University Press: 138–50.

Boon, Richard (1991), *Brenton. The Playwright*, London: Methuen.

Brecht, Bertolt ([1940] 1964), 'Short Description of a New Technique in Acting Which Produces an Alienation Effect', translated by John Willett, in Bertolt Brecht, *Bertolt Brecht on Theatre. The Development of an Aesthetic*, edited by John Willett, London: Methuen: 136–40.

Brecht, Bertolt ([1943] 1980), *The Life of Galileo*, translated by Howard Brenton, London: Methuen.

Bredin, Henrietta (2008), 'Poetry in Motion', *The Spectator*, 17 September 2008. Available online: http://www.spectator.co.uk/arts/arts-feature/2087466/poetry-in-motion/ (accessed 11 March 2014).

Brenton, Howard ([1969] 1986), *Christie in Love*, in Howard Brenton, *Plays 1*, London: Methuen Drama: 1–30.

Brenton, Howard ([1970] 1972), *Wesley*, in Howard Brenton, *Plays for Public Places*, London: Eyre Methuen: 31–70.

Brenton, Howard ([1971] 1972), *Scott of the Antarctic*, in Howard Brenton, *Plays for Public Places*, London: Eyre Methuen: 71–103.

Brenton, Howard (1972), *Plays for Public Places*, London: Eyre Methuen.

Brenton, Howard ([1974 and 1978] 1986), *The Churchill Play*, in Howard Brenton, *Plays 1*, London: Methuen Drama: 107–77.

Brenton, Howard (1980), *Plays for the Poor Theatre*, London: Methuen Drama.

Brenton, Howard ([1980] 1990), *The Romans in Britain*, in Howard Brenton, *Plays II*, London: Methuen Drama: 1–95.

Brenton, Howard ([1981] 1990), *Thirteenth Night*, in Howard Brenton, *Plays II*, London: Methuen Drama: 97–159.

Brenton, Howard (1982), *Hitler Dances*, London: Methuen.

Brenton, Howard ([1983] 1990), *The Genius*, in Howard Brenton, *Plays II*, London: Methuen Drama: 161–232.

Brenton, Howard ([1984] 1990), *Bloody Poetry*, in Howard Brenton, *Plays II*, London: Methuen Drama: 233–310.

Brenton, Howard (1986a), '"The Best We Have, Alas": A Note on Brecht', *Theater*, 17(2): 5–7.

Brenton, Howard (1986b), 'Preface', in Howard Brenton, *Plays 1*, London and New York: Methuen: vii–xv.

Brenton, Howard ([1988] 1990), *Greenland*, in Howard Brenton, *Plays II*, London: Methuen Drama: 311–415.

Brenton, Howard (1989), *H.I.D. (Hess Is Dead)*, London: Nick Hern Books.

Brenton, Howard ([2005] 2006), *Paul*, London: Nick Hern Books.

Brenton, Howard (2006), 'Enduring Love', *The Independent*, 29 August 2006: Extra 1–5. Available online: http://www.independent.co.uk/ arts-entertainment/books/features/howard-brentonspassion-for -abeacutelard-and-heloise-413812.html?origin=internalSearch# (accessed 14 October 2013).

Brenton, Howard (2007), 'Playing to the Crowd', *The Guardian*, 12 May 2007. Available online: http://www.guardian.co.uk/books/2007/ may/12/theatre.shakespeare (accessed 11 December 2012).

Brenton, Howard (2008), *Never So Good*, London: Nick Hern Books.

Brenton, Howard (2010), 'Anne Boleyn: Drama Queen', *The Independent*, 23 June 2010, then as 'Will the Real Anne Boleyn Please Take the Stage' in the programme for *Anne Boleyn*, London: Shakespeare's Globe Theatre: 2–5, and in Howard Brenton, *Anne Boleyn*, London: Nick Hern Books: 5–8.

Brenton, Howard (2011), 'He Caught the Orange', *The Guardian*, 9 July 2011: 18.

Brenton, Howard (2012), *55 Days*, London: Nick Hern Books.

Brenton, Howard (2013a), *#aiww The Arrest of Ai Weiwei*, London: Nick Hern Books.

Brenton, Howard (2013b), *Drawing the Line*, London: Nick Hern Books.

Brenton, Howard (2014a), E-mail Interview with the Author, 24 August 2014.

Brenton, Howard (2014b), 'Howard Brenton on "Doctor Scroggy's War" and an Arena of Opportunity', *The Independent*, 10 September 2014. Available online: http://www.independent.co.uk/artsentertainment/ theatre-dance/features/howard-brenton-on-doctor-scroggys-war-and -anarena-of-opportunity-9722094.html?origin=internalSearch (accessed 28 September 2014).

Brenton, Howard (2015), *Ransomed*, in Howard Brenton, Anders Lustgarten, Timberlake Wertenbaker and Sally Woodcock, *The Magna Carta Plays*, London: Oberon Books.

Brenton, Howard (2016), *Lawrence after Arabia*, London: Nick Hern Books.

Brooks, Libby (2011), 'The Taming of Jade Goody', *The Guardian*, 12 February 2011: 38.

Brown, Georgina (2011), 'It's Called Heaven – But It's Pure Hell', *The Mail on Sunday*, 11 September 2011.

Brown, Peter (2006), 'In Extremis at Shakespeare's Globe Theatre', *London Theatre Guide*, 1 September 2006. Available online: http:// www.londontheatre.co.uk/londontheatre/reviews/inextremis06.htm (accessed 4 September 2006).

Bull, John (1984), *New British Political Dramatists. Howard Brenton, David Hare, Trevor Griffiths and David Edgar*, London and Basingstoke: Macmillan.

Bull, John (2013), '"History Repeating Itself?": Text and Image, Theatre and Performance: Howard Brenton and David Edgar's Appropriation of the Historical Drama', *Studies in Theatre & Performance*, 33(2): 169–85.

Canton, Ursula (2011), *Biographical Theatre: Re-Presenting Real People?*, Basingstoke: Palgrave Macmillan.

Carpenter, Julie (2009a), 'The Frontline', *Daily Express*, 15 May 2009: 54.

Carpenter, Julie (2009b), 'Trojan Epic that Fails to Capture the Moment', *Daily Express*, 7 August 2009: 54.

Carroll, Tim (2008), 'Practising Behaviour to His Own Shadow', in Christie Carson and Farah Karim-Cooper (eds), *Shakespeare's Globe. A Theatrical Experiment*, Cambridge: Cambridge University Press: 37–44.

Carson, Christie and Farah Karim-Cooper, eds (2008), *Shakespeare's Globe. A Theatrical Experiment*, Cambridge: Cambridge University Press.

Cavendish, Dominic (2006), 'Cutting-Edge in the 12th Century', *Daily Telegraph*, 7 September 2006.

Chahidi, Paul (2008), 'Paul Chahidi: Actor and Globe Education Practitioner', in Christie Carson and Farah Karim-Cooper (eds),

*Shakespeare's Globe. A Theatrical Experiment*, Cambridge: Cambridge University Press: 204–10.

Clapp, Susannah (2009), 'Helen', *The Guardian Weekly*, 21 August 2009: 37.

Conkie, Rob (2006), *The Globe Theatre Project. Shakespeare and Authenticity*, Lewiston – Queenston and Lampeter: The Edwin Mellen Press.

Connor, Sheila (2006), 'Under the Black Flag', *Theatreworld Internet Magazine*, 20 July 2006. Clipping available at Shakespeare's Globe Library and Archives.

Cooper, Harry (2007), 'Thoughts on Thoughts on Replication', *Tate Papers*, no. 8. Available online: http://www.tate.org.uk/research/publications/tate-papers/thoughts-on-thoughts-on-replication (accessed 12 June 2014).

Cooper, Paddy (2011), 'In Need of a Little Divine Inspiration', *South London Press*, 9 September 2011.

Cotta Ramusino, Elena (2009), 'The Burial at Thebes: l'Antigone di Seamus Heaney', *Il Confronto Letterario*, 52 (supplement): 199–214.

Coveney, Michael (2011), 'Dominic Posts a Health Warning', *WhatsOnStage*, 2 September 2011. Available online: http://www.whatsonstage.com/west-end-theatre/news/09-2011/dominic-posts-a-health-warning_7166.html (accessed 9 December 2016).

Curtis, Nick (2008), 'Camden's Chronicler', *Evening Standard*, 1 July 2008: 41.

Curtis, Nick (2009), 'The Frontline Brings Modern Edge to The Globe', *London Evening Standard*, 11 May 2009.

Curtis, Nick (2014), 'Harold Gillies, The Man Who Mended Broken Soldiers', *London Evening Standard*, 26 August 2014. Available online: http://www.standard.co.uk/goingout/theatre/harold-gillies-the-man-who-mended-broken-soldiers-9690738.html (accessed 24 January 2015).

Davis, Harriet (2008), 'The Frontline', *Rogues & Vagabonds: Enquire Within*, 11 July 2008. Available online: http://www.roguesandvagabonds.co.uk/cgi-bin/newslist.pl?bid=10837 (accessed 11 July 2008).

Day, Barry (1996), *This Wooden 'O'. Shakespeare's Globe Reborn*, London: Oberon Books.

Debord, Guy (1992), *La société du spectacle*, third edition, Paris: Gallimard.

Debord, Guy (1994), *The Society of the Spectacle*, translated by Donald Nicholson-Smith, New York: Zone Books.

De Marinis, Marco (1982), *Semiotica del teatro: l'analisi testuale dello spettacolo*, Milan: Bompiani.

De Marinis, Marco (1987), 'Dramaturgy of the Spectator', translated by Paul Dwyer, *The Drama Review: TDR*, 31(2): 100–14.

De Sola Pinto, Vivian and Allan Edwin Rodway ([1957] 1965), 'Introduction', in Vivian de Sola Pinto and Allan Edwin Rodway (eds), *The Common Muse. Popular British ballad poetry from the 15th to the 20th Century*, Harmondsworth and Ringwood: Penguin Books: 13–50.

Dessen, Alan C. (2008), '"Original Practices" at the Globe: A Theatre Historian's View', in Christie Carson and Farah Karim-Cooper (eds), *Shakespeare's Globe. A Theatrical Experiment*, Cambridge: Cambridge University Press: 45–53.

Dickson, Andrew (2010), 'A Life in Theatre: Howard Brenton', *The Guardian*, 10 July 2010. Available online: http://www.guardian .co.uk/books/2010/jul/10/howard-brenton-life-in-theatre (accessed 20 September 2013).

Dromgoole, Dominic (2002), 'Howard Brenton', in Dominic Dromgoole, *The Full Room. An A-Z of Contemporary Playwriting*, second edition, London: Methuen Drama, 2002: 34–8.

Dromgoole, Dominic (2008), 'Performance', in *The Shakespeare Globe Trust Annual Review 2007–8*: 6. Available online: http://www .shakespearesglobe.com/about-us/todays-globe/annualreview (accessed 6 August 2013).

Edwardes, Jane (2008), 'The Frontline', *Time Out London*, 17 July 2008, then *Theatre Record*, 28(14): 816.

Elam, Keir (2002), *The Semiotics of Theatre and Drama*, second edition, London and New York: Routledge.

Elkin, Susan (2009), 'Helen', *The Stage*, 13 August 2009: 18–19.

Evans, Lloyd (2011), 'Divine Punishment', *The Spectator*, 10 September 2011: 48.

Evans, Lloyd (2014), 'Charles III Is Made for Numbskulls by Numbskulls', *The Spectator*, 27 September 2014. Available online: http://www.spectator.co.uk/arts/theatre/9323062/charles-iii-is-made -fornumbskulls-by-numbskulls/ (accessed 24 January 2015).

Fallow, Catriona (2014), 'The Plays of Peter Oswald: New Writing at Shakespeare's Globe 1998–2005', *Studies in Theatre and Performance*, 34(1): 90–6.

Feldman, Alexander (2013), *Dramas of the Past on the Twentieth-Century Stage: In History's Wings*, New York and London: Routledge.

Fisher, Philip (2008), 'The Frontline', *British Theatre Guide*. Available online: http://www.britishtheatreguide.info/reviews/frontline-rev.htm (accessed 11 July 2008).

Foucault, Michel ([1967] 1994a), 'Des espaces autres', lecture at the Cercle d'études architecturales, Paris, 14 March 1967, in Michel Foucault, *Dits et écrits 1954–1988*, Paris: Gallimard: vol. 4 (1980–1988), 752–62.

Foucault, Michel ([1967] 1994b), *Different Spaces*, in James B. Faubion (ed.), *Aesthetics, Method, Epistemology*, New York: The New Press: 175–85.

Freshwater, Helen (2009), *Theatre & Audience*, Basingstoke: Palgrave Macmillan.

Fricker, Karen (2008), 'The Frontline', *Variety*, 23 July 2008. Available online: http://www.variety.com/review/VE1117937793 .html?categoryid=33&cs=1 (accessed 1 August 2008).

Fricker, Karen (2009), 'Helen', *Variety*, 17 August 2009: 23.

Gardner, Lyn (2005), 'Rhyme and Punishment', *The Guardian*, 11 July 2005: 16.

Gardner, Lyn (2007), 'In Extremis', *The Guardian*, 24 May 2007.

Gardner, Lyn (2011), 'Anne Boleyn's Feisty Ghost Grabs History by the Scruff of the Neck', *The Guardian*, 19 July 2011: 34.

Gerneke, Gus (1995), 'Expropriating the Unique: Copy, Model, Imitation, Fake', Part 1, *Architecture SA*, (7–8/95): 20–6.

Gerneke, Gus (1996), 'Expropriating the Unique: Copy, Model, Imitation, Fake', Part 2, *Architecture SA*, (1–2/96): 21–7.

Gore-Langton, Robert (2010), 'You'll Lose Your Head over Anne Boleyn', *The Mail on Sunday*, 8 August 2010, then *Theatre Record*, 30(15): 842–3.

Greenfield, Jon (1997), 'Design as Reconstruction: Reconstruction as Design', in J. Ronnie Mulryne and Margaret Shewring (eds), *Shakespeare's Globe Rebuilt*, Cambridge: Cambridge University Press: 81–96.

Gregory, Amber (2008), 'The Frontline', *Extra! Extra!* Available online: http://www.extraextra.org/Review_The_Frontline_08.html (accessed 11 November 2014).

Greimas, Algirdas Julien (1966), *Sémantique structurale: recherche de méthode*, Paris: Larousse.

Gurr, Andrew (1997a), 'Shakespeare's Globe. A History of Reconstructions and Some Reasons for Trying', in J. Ronnie Mulryne and Margaret Shewring (eds), *Shakespeare's Globe Rebuilt*, Cambridge: Cambridge University Press: 26–47.

Gurr, Andrew (1997b), 'Staging at the Globe', in J. Ronnie Mulryne and Margaret Shewring (eds), *Shakespeare's Globe Rebuilt*, Cambridge: Cambridge University Press: 159–68.

Gurr, Andrew (2008), 'Foreword', in Christie Carson and Farah Karim-Cooper (eds), *Shakespeare's Globe. A Theatrical Experiment*, Cambridge: Cambridge University Press: xvii–xx.

Halliburton, Rachel (2013), Review of *Gabriel*, *Time Out London*, 30 July 2013, then *Theatre Record*, 33 (16–17): 775.

Hallissey, Susan (2009), 'Frontline Theatre', *Southwark News*, 14 May 2009: 25.

Hammond, Jonathan (1973), 'Messages First: An Interview with Howard Brenton', *Gambit. International Theatre Review*, 6(23): 24–32.

Hannan, Chris (2011), 'Much Ado about Celebs', *The Independent*, 18 August 2011: 14–15.

Hannan, Chris (2014), E-mail Interview with the Author, 8 September 2014.

Hart, Chrisopher (2006a), 'Rum, Piracy and the Lash', *Sunday Times*, 23 July 2006: 23.

Hart, Christopher (2006b), 'Plenty to Get Your Teeth Into', *Sunday Times*, 9 September 2006: 19.

Hay, Malcolm and Philip Roberts (1979), 'Howard Brenton: An Introduction and Interview', *Performing Arts Journal*, 3(3): 132–41.

Hayman, Ronald (1976), 'Howard Brenton in Conversation with Ronald Hayman', *The New Review*, 3(29): 56–8.

Hellmann, Marie-Christine (1988), 'Vrai ou faux? De l'original à la falsification les multiples facettes de la copie', *Archeologia*, (236): 43–4.

Hemming, Sarah (2009), 'Helen', *Financial Times*, 8/9 August 2009: 8.

Hemming, Sarah (2012), 'Questions of Faith', *Financial Times*, 6 October 2012. Available online: http://www.ft.com/cms/s/2/0e3cf776-0c93 -11e2-a776-00144feabdc0.html (accessed 17 September 2013).

Hemming, Sarah (2013), Review of *Gabriel*, *Financial Times*, 23 July 2013, then *Theatre Record*, 33(15): 703.

Hernadi, Paul (1976), 'Re-Presenting the Past: A Note on Narrative Historiography and Historical Drama', *History and Theory*, 15(1): 45–51.

Hildy, Franklin J. (2008), 'The "Essence of Globeness": Authenticity, and the Search for Shakespeare's Stagecraft', in Christie Carson and Farah Karim-Cooper (eds), *Shakespeare's Globe. A Theatrical Experiment*, Cambridge: Cambridge University Press: 13–25.

Hitchings, Henry (2009), 'The Pratfall of Troy', *London Evening Standard*, 6 August 2009: 35.

Hobsbawm, Eric (1983), 'Introduction: Inventing Traditions', in Eric Hobsbawm and Terence Ranger (eds), *The Invention of Tradition*, Cambridge: Cambridge University Press: 1–14.

Howard, Jean E. (1984), *Shakespeare's Art of Orchestration. Stage Technique and Audience Response*, Urbana and Chicago: University of Illinois Press.

Howey-Nunn, Sam (2002), *The Golden Ass*, Shakespeare's Globe Research Bulletin no. 27. Available online: http://www .shakespearesglobe.com/uploads/ffiles/2012/03/545849.pdf (accessed 25 November 2014).

Hutcheon, Linda (1988), *A Poetics of Postmodernism. History, Theory, Fiction*, London: Routledge.

Irvine, Susan (2006), 'One-legged Action', *Sunday Telegraph*, 23 July 2006: 27, then *Theatre Record*, 26(15): 842.

Itzin, Catherine and Simon Trussler (1975), 'Petrol Bombs through the Proscenium Arch', *Theatre Quarterly*, 5(17): 4–20.

Itzin, Catherine and Simon Trussler (1981), 'Petrol Bombs through the Proscenium Arch', in Simon Trussler (ed.), *New Theatre Voices of the Seventies: Sixteen Interviews from Theatre Quarterly, 1970–1980*, London: Eyre Methuen: 85–97.

Jacobson, Rivka (2011), 'The God of Soho', *Plays to See*. Available online: http://playstosee.com/page.php?sad=play&id=248 (accessed 13 September 2011).

John, Emma (2007), 'In Extremis', *Time Out London*, 23 May 2007: 124.

Jury, Louise (2011), 'Jordan and Jade, The Unlikely Role Models for Shakespeare's theatre', *London Evening Standard*, 11 February 2011: 37.

Keenan, Siobhan and Peter Davidson (1997), 'The Iconography of the Globe', in J. Ronnie Mulryne and Margaret Shewring (eds), *Shakespeare's Globe Rebuilt*, Cambridge: Cambridge University Press: 147–56.

Kennedy, Dennis (1998), 'Shakespeare and Cultural Tourism', *Theatre Journal*, 50(2): 175–88.

Kennedy, Dennis (2009), *The Spectator and the Spectacle: Audiences in Modernity and Postmodernity*, Cambridge: Cambridge University Press.

Kiernan, Pauline (1999), *Staging Shakespeare at the New Globe*, Basingstoke: Palgrave Macmillan.

Labadi, Sophia (2010), 'World Heritage, Authenticity and Post-Authenticity: International and National Perspectives', in Sophia Labadi and Colin Long (eds), *Heritage and Globalisation*, Oxon and New York: Routledge: 66–84.

Leyshon, Nell (2010), 'Mad World', *The Guardian*, 4 September 2010: 17.

Lichtig, Toby (2008), 'A Lovely Wee Jape', *The Times Literary Supplement*, 18 July 2008: 18.

Lindley, David (2008), 'Music, Authenticity and Audience', in Christie Carson and Farah Karim-Cooper (eds), *Shakespeare's Globe. A Theatrical Experiment*, Cambridge: Cambridge University Press: 99–100.

Logan, Brian (2009), 'Dominic Dromgoole: "Cheap Jokes? Bring 'em on"', *The Independent*, 3 May 2009: 20.

Lukowski, Andrzej (2014), 'Doctor Scroggy's War', *Time Out London*, 18 September 2014. Available online: http://www.timeout.com/london/theatre/doctor-scroggys-war (accessed 24 January 2015).

McGinn, Caroline (2007), 'Love-Crossed Scholars', *The London Paper*, 22 May 2007.

McGinn, Caroline (2011), 'Anne Boleyn', *Time Out London*, 20 July 2011.

McMullan, Gordon (2008), 'Afterword', in Christie Carson and Farah Karim-Cooper (eds), *Shakespeare's Globe. A Theatrical Experiment*, Cambridge: Cambridge University Press: 230–3.

Marlowe, Sam (2007), 'In Extremis', *The Times*, 22 May 2007: 18.

Marlowe, Sam (2010a), 'Anne Boleyn', *Time Out London*, 5 August 2010, then *Theatre Record*, 30(15): 842.

Marlowe, Sam (2010b), 'The Globe's Shocking New Play', *Time Out London*, 2 September 2010: 108.

Matthews, Jo and Minna Sharpe (2007), 'We, the Unquiet Americans', *Cuesheet*, Autumn 2007: 1, 4.

Meeke, Kieran (1999), 'Augustine's Oak – Globe', *West End Extra*, 27 August 1999: 11.

Megson, Chris (2012), *Modern British Playwriting: The 1970s. Voices Documents New Interpretations*, London: Methuen Drama.

Milhous, Judith and Robert D. Hume (1985), *Producible Interpretation: Eight English Plays, 1675–1707*, Carbondale: Southern Illinois University Press.

Mitchell, Tony (1987), *File on Brenton*, London and New York: Methuen.

Morrison, Richard (2008), 'A Great Tragedy That This Was Ever Staged', *The Times*, 14 October 2008: 32.

Mountford, Fiona (2013), Review of *The Lightning Child*, *London Evening Standard*, 19 September 2013, then *Theatre Record*, 33(19): 847.

Mullarkey, Rory (2015), 'The Oresteia: Translator's Note', in Rory Mullarkey, *The Oresteia*, London: Bloomsbury Methuen Drama: unnumbered pages.

Mulryne, J. Ronnie and Margaret Shewring, eds (1997), *Shakespeare's Globe Rebuilt*, Cambridge: Cambridge University Press.

*Nara Document on Authenticity* (1993). Available online: http://whc .unesco.org/document/9379 (accessed 3 June 2014).

Nathan, John (2011), 'Cheap Thrills', *Theater News Online*. Available online: http://www.theaternewsonline.com/LondonTheatreReviews/ CHEAPTHRILLS.cfm (accessed 9 December 2016).

Neill, Heather (1999a), 'Scanning Oswald', *Around the Globe* (10): 14–15.

Neill, Heather (1999b), 'Master Pieces, Interview with Director Tim Carroll', in the programme for *Augustine's Oak*, London: Shakespeare's Globe Theatre: [4–5].

Neill, Heather (2006), 'The Brilliant Couple', in the programme for *In Extremis*, London: Shakespeare's Globe Theatre: 7–9.

Neill, Heather (2008), 'Going Underground', in the programme for *The Frontline*, London: Shakespeare's Globe Theatre: 2–4, and *Around the Globe* (38): 14–16.

Neill, Heather (2009), 'Revealing the Real Helen', in the programme for *Helen*, London: Shakespeare's Globe Theatre: 2–4, and *Around the Globe* (42): 12–13.

Neill, Heather (2010), 'Bringing Bedlam to Bankside', in the programme for *Bedlam*, London: Shakespeare's Globe Theatre: 2–5.

Neill, Heather (2013), 'A Most Gracious and Most Terrible God', in the programme for *The Lightning Child*, London: Shakespeare's Globe Theatre: 2–4, and with minor differences as 'Honouring a Most Gracious and Most Terrible God', *Around the Globe* (53): 18–19.

Nightingale, Benedict (1999), 'Distracted by History', *The Times*, 16 August 1999: 42.

Nightingale, Benedict (2006), 'Soulful Take on When Abélard Met Heloïse', *The Times*, 5 September 2006: 28.

Nightingale, Benedict (2009), '2,400 Years On, Tale Has Never Felt More Topical', *The Times*, 7 August 2009: 30.

Nora, Pierre (1989), 'Between Memory and History: Les Lieux de Mémoire', *Representations*, (26): 7–24.

O'Connor, John (2001), 'Disrupting the Spectacle. French Situationist Political Theory and the Plays of Howard Brenton', in John C. Countryman and Noreen Barnes-McLain (eds), *Theatre and Politics in the Twentieth Century*, Tuscaloosa: Southeastern Theatre Conference and the University of Alabama Press: 86–94.

*Operational Guidelines for the Implementation of the World Heritage Convention* (2013), available online: http://whc.unesco.org/archive/opguide13-en.pdf (accessed 9 June 2014).

Orgel, Stephen (1998), 'What's the Globe Good For?', *Shakespeare Quarterly*, 49(2): 191–4.

Oswald, Peter (2005), 'The Playwright Always Thinks Twice', *Around the Globe* (30): 8–9.

Palmer, Richard H. (1998), *The Contemporary British History Play*, Westport and London: Greenwood Press.

Pasternak Slater, Ann (1982), *Shakespeare the Director*, Brighton: Harvester.

Perniola, Mario (1994), 'Celebrare la città', in Michel Foucault, *Eterotopia. Luoghi e non-luoghi metropolitani*, Milan: Mimesis: 53–61.

Prescott, Paul (2008), 'Inheriting the Globe: The Reception of Shakespearean Space and Audience in Contemporary Reviewing', in Barbara Hodgdon and W. B. Worthen (eds), *A Companion to Shakespeare and Performance*, Chichester: Wiley-Blackwell: 359–75.

Purves, Libby (2014), 'A Gallant Sadness: Faces of War', *theatre Cat*, 18 September 2014. Available online: http://theatrecat.com/2014/09/18/doctor-scroggys-war-shakespeares-globe-se1/ (accessed 24 January 2015).

Reinelt, Janelle (1985), 'Bertolt Brecht and Howard Brenton: The Common Task', *Pacific Coast Philology*, 20(1–2): 46–52.

Reinelt, Janelle (1992), 'Selected Affinities: Bertolt Brecht and Howard Brenton', in Ann Wilson (ed.), *Howard Brenton. A Casebook*, New York and London: Garland Publishing: 39–57.

Reinelt, Janelle (1994), *After Brecht: British Epic Theatre*, Ann Arbor: The University of Michigan Press.

Reinelt, Janelle (2007), 'The "Rehabilitation" of Howard Brenton', *TDR*, 51(3): 167–74.

Riegl, Alois (1903), *Der moderne Denkmalkultus. Sein Wesen und seine Entstehung*, Vienna and Leipzig: Verlage von W. Barumüller.

Riegl, Alois ([1903] 1982), 'The Modern Cult of Monuments: Its Character and Its Origin', translated by Kurt W. Forster and Diane Ghirardo, *Oppositions* (25): 20–51.

Righter, Anne (1962), *Shakespeare and the Idea of the Play*, Harmondsworth: Penguin.

Roberts, Philip (1992), 'The Trials of "The Romans in Britain"', in Ann Wilson (ed.), *Howard Brenton. A Casebook*, New York and London: Garland Publishing: 59–70.

Robins, Nicholas (2008), 'Liberty and Terror', in the programme for *Liberty*, London: Shakespeare's Globe Theatre: 9–15, and *Around the Globe* (38): 17–20.

Robins, Nicholas (2009), 'Paine Got it Right', in the programme for *A New World*, London: Shakespeare's Globe Theatre: 2–4, and as 'He Got It Right', *Around the Globe* (42): 10–11.

Robins, Nicholas (2013), 'Sound the Trumpet', *Around the Globe* (53): 22–3.

Rokem, Freddie (2000), *Performing History. Theatrical Representations of the Past in Contemporary Theatre*, Iowa City: University of Iowa Press.

Rose, Margaret (2011), 'Il caso inglese', in Francesca Grassi and A. Magli (eds), *Paolo Grassi: il teatro come bene pubblico*, Bagni a Ripoli: Passigli: 27–33.

Rowley, Anne (2013), 'Out of a Hat Memories', *Cuesheet*, Autumn 2013: [4].

Russell Brown, John (1981), 'Modern Uses for a Globe Theatre', in C. Walter Hodges, S. Schoenbaum and Leonard Leon (eds), *The Third Globe. Symposium for the Reconstruction of the Globe Playhouse, Wayne State University, 1979*, Detroit: Wayne State University Press: 14–28.

Rylance, Mark (1997), 'Playing the Globe. Artistic Policy and Practice', in J. Ronnie Mulryne and Margaret Shewring (eds), *Shakespeare's Globe Rebuilt*, Cambridge: Cambridge University Press: 169–76.

Rylance, Mark (2008), 'Research, Materials, Craft: Principles of Performance at Shakespeare's Globe', in Christie Carson and Farah

Karim-Cooper (eds), *Shakespeare's Globe. A Theatrical Experiment*, Cambridge: Cambridge University Press: 103–14.

Schechter, Joel (1983), 'Beyond Brecht: New Authors, New Spectators', in John Fuegi, Gisela Bahr and John Willett (eds), *Beyond Brecht*, Detroit: Wayne State University Press: 43–53.

Shakespeare, William (2005), *The Complete Works*, second edition, edited by John Jowett, William Montgomery, Gary Taylor and Stanley Wells, Oxford: Oxford University Press.

*Shakespeare's Globe Annual Review* 2012. Available online: http://www.shakespearesglobe.com/about-us/todays-globe/annual-review (accessed 23 November 2016).

*Shakespeare's Globe Annual Review* 2013. Available online: http://www.shakespearesglobe.com/about-us/todays-globe/annual-review (accessed 23 November 2016).

*Shakespeare's Globe Annual Review* 2015. Available online: http://www.shakespearesglobe.com/about-us/todays-globe/annual-review (accessed 23 November 2016).

Sharp, Rob (2011), 'Jade Goody's Tragic Life Inspires Play at Shakespeare's Globe', *The Independent*, 11 February 2011.

Shore, Robert (2006a), 'Not So Jolly Roger', *Metro (London)*, 21 July 2006: 32–3.

Shore, Robert (2006b), 'In Extremis', *Time Out London*, 6 September 2006: 129.

Shore, Robert (2010), Review of *Anne Boleyn*, *Metro – London*, 2 August 2010, then *Theatre Record*, 30(15): 842.

Shuttleworth, Ian (2006), 'Under the Black Flag', *Financial Times*, 21 July 2006: 9, then *Theatre Record*, 26(15): 841.

Shuttleworth, Ian (2008), 'The World at Camden Town', *Financial Times*, 15 July 2008: 17.

Shuttleworth, Ian (2010), 'Anne Boleyn, Shakespeare's Globe, London', *Financial Times*, 30 July 2010, then *Theatre Record*, 30(15): 840–41.

Sierz, Aleks (2006), 'Big, Bold and Public or Small and Personal?', *Tribune*, 22 September 2006: 37.

Smith, Alistair (2008), 'Bards of Camden Grace the Globe', *The London Paper*, 3 July 2008: 14.

Spencer, Charles (2006), 'Long John's All at Sea', *Daily Telegraph*, 20 July 2006: 26.

Swale, Jessica (2013), 'College Girls Go Wild', *London Evening Standard*, 6 August 2013. Available online: http://www.standard.co.uk/goingout/theatre/college-girlsgo-wild-jessica-swale-on-her-new-globe-play-blue-stockings-8747701.html (accessed 7 April 2014).

Swale, Jessica (2014), telephone interview with the author, 11 September 2014.

Szalwinska, Maxie (2010), Review of *Anne Boleyn*, *Sunday Times*, 8 August 2010, then *Theatre Record*, 30(15): 843.

Tait, Simon (2008), 'Premiere of the Fortnight', *Classical Music*, 27 September 2008: 15.

Tanitch, Robert (2008), 'Dramatic Hustle and Bustle', *Morning Star*, 24 July 2008: 9.

Taylor, Paul (2006a), 'Silver's Original Pirate Material', *The Independent*, 21 July 2006: 15.

Taylor, Paul (2006b), 'Warrior Spirits in a Dark Age', *The Independent*, 6 September 2006: Extra 20.

Taylor, Paul (2008), 'Is This a Play, or a Group Hug?', *The Independent*, 11 July 2008: 15, then *Theatre Record*, 28(14): 815.

Taylor, Paul (2010), 'Anne Boleyn, Shakespeare's Globe, London', *The Independent*, 2 August 2010, then *Theatre Record*, 30(15): 842.

Taylor, Paul (2013), Review of *Gabriel*, *The Independent*, 25 July 2013, then *Theatre Record*, 33(15): 703.

Thaxter, John (2006), 'Under the Black Flag', *British Theatre Guide*. Available online: http://www.britishtheatreguide.info/reviews/blackflag-rev.htm (accessed 20 July 2006).

Tiramani, Jenny (2008), 'Exploring Early Modern Stage and Costume Design', in Christie Carson and Farah Karim-Cooper (eds), *Shakespeare's Globe. A Theatrical Experiment*, Cambridge: Cambridge University Press: 57–65.

Tripney, Natasha (2008), 'Interview: Ché Walker', *music OMH*, June 2008. Available online: http://www.musicomh.com/theatre/features/che-walker_0608.htm (accessed 30 June 2008).

Trussler, Simon, ed. (1981), *New Theatre Voices of the Seventies: Sixteen Interviews from Theatre Quarterly, 1970–1980*, London: Eyre Methuen.

Van Kampen, Claire (2008a), 'Music and Aural Texture at Shakespeare's Globe', in Christie Carson and Farah Karim-Cooper (eds), *Shakespeare's Globe. A Theatrical Experiment*, Cambridge: Cambridge University Press: 79–89.

Van Kampen, Claire (2008b), 'Claire van Kempen on Creating a Working Definition of "Authenticity"', in Christie Carson and Farah Karim-Cooper (eds), *Shakespeare's Globe. A Theatrical Experiment*, Cambridge: Cambridge University Press: 183–5.

Von der Goltz, Michael (2010), 'Alois Riegl's Denkmalswerte: A Decision Chart Model for Modern and Contemporary Art Conservation?', in Ursula Schädler-Saub and Angela Weyer (eds), *Theory and Practice in the Conservation of Modern and Contemporary Art. Reflections on the Roots and the Perspectives. Proceedings of the International Symposium held 13–14 January 2009 at the University of Applied Sciences and Arts, Faculty Preservation of Cultural Heritage, Hildesheim*, London: Archetype Publications: 50–61.

Walker, Ché (2009), 'On ... Returning to the Frontline', *WhatsOnStage*,
    11 May 2009. Available online: http://www.whatsonstage.com/
    west-end-theatre/news/05-2009/che-walker-on-returning-to-the
    -frontline_17165.html (accessed 9 December 2016).
Walker, Tim (2006), 'Anything But the Girl', *Sunday Telegraph*, 10
    September 2006.
Walker, Tim (2007), 'Big Worthy Issues', *Sunday Telegraph*, 27 May
    2007: 42.
Westenberg, Kelsey (2009), 'Ché Walker: Camden Market', *NW
    Magazine*, clipping available at Shakespeare's Globe Library and
    Archives.
Whalen, Jeanne (2008), 'The Globe beyond the Bard', *The Wall Street
    Journal – Europe*, 25 July 2008: 8.
White, Martin (2008), 'Research and the Globe', in Christie Carson
    and Farah Karim-Cooper (eds), *Shakespeare's Globe. A Theatrical
    Experiment*, Cambridge: Cambridge University Press: 166–74.
Wilkinson, Chris (2006), 'A Medieval Light on the Modern World',
    *Financial Times*, 22 August 2006. Available online: http://www.ft.com/
    cms/s/2/88ede022-31ff-11db-ab06-0000779e2340.html (accessed 17
    September 2013).
Williams, Karla (2009), 'The Frontline, Globe Theatre', *Afridiziak's
    Theatre News*, 26 May 2009. Available online: http://www.afridiziak
    .com/theatrenews/reviews/review-the-frontline.html (accessed 9
    December 2016).
Wilson, Ann, ed. (1992), *Howard Brenton. A Casebook*, New York and
    London: Garland Publishing.
Woddis, Carole (2005), 'Writing the Storm', in the programme for *The
    Storm*, London: Shakespeare's Globe Theatre: 24–5.
Woddis, Carole (2006), 'In the Wake of Young John Silver', in the
    programme for *Under the Black Flag*, London: Shakespeare's Globe
    Theatre: 8–9, and *Around the Globe* (33): 16–17.
Woddis, Carole (2010), 'theartsdesk Q&A: Playwright Howard Brenton',
    *theartsdesk.com*, 17 July 2010. Available online: http://www
    .theartsdesk.com/theatre/theartsdesk-qa-playwright-howard-brenton
    (accessed 18 September 2013).
Woddis, Carole (2011), 'Shades of a Darker Carnival', *Herald*, 30 August
    2011: 17.
Woods, Penelope (2012), 'Globe Audiences: Spectatorship and
    Reconstruction at Shakespeare's Globe', PhD thesis, London: Queen
    Mary, University of London and Shakespeare's Globe, 2012.
Woolf, Alexa (2009), 'The Frontline by Ché Walker', *Musical Pointers*,
    8 May 2009. Available online: http://www.musicalpointers.co.uk/
    reviews/liveevents09/GlobeFrontline.html (accessed 12 May 2009).

Worthen, W. B. (2003), *Shakespeare and the Force of Modern Performance*, Cambridge: Cambridge University Press.

Wu, Duncan (2000), *Making Plays: Interviews with Contemporary British Dramatists and Their Directors*, New York: St. Martin's Press.

# INDEX

Note: Page references with letter 'n' followed by locators denote note numbers.

Lightning Source UK Ltd.
Milton Keynes UK
UKHW040724050119
334830UK00003B/62/P